Phraseologie und Parömiologie

Herausgegeben von
Wolfgang Eismann (Graz)
Peter Grzybek (Graz)
Wolfgang Mieder (Burlington VT, USA)

In Zusammenarbeit mit der
Europäischen Gesellschaft für Phraseologie
vertreten durch:

Harald Burger (Zürich), Wolfgang Eismann (Graz)
Peter Ďurčo (Bratislava), Gertrud Gréciano (Strasbourg)
Jarmo Korhonen (Helsinki), Christine Palm (Uppsala), Jan Wirrer (Bielefeld)

Band 12

Schriftleitung / Anschrift der Redaktion

Christoph Chlosta
Universität GH Essen
FB 3 Literatur- und Sprachwissenschaften
D-45117 Essen

Proverbs and the Social Sciences

An Annotated International Bibliography

Wolfgang Mieder
and
Janet Sobieski

Schneider Verlag Hohengehren GmbH

Gedruckt auf umweltfreundlichem Papier (chlor- und säurefrei hergestellt).

Bibliografische Information Der Deutschen Bibliothek

Die Deutsche Bibliothek verzeichnet diese Publikation in der Deutschen Nationalbibliografie; detaillierte bibliografische Daten sind im Internet über ›http://dnb.ddb.de› abrufbar.

Phraseologie und Parömiologie ; Bd. 12
ISBN 3-89676-667-8

Alle Rechte, insbesondere das Recht der Vervielfältigung sowie der Übersetzung, vorbehalten. Kein Teil des Werkes darf in irgendeiner Form (durch Fotokopie, Mikrofilm oder ein anderes Verfahren) ohne schriftliche Genehmigung des Verlages reproduziert werden.
© Schneider Verlag Hohengehren, Baltmannsweiler 2003.
  Printed in Germany.

TABLE OF CONTENTS

Introduction	vii
Bibliography	1
Name Index	197
Subject Index	203
Proverb Index	231

INTRODUCTION

During the past two decades I have expended much energy into assembling a series of international bibliographies on paremiology (the study of proverbs). Still working without a computer, I published the first volume of my *International Proverb Scholarship: An Annotated Bibliography* in 1982. Two supplementary volumes followed in 1990 and 1993, both once again with Garland Publishing in New York. By the time I put together a third supplement with the title *International Proverb Scholarship: An Annotated Bibliography. Supplement III (1990–2000)*, the Garland company had unfortunately changed hands as well as interest in folklore studies. Luckily Peter Lang Publishing of New York put this fourth volume into print in 2001, even though the previous three volumes of my *International Proverb Scholarship* bibliography had long gone out of print. These volumes contain a total of 7368 entries and represent the largest annotated bibliography ever assembled for one particular folklore genre.

In addition to these volumes, it has also been my task as editor of *Proverbium: Yearbook of International Proverb Scholarship* since 1984 to put together two annual bibliographies, namely "International Bibliography of New and Reprinted Proverb Collections" (paremiography) and "International Proverb Scholarship: An Updated Bibliography" (paremiology). Valuable as these yearly updates with their about four to five hundred titles might be, they nevertheless lack a number of desirable components that would make them more useful to proverb scholars. Due to space restrictions in the yearbook, there are no annotations, and there is also no space for name, subject, and proverb indices. In addition, scholars literally have to peruse the bibliographies of all volumes to locate a particular publication. These bibliographies are simply meant to communicate the newest publications on proverb matters each year, but they do not serve the role of comprehensive reference works with the appropriate apparatus that describes the content of each article, dissertation, essay volume, or book. This information is, of course, of particular value in the case of the vast scholarship in various foreign languages. It is with some feeling of pride that I can claim that my bibliographies are indeed international in scope.

Having assembled large proverb bibliographies both as massive books and as annual updates, I have also realized the need for specialized bibliographies that help scholars of certain disciplines to locate publications that deal especially with their interest. To accomplish this significant goal, it has been my good fortune to be able to engage the help of two wonderful colleagues and friends. Together with George B. Bryan (1939–1996) I put together *Proverbs in World Literature: A Bibliography* (New York: Peter Lang, 1996), and Janet Sobieski and I teamed up to produce *Proverb Iconography: An International Bibliography* (New York: Peter Lang, 1999). Supposedly all good things come in the proverbial three, and thus Janet Sobieski and I are now pleased to offer a long overdue volume on *Proverbs and the Social Sciences: An Annotated International Bibliography* that should enable scholars of the social sciences to have the most important proverb scholarship relating to their particular disciplines at their fingertips.

We have interpreted the social sciences in the widest sense of that conglomerate of individual disciplines. As one glance into the subject index will reveal, there are many entries for anthropology, ethnography, folklore, linguistics (neuro-, psycho-, and sociolinguistics), pedagogy (education and teaching), political science, psychiatry, psychology, and sociology. But the same is true for art (iconography), communication (mass media), history, law, literature, medicine (health), philosophy, and religion as they relate to aspects of the social sciences. In modern scholarship it is ever more difficult to separate publications by strict adherence to traditional disciplines. As scholars expand their interdisciplinary interests, the social sciences and the arts and humanities tend to be considered together to a certain degree.

The subject index contains dozens of key–words that indicate the pervasiveness of proverbs and proverbial expressions as well as various types of phraseologisms (idioms, routine formulas, wellerisms, etc.). The following concepts, for which the bibliography contains numerous entries, are clear indications of the multi–faceted characteristics, uses, and functions of proverbs: abstraction, acquisition, ambiguity, analogy, attitude, behavior, character, cognition, communication, competence, comprehension, culture, currency, didacticism, discourse, empiricism, ethics, ethnicity, experience, familiarity, feminism, gender, health, imagery, indirection, intelligence, interpretation, knowledge, language, life, logic, meaning, memory, mentality, metaphor, misogyny, morality, motivation, national character, obscenity, orality, paradox, performance, perception, personality, politics, pragmatics, prejudice, proverbs test, race, rhetoric, schizophrenia, semantics, semiotics, sex, socialization, society, speech act, stereotype, structure, symbol, syntax, tradition, transmission, truth, universality, validity, variability, wisdom, worldview, etc. But there are literally hundreds of additional key–words in the subject index that will refer scholars to studies that deal with such specific aspects as for example adultery, alcoholism, Alzheimer's, caregiving, chauvinism, concentration camp, defloration, disability, enculturation, fatalism, gerontology, humor, idiomaticity, justice, loafing, maturity, nonsense, obsoleteness, patriarchy, projection, rape, scatology, subversion, taboo, time, uniformity, verbal dueling, virtue, war, and youth. The topics are indeed endless, yet another proof for the ubiquity of proverbs in social communication of all types.

This bibliography also contains a list of those proverbs from a number of cultures and languages for which scholars have published entire monographs. Such detailed studies of but one proverb or proverbial expression show the complexity of the origin, transmission, history, and meaning of phraseologism in various oral and written contexts ranging from literature to the mass media, including caricatures, cartoons, greeting cards, and advertisements. But speaking of different languages and ethnic groups, it should be noted that there are many entries that deal specifically with numerous proverbs from the African, American, Arabic, Croatian, Brazilian, Dutch, English, Finnish, French, German, Greek, Indian, Italian, Jewish, Native American, Rumanian, Russian, Spanish, and Turkish tradition. As already mentioned, special care has been taken to make this bibliography as international as possible.

A few comments regarding the organization of our bibliography are in order at the end of this succinct introduction. It is arranged alphabetically according to the last name of the author. If there is more than one author, the additional name(s) are listed in the name index following the bibliographical entries. This index also contains all the names mentioned both in the titles and the annotations. As mentioned, the volume also includes subject and proverb indices. It should be observed that the numbers in the three indices refer to the bibliographical entries and not to pages. On the average, every bibliographical reference is followed by one to two lines of key–words (about six to fourteen terms) set off in smaller italicized print. Occasionally a few more lines of key–words are added, notably in the case of essay volumes. The individual entries of such essays contain, of course, more precise key–words. The 1169 bibliographical entries in our volume on *Proverbs and the Social Sciences: An Annotated International Bibliography* bear witness to the truly impressive scholarship of paremiology and phraseology (excluding any collections). It is also with much excitement that we can state that every publication listed in our bibliography is part of an international proverb archive that has been established here at the University of Vermont.

Bibliographies are meant to serve others, and for us the considerable amount of work that it took to put this volume together was a labor of love in the service of proverb scholars everywhere. We hope that our compilation will be of considerable use to colleagues and students from the social sciences in particular. Should there be difficulties in obtaining one or the other of the registered publications, we would be glad to be of assistance in making copies available. International scholarship means sharing information and resources, and we want to be of help in making these important materials available throughout the world.

We would like to dedicate this book to our respective spouses, William Doucette and Barbara Mieder, who show so much understanding for our scholarly passion for those small gems of human wisdom. Proverbs are not absolute truths, but they certainly encapsulate life in all of its challenges and pleasures.

January 2003

Wolfgang Mieder
Janet Sobieski

BIBLIOGRAPHY

A

1. Abel, Ernest L. "'Who Goes Drunk to Bed Begets but a Girl': The History of a Renaissance Medical Proverb." *Journal of the History of Medicine and Allied Sciences*, 54, no. 1 (1999), 5–22.
Alcohol / Francis Bacon / George Herbert / history / medicine / Renaissance / sex / William Shakespeare / "Who goes drunk to bed begets but a girl."

2. Abiodun, Michael A. "Acknowledgement and the Use of Proverbs in Yoruba: A Sociolinguistic Overview." *Proverbium*, 17 (2000), 23–26.
Acknowledgement / African / context / introductory formula / sociolinguistics / speech act / Yoruba.

3. Abrahams, Roger D. "A Rhetoric of Everyday Life: Traditional Conversational Genres." *Southern Folklore Quarterly*, 32 (1968), 44–59.
Behavior / context / conversation / genre / life / rhetoric / society / superstition / tradition.

4. Abrahams, Roger D., and Barbara Babcock–Abrahams. "A Sociolinguistic Approach to Proverbs." *Midwestern Journal of Language and Folklore*, 1 (1975), 60–64.
Behavior / communication / poetics / society / sociolinguistics / speech / "A rolling stone gathers no moss."

5. Ackerman, Brian. "On Comprehending Idioms: Do Children Get the Picture?" *Journal of Experimental Child Psychology*, 33, no. 3 (1982), 439–454.
Children / cognition / comprehension / idiom / interpretation / psychology.

6. Al–Jamal, Ziad. "Frauen in patriarchalischen 'Spruchweisheiten': Ein Beitrag zur Stellung der Frau in deutschen bzw. jordanisch–arabischen Sprichwörtern und anderen Spruchgattungen." *Kairoer Germanistische Studien*, 10 (1997), 89–112.
Anti–feminism / Arabic / genre / German / Jordanian / misogyny / patriarchy / wisdom / women.

7. Alagoa, E.J. "Proverbs as Contested Texts: The Construction of a Philosophy of History from African Proverbs." *Embracing the Baobab Tree: The African Proverb in the 21st Century.* Ed. Willem Saayman. Pretoria: University of South Africa, 1997. 84–93.
   African / culture / elder / history / Nembe / philosophy / truth / wisdom.

8. Albig, William. "Proverbs and Social Control." *Sociology and Social Research*, 15 (1931), 527–535.
   American / change / control / culture / empiricism / popularity / society / sociology / validity.

9. Aldridge, Mavis. *Critical Thinking: Thinking with Proverbs. Reasoning with Analogies.* Dubuque, Iowa: Kendall/Hunt Publishing, 1997. 102 pp.
   Analogy / contradiction / culture / experience / logic / meaning / paradox / reasoning.

10. Alexander, Tamar, and Galit Hasan–Rokem. "Games of Identity in Proverb Usage: Proverbs of a Sephardic–Jewish Woman." *Proverbium*, 5 (1988), 1–14.
    Competence / context / field research / identity / informant / interview / Jewish / pragmatics / repertoire / semantics / Sephardic / Spanish / speech act.

11. Alexander, Tamar, and Galit Hasan–Rokem. "Yesodot shel makom b'fitgamim shel yehudey turkia: Haolam vehabayit." *Pe'amim: Studies in Oriental Jewry*, 41 (1989), 112–133 (in Hebrew).
    Anthropocentrism / home / Jewish / semiotics / society / sociology / strategy / tradition / Turkish / world.

12. Allan, Keith, and Kate Burridge. *Euphemism & Dysphemism: Language Used as Shield and Weapon.* New York: Oxford University Press, 1991. 263 pp.
    Dysphemism / ethnicity / euphemism / jargon / language / obscenity / sex / slur / stereotype / taboo.

13. Allinson, Robert E., and A.L. Minkes. "Principles, Proverbs and Shibboleths of Administration." *International Journal [of] Technology Management*, 5, no. 2 (1990), 179–187.
    Administration / management / principle / shibboleth / truth / universality / "The buck stops here."

14. Almela Pérez, Ramón. "Son los refranes un reflejo de la sabiduría popular?" *Paremia*, 5 (1996), 143–145.
    Culture / mentality / people / science / society / wisdom / worldview.

15. Alster, Bendt. "Proverbs from Ancient Mesopotamia: Their History and Social Implications." *Proverbium*, 10 (1993), 1–20.
    Akkadian / content / history / meaning / Mesopotamia / society / Sumerian / wellerism.

16. Altunjan, Alexandr. "The Slogan in Political Discourse." *Totalitäre Sprache – Langue de bois – Language of Dictatorship*. Eds. Ruth Wodak and Fritz Peter Kirsch. Wien: Passagen Verlag, 1995. 59–69.
    Argument / discourse / ideology / language / politics / rhetoric / Russian / semantics / slogan.

17. Amali, Idris O.O. "The Image of Women in a Traditional African Society: A Case Study of Idoma Proverbs on Women." *Proverbium*, 17 (2000), 27–42.
    African / anti-feminism / gender / Idoma / men / misogyny / society / tradition / women.

18. Amali, Idris O.O. "Linguistic and Semantic Aspects of Obscene Idoma Proverbs." *Proverbium*, 18 (2001), 1–14.
    African / Idoma / linguistics / metaphor / obscenity / scatology / semantics / sex / society.

19. Aman, Reinhold (ed.). *Opus Maledictorum: A Book of Bad Words*. New York: Marlowe & Company, 1996. 364 pp.
    Abuse / aggression / blasphemy / ethnicity / euphemism / insult / malediction / obscenity / prejudice / sex / slang / slogan / slur / stereotype.

20. Ammons, R.B., and C.H. Ammons. "Use and Evaluation of Proverbs Test: Partial Summary through March, 1976." *Perceptual and Motor Skills*, 47 (1978), 1044–1046.
    Bibliography / brain / Donald R. Gorham / proverbs test / psychiatry / psychology / schizophrenia / testing.

21. Anada, Yoshiyuki. *Kotowaza, shakai shinrigaku*. [Proverbs – Social Psychology]. Tokyo: Shinsohan, 1996. 275 pp. (in Japanese).

Content / culture / Japanese / mentality / psychology / society / sociology / tradition / worldview.

22. Anders, Heidi. *"Never say die": Englische Idiome um den Tod und das Sterben.* Frankfurt am Main: Peter Lang, 1995. 342 pp.
Death / dying / English / euphemism / idiom / literature / psychology / semantics / sociology / syntax.

23. Andreason, Nancy C. "Reliability and Validity of Proverb Interpretation to Assess Mental Status." *Comprehensive Psychiatry*, 18 (1977), 465–472. Also in *The Wisdom of Many. Essays on the Proverb.* Eds. Wolfgang Mieder and Alan Dundes. New York: Garland Publishing, 1981. 218–229.
Brain / disorder / interpretation / mentality / proverbs test / psychiatry / psychology / validity.

24. Andreesco–Miereanu, Ioana. "Souvenirs en proverbes." *Cahiers de littérature orale*, no. 13 (1983), 171–173.
African / dialogue / didacticism / generation / informant / transmission / validity / wisdom.

25. Andrzejewski, B.W. "Reflections on the Nature and Social Function of Somali Proverbs." *African Language Review*, 7 (1968), 74–85.
African / animal / family / function / life / rhetoric / society / Somali / speech act.

26. Angenot, Marc. "'La lutte pour la vie': Migrations et usages d'un idéologème." *La locution. Actes du colloque international Université McGill, Montréal, 15–16 octobre 1984.* Eds. Giuseppe Di Stefano and Russell G. McGillivray. Montréal: Editions CERES, 1984. 171–190.
Charles Darwin / Alphonse Daudet / French / ideology / littérature / science / slogan / Herbert Spencer / "La lutte pour la vie."

27. Anido, Naiade. "Le proverbe: clé de la sagesse et clé des champs de la société gaucha." *Cahiers de littérature orale*, no. 13 (1983), 127–141.
Brazilian / definition / duel / Gauchos / improvisation / society / speech act / tradition / wisdom.

28. Anscombre, Jean–Claude. "Proverbes et formes proverbiales: Valeur évidentielle et argumentative." *Langue française*, 102 (1994), 95–107.
Argumentation / definition / fixidity / form / French / linguistics / morphology / proverbiality / semantics / syntax / validity.
29. Appiah, Michael Anthony. *Okyeame: An Integrative Model of Communication Behavior.* Diss. State University of New York at Buffalo, 1979. 157 pp.
African / Akan / behavior / communication / culture / ideology / philosophy / religion / society / tradition / worldview.
30. Arewa, E. Ojo, and Alan Dundes. "Proverbs and the Ethnography of Speaking Folklore." *American Anthropologist*, 66, part 2, no. 6 (1964), 70–85. Also in A. Dundes. *Analytic Essays in Folklore.* The Hague: Mouton, 1975. 35–49.
African / anthropology / context / ethnography / folklore / speech act / Yoruba.
31. Arkush, R. David. "'If Man Works Hard the Land Will not Be Lazy'. Entrepreneurial Values in North Chinese Peasant Proverbs." *Modern China*, 10, no. 4 (1984), 461–479.
Chinese / entrepreneurship / fatalism / life / peasant / society / value / worldview.
32. Arkush, R. David. "Orthodoxy and Heterodoxy in Twentieth–Century Chinese Peasant Proverbs." *Orthodoxy in Late Imperial China.* Ed. Kwang–Ching Liu. Berkeley, California: University of California Press, 1990. 311–331.
Chinese / collection / content / heterodoxy / morality / orthodoxy / peasant / society / tradition / worldview.
33. Arora, Shirley L. "'El que nace para tamal…': A Study in Proverb Patterning." *Folklore Americas*, 28 (1968), 55–79.
Destiny / introductory formula / life / pattern / structure / type / "El que nace…"
34. Arora, Shirley L. "The 'El que nace' Proverbs: A Supplement." *Journal of Latin American Lore*, 1 (1975), 185–198.
Destiny / introductory formula / life / pattern / structure / type / "El que nace…"
35. Arora, Shirley L. "The Perception of Proverbiality." *Proverbium*, 1 (1984), 1–38. Also in *Wise Words: Essays on the Proverb.* Ed. Wolfgang Mieder. New York: Garland Publishing, 1994. 3–29. Also in Spanish translation as "El reconoci-

miento del refrán." *Lingüística y Literatura*, 18, no. 31 (1997), 77–96.
Currency / definition / empiricism / marker / metaphor / native speaker / poetics / proverbiality / repetition / semantics / statistics / syntax / traditionality.

36. Arora, Shirley L. "'No Tickee, No Shirtee'. Proverbial Speech and Leadership in Academe." *Inside Organizations. Understanding the Human Dimension*. Eds. Michael Owen Jones, Michael Dane Moore, and Richard Christopher Snyder. Newbury Park, California: Sage Publishers, 1988. 179–189.
Academe / American / committee / communication / debate / familiarity / field research / function / humor / intelligentsia / persuasion / professor / speech act.

37. Arora, Shirley L. "A Woman and a Guitar: Variations on a Folk Metaphor." *Proverbium*, 10 (1993), 21–36.
Gender / guitar / instrument / metaphor / misogyny / music / riddle / sex / Spanish / stereotype / variant / women.

38. Arora, Shirley L. "Proverbs and Prejudice: *El Indio* in Hispanic Proverbial Speech." *Proverbium*, 11 (1994), 27–46.
Caribbean / Central American / ethnicity / Native American / prejudice / slur / South American / Spanish / speech / stereotype.

39. Arthurs, Jeffrey D. "Proverbs in Inspirational Literature: Sanctioning the American Dream." *Journal of Communication and Religion*, 17, no. 2 (1994), 1–15.
American / authority / communication / didacticism / inspiration / literature / religion / self–help book / value.

40. Ayanga, Hazel O. "Violence against Women in African Oral Literature as Portrayed in Proverbs." *Violence against Women: Reflections by Kenyan Women Theologians*. Eds. Grace Wamue and Mary Getui. Nairobi: Acton, 1996. 13–20.
African / anti–feminism / Kenyan / literature / misogyny / orality / violence / women.

41. Ayaß, Ruth. "Entstehen Sprichwörter aus Kategorischen Formulierungen?" *Sociologia Internationalis*, 32, no. 2 (1994), 227–252.
Categorical formulation / empiricism / familiarity / form / marker / metaphor / origin / poetics / sociology / structure.

42. Ayaß, Ruth. "'Wer das verschweigt, handelt eigentlich in böser Absicht': Zu Form und Funktion Kategorischer Formulierungen." *Linguistische Berichte*, no. 162 (1996), 137–160.
    Categorical formulation / didacticism / empiricism / form / function / indirection / poetics / structure.

43. Ayaß, Ruth. "Form und Funktion Katergorischer Formulierungen." *Kommunikative Konstruktion von Moral: Struktur und Dynamik der Formen moralischer Kommunikation.* Eds. Jörg Bergmann and Thomas Luckmann. Opladen: Westdeutscher Verlag, 1999. 106–124.
    Categorical formulation / didacticism / empiricism / form / function / indirection / morality / poetics / structure.

44. Ayaß, Ruth. "Vom Ursprung der Sprichwörter und ihrem Schicksal." *Kommunikative Konstruktion von Moral: Struktur und Dynamik der Formen moralischer Kommunikation.* Eds. Jörg Bergmann and Thomas Luckmann. Opladen: Westdeutscher Verlag, 1999. 127–150.
    Categorical formulation / communication / familiarity / form / metaphor / morality / origin / poetics.

45. Ayaß, Ruth. "On the Genesis and the Destiny of Proverbs." *Verbal Art across Cultures: The Aesthetics and Proto–Aesthetics of Communication.* Eds. Hubert Knoblauch and Helga Kotthoff. Tübingen: Gunter Narr, 2001. 237–254 (English version of previous essay).
    Categorical formulation / communication / familiarity / form / metaphor / morality / origin / poetics.

B

46. Bailey, Larry W., and Darrel Edwards. "Use of Meaningless and Novel Proverbs as a Projective Technique." *Journal of Personality Assessment*, 37 (1973), 527–530.
Abstraction / behavior / disorder / projection / proverbs test / psychology / schizophrenia.

47. Bain, Read. "Verbal Stereotypes and Social Control." *Sociology and Social Research*, 23 (1939), 431–446.
Control / society / sociology / stereotype / student / truth / validity.

48. Bambeck, Manfred. "'Malin comme un singe': Oder Physiognomik und Sprache." *Archiv für Kulturgeschichte*, 61 (1979), 292–316.
Animal / Aristotle / behavior / culture / French / language / life / monkey / physiognomy / "Malin comme un singe."

49. Baños, Josep–Eladio, and Elena Guardiola. "Verdades y falacias en los refranes españoles sobre el dolor de cabeza y el dolor odontológico." *Paremia*, 6 (1997), 77–84.
Content / fallacy / headache / health / medicine / Spanish / toothache / truth.

50. Bar–Sela, Ariel, and Hebbel E. Hoff. "Maimonides' Interpretation of the First Aphorism of Hippocrates." *Bulletin of the History of Medicine*, 37 (1963), 347–354.
Aphorism / Hippocrates / interpretation / Moses Maimonides / medicine / "Life is short, and the art is long."

51. Baranov, Anatolij, and Dmitrij Dobrovol'skij. "Kognitive Modellierung in der Phraseologie: Zum Problem der aktuellen Bedeutung." *Beiträge zur Erforschung der deutschen Sprache*, 10 (1991), 112–123.
Cognition / lexicology / phraseology / semantics / semiotics / structure.

52. Barley, Nigel. "A Structural Approach to the Proverb and Maxim with Special Reference to the Anglo–Saxon Corpus." *Proverbium*, 20 (1972), 737–750.
Context / definition / English / function / genre / logic / maxim / meaning / metaphor / structure / variation / wellerism.

53. Barnard, P.J., N.V. Hammond, A. MacLean, and J. Morton. "Learning and Remembering Interactive Commands in a Text–Editing Task." *Behaviour and Information Technology*, 1 (1982), 347–358.
Computer / informant / learning / memory / proverbs test / semantics / vocabulary.

54. Barnes–Harden, Alene Leett. *African American Verbal Arts: Their Nature and Communicative Interpretation (A Thematic Analysis)*. Diss. State University of New York at Buffalo, 1980. 186 pp.
African American / amusement / communication / conformity / culture / education / field research / function / interpretation / interview / society / validity / value.

55. Bartlotti, Leonard N. *Negotiating Pakhto [Pashto]: Proverbs, Islam and the Construction of Identity among Pashtuns*. Diss. University of Wales, 2000. Oxford: Oxford Centre for Mission Studies, 2000. 445 pp.
Afghanistan / context / ethnography / folklore / function / identity / indirection / Islam / literacy / metaphor / orality / religion / semantics / society.

56. Başgöz, Ilhan. "Proverbs about Proverbs or Folk Definitions of Proverb." *Proverbium*, 7 (1990), 1–17.
Selwyn Champion / collection / content / definition / discourse / form / function / meta–proverb / origin / power / speech / transmission / Turkish.

57. Başgöz, Ilhan. "Proverb Image, Proverb Message, and Social Change." *Journal of Folklore Research*, 30, nos. 2–3 (1993), 127–142.
Change / content / culture / folklore / image / message / metaphor / realia / semantics / semiotics / sex / society / Turkish.

58. Bass, Bernard M. "Development and Evaluation of a Scale for Measuring Social Acquiescence." *Journal of Abnormal and Social Psychology*, 53 (1956), 296–299.
Acquiescence / attitude / behavior / generalization / proverbs test / psychology / society / truth.

59. Bass, Bernard M. "Development of a Structured Disguised Personality Test." *Journal of Applied Psychology*, 40 (1956), 393–397.

Attitude / occupation / mores / personality / proverbs test / psychology / society / value.

60. Bass, Bernard M. "Validity Studies of a Proverbs Personality Test." *Journal of Applied Psychology*, 41 (1957), 158–160.
Achievement / aggression / attitude / occupation / informant / personality / proverbs test / psychology / sex / student / validity.

61. Bassin, Alexander. "Proverbs, Slogans and Folk Sayings in the Therapeutic Community: A Neglected Therapeutic Tool." *Journal of Psychoactive Drugs*, 16 (1984), 51–56.
Addiction / alcoholism / behavior / community / drug / intervention / psychology / psychotherapy / slogan / therapy.

62. Baum, Martha, and Mary Page. "Caregiving and Multigenerational Families." *The Gerontologist*, 31, no. 6 (1991), 762–769.
Caregiving / family / generation / gerontology / health / proverbs test / psychology / women.

63. Bauman, Richard, and Neil McCabe. "Proverbs in an LSD Cult." *Journal of American Folklore*, 83 (1970), 318–324.
American / cult / drug / folklore / function / litany / LSD (drug) / parody / rhetoric / sanction.

64. Baumgarten, Franziska. "A Proverb Test for Attitude Measurement." *Personnel Psychology*, 5 (1952), 249–261. Also in *The Wisdom of Many. Essays on the Proverb*. Eds. Wolfgang Mieder and Alan Dundes. New York: Garland Publishing, 1981. 230–241.
Attitude / emotion / experience / personality / proverbs test / psychology / Swiss / work.

65. Baur, Rupprecht S., and Torsten Ostermann. "Erwerb von Phraseologismen bei Aussiedlern aus Rußland." *Wörter in Bildern – Bilder in Wörtern: Beiträge zur Phraseologie und Sprichwortforschung aus dem Westfälischen Arbeitskreis*. Eds. Rupprecht S. Baur, Christoph Chlosta, and Elisabeth Piirainen. Baltmannsweiler: Schneider Verlag Hohengehren, 1999. 47–70.
Acquisition / archive / emigrant / empiricism / familiarity / foreign language / German / informant / interview / phraseologism / Russian.

66. Beaumatin, Eric. "El papel de la distinción lengua/discurso en la tipología paremiológica, con especial atención al problema de las *maledicta*." *Paremia*, 6 (1997), 101–106.
Aggression / discourse / language / malediction / prejudice / stereotype.

67. Becker, Wesley Clemence. *The Relation of Severity of Thinking Disorder to the Process–Reactive Concept of Schizophrenia.* Diss. Stanford University, 1955. 125 pp.
Abstraction / John D. Benjamin / brain / disorder / proverbs test / psychiatry / psychology / schizophrenia.

68. Becker, Wesley Clemence. "A Genetic Approach to the Interpretation and Evaluation of the Process–Reactive Distinction in Schizophrenia." *Journal of Abnormal and Social Psychology*, 53 (1956), 229–236.
Abstraction / John D. Benjamin / brain / disorder / interpretation / proverbs test / psychiatry / psychology / schizophrenia.

69. Beckmann, Susanne. "'So wie man ist, ist man': Zur Funktion von Phraseologismen in argumentativen Zusammenhängen." *Neue Fragen der Linguistik. Akten des 25. Linguistischen Kolloquiums, Paderborn 1990.* Eds. Elisabeth Feldbusch, Reiner Pogarell and Cornelia Weiß. Tübingen: Max Niemeyer, 1991. II, 85–91.
Argumentation / discourse / function / phraseologism / rhetoric / speech act.

70. Bellmann, Günter. "Sprechsprachliche Phraseologismen: Forschungsdesiderate und Forschungsansätze." *Beiträge zur Phraseologie, Wortbildung, Lexikologie. Festschrift für Wolfgang Fleischer.* Eds. Rudolf Grosse, Gotthard Lerchner, and Marianne Schröder. Frankfurt am Main: Peter Lang, 1992. 37–49.
Acoustics / codification / competence / idiomaticity / linguistics / phraseologism / speech act.

71. Benjafield, John, and Eleanor Carson. "The Image–Arousing Potential of Proverbs as a Function of Source and Mode." *British Journal of Social Psychology*, 25 (1986), 51–56.
Anonymity / communication / education / function / imagery / memorability / origin / psychology / society.

72. Benjafield, John, Kris Frommhold, Tom Keenan, Ron Muckenheim, and Dierk Mueller. "Imagery, Concreteness, Good-

ness, and Familiarity Ratings for 500 Proverbs Sampled from the 'Oxford Dictionary of English Proverbs'." *Behavior Research Methods, Instruments, & Computers*, 25, no. 1 (1993), 27–40.
Behavior / collection / concreteness / empiricism / English / familiarity / goodness / imagery.

73. Benjamin, John D. "A Method for Distinguishing and Evaluating Formal Thinking Disorders in Schizophrenia." *Language and Thought in Schizophrenia.* Ed. Jacob Kasanin. Berkeley, California: University of California Press, 1944; rpt. New York: W. Norton, 1964. 65–90.
Abstraction / brain / disorder / literalness / proverbs test / psychiatry / psychology / schizophrenia / "A rolling stone gathers no moss."

74. Bergsma, Harold M. "Tiv Proverbs as a Means of Social Control." *Africa*, 40 (1970), 151–163.
African / anthropology / approbation / behavior / control / society / Tiv.

75. Berman, Louis A. "Using Proverbs to Test Readiness for College Composition." *Proverbium*, 7 (1990), 19–36.
Assessment / composition / education / familiarity / foreign language / interpretation / proverbs test / student.

76. Billow, Richard M. "A Cognitive Development Study of Metaphor Comprehension." *Developmental Psychology*, 11, no. 4 (1975), 415–423.
Age / children / cognition / comprehension / development / metaphor / psycholinguistics / psychology.

77. Birnbaum, Mariana D. "On the Language of Prejudice." *Western Folklore*, 30 (1971), 247–268.
Blason populaire / ethnicity / folklore / immigrant / Jewish / language / minority / nationalism / prejudice / slur / stereotype.

78. Bleton, Paul. "C'est juste une façon de parler: les locutions métalinguistiques." *La locution. Actes du colloque international Université McGill, Montréal, 15–16 octobre 1984.* Eds. Giuseppe Di Stefano and Russell G. McGillivray. Montréal: Editions CERES, 1984. 3–18.
Communication / figurativeness / French / meta–linguistic / metaphor / phraseologism / speech act / worldview.

79. Bloc–Duraffour, Catherine. "Traitement de la logique des rôles narratifs dans les proverbes italiens." *Richesse du proverbe*. Eds. François Suard and Claude Buridant. Lille: Université de Lille, 1984. II, 37–49.
Content / Italian / logic / narrative / realia / semiotics / structure.

80. Bobrow, Samuel A., and Susan M. Bell. "On Catching on to Idiomatic Expressions." *Memory & Cognition*, 1 (1973), 343–346.
Ambiguity / cognition / comprehension / figurativeness / idiom / literalness / proverbs test / psycholinguistics / psychology / sentence / student.

81. Bock, J. Kathryn, and William F. Brewer. "Comprehension and Memory of the Literal and Figurative Meaning of Proverbs." *Journal of Psycholinguistic Research*, 9 (1980), 59–72.
Comprehension / figurativeness / literalness / meaning / memory / proverbs test / psycholinguistics / psychology / student.

82. Boesky, Dale. "Proverbs and Psychoanalysis." *Psychoanalytic Quarterly*, 45 (1976), 539–564.
Dream / folklore / Sigmund Freud / myth / psychoanalysis / psychology / riddle.

83. Bogardus, Emory S. "Earliest Social Thought." In E. Bogardus. *Development of Social Thought.* New York: Longmans, Green and Co., 1940; rpt. New York: David McKay, 1968. 10–27.
Culture / folklore / society / sociology / uniformity / wisdom / worldview.

84. Bohmer–Wood, Christine. *Flexibility in Language Comprehension: Paraphrasing Metaphors, Proverbs, and Vague Sentences*. Diss. Kent State University, 1978. 101 pp.
Comprehension / context / language / meaning / metaphor / psycholinguistics / psychology / sentence / structure.

85. Boller, Paul F. *Quotemanship: The Use and Abuse of Quotations for Polemical and Other Purposes*. Dallas, Texas: Southern Methodist University Press, 1967. 454 pp.
American / authority / context / function / Lyndon Baines Johnson / meaning / polemics / politics / quotation / rhetoric.

86. Bon, Michel, and Roland Colin. "Les proverbes sara et la pédagogie du développement." *Recherche, Pédagogie et Culture*, 21 (1976), 36–40.
    African / Chad / children / development / education / pedagogy / teaching.

87. Bonis, Monique de, Catherine Epelbaum, and André Féline. "Cognitive Processing of Contradictory Statements: An Experimental Study of Reasoning on Proverbs in Schizophrenia." *Psychopathology*, 25, no. 2 (1992), 100–108.
    Brain / cognition / contradiction / proverbs test / psychiatry / psychology / reasoning / schizophrenia.

88. Bornstein, Valerie. "A Case Study and Analysis of Family Proverb Use." *Proverbium*, 8 (1991), 19–28.
    American / authority / context / didacticism / family / family proverb / function / immigrant / meaning / socialization / society / use.

89. Borrajo, Daniel, Juan Ríos, M. Alicia Pérez, and Juan Pazos. "Dominoes as a Domain Where to Use Proverbs as Heuristics." *Data & Knowledge Engineering*, 5, no. 2 (1990), 129–137.
    Computer / dominoes / game / heuristics / meaning / prediction / utility.

90. Botelho da Silva, Teresa, and Anne Cutler. "Ill–Formedness and Transformability in Portuguese Idioms." *Idioms: Processing, Structure, and Interpretation*. Eds. Cristina Cacciari and Patrizia Tabossi. Hillsdale, New Jersey: Lawrence Erlbaum Associates, 1993. 129–143.
    Idiom / ill–formedness / memory / Portuguese / psycholinguistics / recall / semantics / transformability.

91. Bouissou, R. "Medical Proverbs. The Common Sense of Centuries." *World Health. The Magazine of the World Health Organization*, no volume given (July 1971), 2–26.
    Common sense / content / disease / health / medicine / prevention / value.

92. Bowden, Betsy. "A Modest Proposal, Relating Four Millennia of Proverb Collections to Chemistry within the Human Brain." *Journal of American Folklore*, 109, no. 434 (1996), 440–449.

Alzheimer's / antiquity / brain / chemistry / collection / culture / folklore / literacy / memory / Middle Ages / orality / poetics / religion / semantics.

93. Braekman, Willy L., and Peter S. Macaulay. "The Story of the Cat and the Candle in Middle English Literature." *Neuphilologische Mitteilungen*, 70 (1969), 690–702.
Animal / behavior / cat / education / instinct / literature / mouse / narrative / nature / nurture / "Nature passes nurture."

94. Braff, David L., Ira D. Glick, and Peggy Griffin. "Thought Disorder and Depression in Psychiatric Patients." *Comprehensive Psychiatry*, 24 (1983), 57–64.
Abstraction / depression / disorder / Donald R. Gorham / psychiatry / psychology / schizophrenia.

95. Brandes, Stanley H. "The Selection Process in Proverb Use: A Spanish Example." *Southern Folklore Quarterly*, 38 (1974), 167–186.
Anthropology / experience / field research / folklore / function / informant / repertoire / selection / society / Spanish / use / village.

96. Brannon, Linda Lorraine. *On the Understanding of Idiomatic Expressions*. Diss. University of Texas at Austin, 1975. 122 pp.
Ambiguity / cognition / comprehension / grammar / idiom / psycholinguistics / psychology.

97. Brasseur, Judith, and Beatrice C. Jimenez. "Performance of University Students on the Fullerton Subtest of Idioms." *Journal of Communication Disorders*, 22 (1989), 351–359.
Competence / familiarity / idiom / informant / proverbs test / psychology / student.

98. Brattemo, Carl–Erik. "Interpretations of Proverbs in Schizophrenic and Depressive Patients." *Acta Psychiatrica Scandinavica*, 37 (1961), 193–197.
Abstraction / comprehension / depression / generalization / interpretation / metaphor / proverbs test / psychiatry / psychology / schizophrenia / Swedish.

99. Brattemo, Carl–Erik. "Interpretations of Proverbs in Schizophrenic and Depressive Patients." *Acta Psychologica*, 18 (1961), 342–350.

Abstraction / autism / comprehension / depression / generalization / Donald R. Gorham / interpretation / metaphor / proverbs test / psychiatry / psychology / schizophrenia / Swedish.

100. Brattemo, Carl–Erik. "Interpretations of Proverbs in Schizophrenic Patients. Further Studies." *Acta Psychologica*, 20 (1962), 254–263.
Abstraction / age / cognition / comprehension / depression / intelligence / interpretation / proverbs test / psychiatry / psychology / schizophrenia / Swedish / verbalization.

101. Brattemo, Carl–Erik. "Effects of Lobotomy Operation in Schizophrenics and Electroshock Treatment in Depressives on Interpretation of Proverbs." *Acta Psychologica*, 20 (1962), 264–268.
Age / depression / intelligence / interpretation / lobotomy / metaphor / proverbs test / psychiatry / psychology / schizophrenia / Swedish.

102. Brattemo, Carl–Erik. "Changes in Interpretations of Proverbs in Schizophrenic Patients." *Acta Psychologica*, 20 (1962), 269–278.
Age / change / intelligence / interpretation / proverbs test / psychiatry / psychology / schizophrenia / Swedish.

103. Brattemo, Carl–Erik. "Differentiating Border–Line Schizophrenics from other Diagnostic Groups by Use of the Proverbs Test." *Acta Psychologica*, 20 (1962), 279–284.
Abstraction / interpretation / metaphor / proverbs test / psychiatry / psychology / schizophrenia / Swedish.

104. Brattemo, Carl–Erik. "The Effectiveness of Non–Standardized Categorization in Differentiating Schizophrenic Patients of Various Levels of Abstracting Functioning." *Acta Psychologica*, 24 (1965), 314–328.
Abstraction / interpretation / proverbs test / psychiatry / psychology / schizophrenia / Swedish / verbalization.

105. Brattemo, Carl–Erik. "Impairment and Improvement of the Abstracting Ability in Schizophrenic Patients." *Acta Psychologica*, 24 (1965), 387–397.
Abstraction / bibliography / concreteness / intelligence / metaphor / proverbs test / psychiatry / psychology / schizophrenia / Swedish.

106. Brattemo, Carl–Erik. *Studies in Metaphoric Verbal Behavior in Patients with a Psychiatric Diagnosis of Schizophrenia.* Sundsvall: Boktryckeri Aktiebolaget, 1968. 125 pp.
Abstraction / age / behavior / bibliography / brain / concreteness / depression / gender / intelligence / interpretation / metaphor / proverbs test / psychiatry / psychology / schizophrenia / Swedish / verbalization.

107. Brattemo, Carl–Erik, and C. Perris. "Relations entre le rythme alpha et l'aptitude à l'abstraction mesurée par des proverbes." *Revue de psychologie appliquée,* 16, no. 3 (1966), 129–139.
Abstraction / age / disorder / interpretation / meaning / proverbs test / psychiatry / psychology / schizophrenia / Swedish.

108. Brewer, Patricia J. *Age, Language, Culture, Previous Knowledge and the Proverb as Social Metaphor: A Study in Relationships.* Diss. University of Pennsylvania, 1973. 208 pp.
Acquisition / age / children / comprehension / context / culture / empiricism / familiarity / knowledge / language / metaphor / performance / production / society.

109. Briggs, Charles L. "The Pragmatics of Proverb Performances in New Mexican Spanish." *American Anthropologist,* 87, no. 4 (1985), 793–810. Also in *Wise Words: Essays on the Proverb.* Ed. Wolfgang Mieder. New York: Garland Publishing, 1994. 317–349. See also the expanded version with the title "Proverbs" in C. Briggs. *Competence in Performance. The Creativity of Tradition in Mexicano Verbal Art.* Philadelphia: University of Pennsylvania Press, 1988. 101–135 and 380 (notes).
Anthropology / context / field research / function / introductory formula / meaning / New Mexico / orality / performance / pragmatics / Spanish / speech act / validation.

110. Brinton, Bonnie, Martin Fujiki, and Teresa A. Mackey. "Elementary School Age Children's Comprehension of Specific Idiomatic Expressions." *Journal of Communication Disorders,* 18 (1985), 245–257.
Age / children / comprehension / idiom / language / psycholinguistics.

111. Bronner, Simon J. "The Haptic Experience of Culture ['Seeing is Believing, but Feeling is the Truth']." *Anthropos,* 77 (1982), 351–362.
American / culture / experience / haptics / meaning / perception / reality / "Seeing is believing, but feeling is the truth."

112. Bronner, Simon J. "['Seeing is Believing']… but 'Feeling's the Truth'." *Tennessee Folklore Society Bulletin*, 48, no. 4 (1982), 117–124 (somewhat shortened version of previous entry).
American / culture / experience / haptics / meaning / perception / reality / "Seeing is believing, but feeling is the truth."

113. Bronzini, Giovanni Battista. "La logica del proverbio. Problemi e prospettive di classificazione e analisi." *Proverbi locuzioni modi di dire nel dominio linguistico italiano*. Ed. Salvatore C. Trovato. Rome: Editrice "il Calamo," 1999. 45–55.
Analogy / classification / culture / ethnology / Italian / logic / society.

114. Brown, Warren S. (ed.). *Understanding Wisdom: Sources, Science & Society*. Philadelphia: Templeton Foundation Press, 2000. 445 pp.
African / Akan / anthropology / belief / Bemba / communication / Dangme / definition / education / epistemology / ethics / evangelization / feminism / folklore / function / Ga / Gikuyu / history / inculturation / Kaguru / literature / Malawi / marriage / Mossi / orality / paremiology / philosophy / religion / science / society / tradition / wisdom / women / Xhosa / Yoruba.

115. Brundage, Shelley Brown. *Comparison of Proverb Interpretations Provided by Non–Brain–Damaged Adults, Aphasic Adults, Right–Hemisphere–Damaged Adults, and Adults with Probable Dementia*. Diss. University of Minnesota, 1993. 121 pp.
Abstraction / aphasia / brain / dementia / disorder / informant / interpretation / proverbs test / psychiatry / psychology.

116. Brunvand, Jan Harold. "Folklore in the News (and, Incidentally, on the Net)." *Western Folklore*, 60, no. 1 (2001), 47–66.
American / folk speech / folklore / function / innovation / mass media / meaning / news / origin / politics / society.

117. Bruster, Douglas. "The Horn of Plenty – Cuckoldry and Capital in the Drama of the Age of Shakespeare." *Studies in English Literature 1500–1900*, 30, no. 2 (1990), 195–215.
Animal / cuckoldry / gender / literature / sex / William Shakespeare / "To wear the breeches" / "To be a cuckold."

118. Bühler, Karl. "Über Gedankenerinnerungen." *Archiv für die gesamte Psychologie*, 12 (1908), 24–92.

Analogy / German / intelligence / memorability / memory / performance / production / proverbs test / psychology.

119. Bühler, Karl. "Nachtrag. Antwort auf die von W. Wundt erhobenen Einwände gegen die Methode der Selbstbeobachtung an experimentell erzeugten Erlebnissen." *Archiv für die gesamte Psychologie*, 12 (1908), 93–123.
Analogy / cognition / German / intelligence / memorability / memory / performance / production / psychology / Wilhelm Wundt.

120. Buhofer, Annelies. *Der Spracherwerb von phraseologischen Wortverbindungen. Eine psycholinguistische Untersuchung an schweizerdeutschem Material*. Frauenfeld: Huber, 1980. 320 pp.
Acquisition / children / cognition / comprehension / dialect / function / German / language / meaning / metaphor / phraseologism / production / psycholinguistics / psychology / Swiss German / use.

121. Buhofer, Annelies. "Alltägliche Verstehens- und Erklärungsstrategien bei Phraseologismen." *Aktuelle Probleme der Phraseologie*. Eds. Harald Burger and Robert Zett. Bern: Peter Lang, 1987. 59–77.
Bible / children / comprehension / explanation / German / history / language / meaning / meta–linguistic / metaphor / psycholinguistics / strategy / Swiss German.

122. Burger, Harald. "Redensarten 'auf der Goldwaage'." *Deutsche Sprache: Geschichte und Gegenwart. Festschrift für Friedrich Maurer*. Eds. Hugo Moser, Heinz Rupp and Hugo Steger. Bern: Francke, 1978. 55–68.
Folklore / history / linguistics / philology / phraseologism / psychology / sociology.

123. Burger, Harald. "Phraseologie und Spracherwerb." *Akten des VI. Internationalen Germanisten–Kongresses (Basel 1980)*. Eds. Heinz Rupp and Hans–Gert Roloff. Bern: Peter Lang, 1980. II, 337–344.
Acquisition / children / competence / comprehension / context / development / discourse / German / performance / phraseology / production / psycholinguistics / speech act.

124. Burger, Harald. "Sprache als Spiegel ihrer Zeit: Synchronie und Diachronie in der Phraseologie." *Fremdsprache Deutsch*, no volume given, no. 15 (1996), 25–30.
    Culture / diachronic / etymology / history / language / phraseology / synchronic.

125. Burger, Harald. "Phraseologie im Kinder- und Jugendbuch." *Wortbildung und Phraseologie*. Eds. Rainer Wimmer and Franz–Josef Berens. Tübingen: Gunter Narr, 1997. 233–254.
    Acquisition / children / competence / cognition / context / function / German / literature / phraseologism.

126. Burger, Harald. "Idiom and Metaphor: Their Theory and Text." *Europhras 97: Phraseology and Paremiology*. Ed. Peter Ďurčo. Bratislava: Akadémia PZ, 1998. 30–36.
    Advertisement / context / idiom / mass media / metaphor / phraseologism.

127. Burger, Harald. *Phraseologie: Eine Einführung am Beispiel des Deutschen*. Berlin: Erich Schmidt, 1998. 224 pp.
    Classification / context / diachronic / dictionary / fixity / idiomaticity / mass media / metaphor / orality / phraseology / regionalism / semantics / terminology / variation.

128. Burger, Harald. "Problembereiche einer historischen Phraseologie." *Europhras 95: Europäische Phraseologie im Vergleich: Gemeinsames Erbe und kulturelle Vielfalt*. Ed. Wolfgang Eismann. Bochum: Norbert Brockmeyer, 1998. 79–108.
    Culture / diachronic / dictionary / etymology / history / idiomatization / origin / phraseology / psycholinguistics / variation.

129. Burger, Harald. "Dialektale Phraseologie – am Beispiel des Schweizerdeutschen." *Phraseologie in Raum und Zeit: Akten der 10. Tagung des Westfälischen Arbeitskreises "Phraseologie/Parömiologie" (Münster 2001)*. Eds. Elisabeth and Ilpo Tapani Piirainen. Baltmannsweiler: Schneider Verlag Hohengehren, 2002. 11–29.
    Dialect / empiricism / familiarity / frequency / German / linguistics / phraseography / phraseologism / phraseology / sociolinguistics / Swiss German.

130. Burger, Harald, Annelies Buhofer, and Ambros Sialm. *Handbuch der Phraseologie*. Berlin: Walter de Gruyter, 1982. 435 pp.

Children / classification / comprehension / context / diachronic / dialect / etymology / folklore / foreign language / form / German / history / language / linguistics / literature / philology / phraseology / pragmatics / psycholinguistics / semantics / society / speech act / structure / Swiss German / synchronic / variability.

131. Burgos, Luis Antonio. *Inter–Rater Reliability and the Use of Proverb Interpretation in the Detection of Disordered Thinking.* Diss. United States International University, 1985. 89 pp.
Bibliography / brain / cognition / disorder / interpretation / proverbs test / psychology / schizophrenia.

132. Burke, Kenneth. "Literature as Equipment for Living." In K. Burke. *The Philosophy of Literary Form. Studies in Symbolic Action.* Baton Rouge: Louisiana University Press, 1941. 253–262.
Attitude / contradiction / experience / function / life / literature / society / strategy / use.

133. Burkhart, Dagmar. "Das Sprichwort als Faktum der Kommunikationswissenschaft und der Semiotik." *Proverbium Paratum*, 2 (1981), 141–172.
Communication / context / function / logic / meaning / Grigorii L'vovich Permiakov / pragmatics / semiotics / speech act.

134. Burkhart, Dagmar. "Die semiotischen Dimensionen des russischen Sprichworts." *Beiträge zur russischen Volksdichtung.* Ed. Klaus–Dieter Seemann. Wiesbaden: Otto Harrassowitz, 1987. 13–37.
Content / definition / linguistics / national character / paremiology / Grigorii L'vovich Permiakov / poetics / Russian / semiotics / structure.

135. Burns, D.A. "A Potpourri of Parasites in Poetry and Proverbs." *British Medical Journal*, 303 (December 21–28, 1991), 1611–1614.
Animal / disease / health / medicine / parasite / poetry / science.

136. Burton, John D. *An Information Processing Analysis of the Interpretation of Proverbs by Grade Nine Students: An Exploratory Study.* Diss. University of Ottawa, 1989. 195 pp.
Cognition / comprehension / familiarity / informant / interpretation / proverbs test / psycholinguistics / psychology / student.

137. Bychowski, Gustav. "Certain Problems of Schizophrenia in the Light of Cerebral Pathology." *Journal of Nervous and Mental Diseases*, 81 (1935), 280–298.
Abstraction / brain / concreteness / disorder / metaphor / proverbs test / psychiatry / psychology / schizophrenia.

C

138. Cabassut, Erika. "Phraseme in der Kinderwelt." *Phraseme in Kontext und Kontrast.* Eds. Gertrud Gréciano and Annely Rothkegel. Bochum: Norbert Brockmeyer, 1997. 9–15.
Age / children / cognition / comprehension / education / foreign language / idiom / teaching.

139. Cacciari, Cristina. "The Place of Idioms in a Literal and Metaphorical World." *Idioms: Processing, Structure, and Interpretation.* Eds. Cristina Cacciari and Patrizia Tabossi. Hillsdale, New Jersey: Lawrence Erlbaum Associates, 1993. 27–55.
Children / figurativeness / idiom / literalness / meaning / metaphor / motivation.

140. Cacciari, Cristina. "Why Do We Speak Metaphorically? Reflections on the Functions of Metaphor in Discourse and Reasoning." In Albert N. Katz, Cristina Cacciari, Raymond W. Gibbs, and Mark Turner. *Figurative Language and Thought.* New York: Oxford University Press, 1998. 119–157.
Abstraction / cognition / discourse / emotion / experience / figurativeness / function / haptics / indirection / metaphor / perception / psycholinguistics / reasoning.

141. Cacciari, Cristina, and Sam Glucksberg. "Understanding Idiomatic Expressions: The Contribution of Word Meanings." *Understanding Word and Sentence.* Ed. Greg B. Simpson. Amsterdam: North–Holland, 1991. 217–240.
Comprehension / function / idiom / literalness / meaning / psycholinguistics / variability / word.

142. Cacciari, Cristina, and Sam Glucksberg. "Imagining Idiomatic Expressions: Literal or Figurative Meanings?" *Idioms: Structural and Psychological Perspectives.* Eds. Martin Everaert, Erik–Jan van der Linden, André Schenk, and Rob Schreuder. Hillsdale, New Jersey: Lawrence Erlbaum Associates, 1995. 43–56.
Comprehension / familiarity / figurativeness / idiom / imagery / literalness / meaning / psycholinguistics.

143. Cacciari, Cristina, and Patrizia Tabossi. *Idioms: Processing, Structure, and Interpretation.* Hillsdale, New Jersey: Lawrence Erlbaum Associates, 1993. 337 pp.
Acquisition / ambiguity / cognition / comprehension / figurativeness / idiom / idiomaticity / interpretation / linguistics / literal-

ness / meaning / metaphor / neurolinguistics / orality / psycholinguistics / psychology / semantics / structure.

144. Caeneghem, R. van. "De psychologie der Baluba in hun spreekwoorden over de ziekten." *Congo,* 21 (1940), 284–306.
African / Baluba / Congo / disease / medicine / psychology / society / superstition.

145. Cahoon, Delwin, and Ed M. Edmonds. "The Watched Pot Still Won't Boil: Expectancy as a Variable in Estimating the Passage of Time." *Bulletin of the Psychonomic Society,* 16, no. 2 (1980), 115–116.
English / expectancy / interpretation / psychology / time / "A watched pot never boils."

146. Calero Fernández, María Angeles. "El mundo de la prostitución en el refranero español." *Paremia,* 2 (1993), 245–256.
Anti–feminism / misogyny / prostitution / sex / Spanish / stereotype / women.

147. Camacho Villalba, Manuel Ángel. "Otros discriminados: 'El hombre y el oso, cuanto más feo más hermoso'." *Paremia,* 5 (1996), 207–213.
Behavior / content / family / life / occupation / society / worldview.

148. Cancro, Robert. "Abstraction on Proverbs in Process–Reactive Schizophrenia." *Journal of Consulting and Clinical Psychology,* 33 (1969), 267–270.
Abstraction / John D. Benjamin / proverbs test / psychiatry / psychology / schizophrenia / validity.

149. Cancro, Robert. "Clinical Prediction of Outcome in Schizophrenia." *Comprehensive Psychiatry,* 10 (1969), 349–354.
Abstraction / John D. Benjamin / prediction / proverbs test / psychiatry / psychology / schizophrenia / validity.

150. Carey, Timothy A. "'Spare the Rod and Spoil the Child': Is this a Sensible Justification for the Use of Punishment in Child Rearing?" *Child Abuse & Neglect,* 18, no. 12 (1994), 1005–1010.
Bible / children / development / punishment / variation / "Spare the rod and spoil the child."

151. Carnes, Pack. "The Fable and the Proverb: Intertexts and Reception." *Proverbium*, 8 (1991), 55–76. Also in *Wise Words: Essays on the Proverb*. Ed. Wolfgang Mieder. New York: Garland Publishing, 1994. 467–493.
Definition / fable / folklore / function / intertextuality / narrative / reception / semantics.

152. Caro Baroja, Julio. "El socioentrismo de los pueblos españoles." *Homenaje a Fritz Krüger*. Eds. Toribio M. Lucero and Alfredo Dornheim. Mendoza: Universidad Nacional de Cuyo, 1954. II, 457–485.
Blason populaire / culture / ethnicity / folklore / national character / society / Spanish / stereotype.

153. Carpenter, Bruce N., and Loren J. Chapman. "Premorbid Status in Schizophrenia and Abstract, Literal or Autistic Proverb Interpretation." *Journal of Abnormal Psychology*, 91 (1982), 151–156.
Abstraction / autism / brain / Donald R. Gorham / interpretation / literalness / proverbs test / psychiatry / psychology / schizophrenia.

154. Carson, Robert C. "Proverb Interpretation in Acutely Schizophrenic Patients." *Journal of Nervous and Mental Diseases*, 135 (1962), 556–564.
Abstraction / brain / disease / interpretation / literalness / metaphor / proverbs test / psychiatry / psychology / schizophrenia.

155. Carter, Marjorie L. *The Assessment of Thought Disorder in Psychotic Unipolar Depression*. Diss. Catholic University of America, 1983. 197 pp.
John D. Benjamin / depression / disorder / paranoia / proverbs test / psychiatry / psychology / schizophrenia.

156. Cascajero, Juan. "La descalificación de la mujer en la paremiología latina." *Paremia*, 10 (2001), 23–30.
Anti–feminism / gender / Latin / misogyny / society / stereotype / women / worldview.

157. Case, Tammy Jean Smith. *The Role of Literal and Figurative Familiarity in Proverb Comprehension*. Diss. University of Cincinnati, 1991. 109 pp.
Comprehension / context / familiarity / figurativeness / informant / literalness / proverbs test / psycholinguistics.

158. Castillo de Lucas, Antonio. "Selection de refranes de interés médico en la 'philosophia vulgar' de Juan de Mal Lara (siglo XVI)." *Revista de Etnografía* (Porto), 16 (1972), 45–52.
Content / culture / disease / folk medicine / health / history / Juan de Mal Lara / medicine / Spanish.

159. Castillo de Lucas, Antonio. "Refranes de aplicación médica en *El Quijote*." *Paremia*, 5 (1996), 43–48 (published lecture from the year 1943).
Miguel de Cervantes Saavedra / disease / health / literature / medicine / Spanish.

160. Cauvin, Jean. "Les proverbes comme expression privilégiée de la pensée imageante." *Afrique et langage*, no. 6 (1977), 5–34.
African / comprehension / image / mentality / metaphor / semantics / semiotics / symbol.

161. Cauvin, Jean. *Comprendre: Les Proverbes*. Issy les Moulineaux: Les Classiques Africains, 1981. 103 pp.
African / collection / comprehension / content / field research / image / linguistics / metaphor / philosophy / semantics / society / speech act / symbol / tradition.

162. Čermák, František. "Somatic Idioms Revisited." *Europhras 95: Europäische Phraseologie im Vergleich: Gemeinsames Erbe und kulturelle Vielfalt*. Ed. Wolfgang Eismann. Bochum: Norbert Brockmeyer, 1998. 109–119.
Anthropomorphism / Chinese / Czech / gesture / hand / idiom / semantics / semiotics / somatism / universality.

163. Čermák, František. "Substance of Idioms: Perennial Problems, Lack of Data or Theory?" *International Journal of Lexicography*, 14, no. 1 (2001), 1–20.
Dictionary / form / function / idiom / lexicography / linguistics / meaning / phraseologism.

164. Chafe, Wallace L. "Idiomaticity as an Anomaly in the Chomskyan Paradigm." *Foundations in Language*, 4 (1968), 109–127.
Noam Chomsky / frequency / idiomaticity / linguistics / semantics / structure.

165. Chambers, John Wayne. *Proverb Comprehension in Children*. Diss. University of Cincinnati, 1977. 107 pp.

Age / children / comprehension / development / linguistics / production / proverbs test / psycholinguistics / psychology.

166. Chang, Fu–Liang. "Cultural Patterns as Revealed in Chinese Proverbs." *Kentucky Foreign Language Quarterly*, 4 (1957), 171–176.
Attitude / Chinese / culture / semantics / society / tradition / worldview.

167. Chapman, Loren J., Richard Cameron, Joseph G. Cocke, and Thomas Pritchett. "Effects of Phenothiazine Withdrawal on Proverb Interpretation by Chronic Schizophrenics." *Journal of Abnormal Psychology*, 84 (1975), 24–29.
Drug / Donald R. Gorham / interpretation / proverbs test / psychiatry / psychology / schizophrenia.

168. Chapman, Sandra Bond, Hanna K. Ulatowska, L.R. Franklin, A.E. Shobe, J.L. Thompson, and D.D. McIntire. "Proverb Interpretation in Fluent Aphasia and Alzheimer's Disease: Implications beyond Abstract Thinking." *Aphasiology*, 11, nos. 4–5 (1997), 337–350.
Abstraction / Alzheimer's / aphasia / brain / cognition / disease / familiarity / interpretation / proverbs test / psychiatry / psychology.

169. Charteris–Black, Jonathan. "Proverbs in Communication." *Journal of Multilingual and Multicultural Development*, 16, no. 4 (1995), 259–268.
Behavior / communication / culture / discourse / figurativeness / foreign language / metaphor / semiotics / speech act / teaching.

170. Charteris–Black, Jonathan. "'Still Waters Run Deep' – Proverbs about Speech and Silence: A Cross–Linguistic Perspective." *De Proverbio: An Electronic Journal of International Proverb Studies*, 1, no. 2 (1995). 11 pp.
Culture / linguistics / metaphor / psycholinguistics / silence / speech / stereotype / women.

171. Chen, Shing–lung. "Die Redensart 'das Gesicht verlieren' in der chinesischen und deutschen Sprache." *Fu Jen Studies*, 28 (1995), 50–67.
Chinese / culture / diachronic / function / German / semantics / somatism / "Das Gesicht verlieren."

172. Cherubim, Dieter. "Mannomann!" *Muttersprache*, 106 (1996), 117–134.
Chauvinism / culture / euphemism / gender / lexicography / men / stereotype / "Mannomann."

173. Chetrit, Joseph. "Dire proverbial et dire personnel: Pour une socio–pragmatique du proverbe." *Tendances recentes en linguistique française et general.* Eds. Hava Bat–Zeev Shyldkrot and Lucien Kupferman. Amsterdam: John Benjamins, 1995. 121–133.
Discourse / pragmatics / semantics / society / speech act / strategy / structure.

174. Chiang, Alpha C. "Religion, Proverbs, and Economic Mentality." *American Journal of Economics*, 20 (1961), 253–264.
Chinese / economics / mentality / religion / slogan / tradition / worldview.

175. Chiche, Michèle. "Proverbes… et mon enfance embaume ma mémoire." *Cahiers de littérature orale*, no. 13 (1983), 159–161.
Children / didacticism / duel / elder / family / French / teaching / tradition.

176. Chico Ortega, Paloma. "Aplicaciones prácticas de la paremiología. Las pruebas de contenido proverbial como herramienta para el diagnóstico de desórdenes mentales." *Paremia*, 8 (1999), 149–154.
Abstraction / cognition / disorder / figurativeness / paremiology / psychiatry / psycholinguistics / psychology.

177. Chiesa, Alessandra Maria. *Translation and Preliminary Normative Data for the Biber Cognitive Estimation Scale and the California Proverbs Test with a Puerto Rican Population.* Diss. University of Connecticut, 1996. 90 pp.
Abstraction / cognition / foreign language / proverbs test / psycholinguistics / psychology / Puerto Rican / Spanish / translation.

178. Chindongo, Marion. "Grassroot Development Facilitators and Traditional Local Wisdom: The Case of Malawi." *Embracing the Baobab Tree: The African Proverb in the 21st Century.* Ed. Willem Saayman. Pretoria: University of South Africa, 1997. 125–135.

African / culture / development / knowledge / Malawi / tradition / wisdom.

179. Chlosta, Christoph, and Peter Grzybek. "Empirical and Folkloristic Paremiology: Two to Quarrel or to Tango?" *Proverbium*, 12 (1995), 67–85.
Empiricism / extension / familiarity / folklore / informant / paremiological minimum / paremiology / reduction / variant / variation.

180. Chlosta, Christoph, Peter Grzybek, and Undine Roos. "Wer kennt denn heute noch den Simrock? Ergebnisse einer empirischen Untersuchung zur Bekanntheit deutscher Sprichwörter in traditionellen Sammlungen." *Sprachbilder zwischen Theorie und Praxis.* Eds. Christoph Chlosta, Peter Grzybek, and Elisabeth Piirainen. Bochum: Norbert Brockmeyer, 1994. 31–60.
Collection / empiricism / familiarity / geography / German / informant / paremiological minimum / Karl Simrock.

181. Chlosta, Christoph, and Torsten Ostermann. "Suche *Apfel* finde *Stamm*: Überlegungen zur Nutzung des Internets in der Sprichwortforschung." *"Wer A sägt, muss auch B sägen": Beiträge zur Phraseologie und Sprichwortforschung aus dem Westfälischen Arbeitskreis.* Eds. Dietrich Hartmann and Jan Wirrer. Baltmannsweiler: Schneider Verlag Hohengehren, 2002. 39–56.
Computer / empiricism / internet / lexicography / structure / variant.

182. Chong–ho, Ch'oe. "The Concept of Language in the Traditional Korean Thought." *Korea Journal*, 25, no. 10 (1985), 18–32.
Attitude / discourse / Korean / language / orality / psycholinguistics / speech / tradition / value / worldview.

183. Choul, Jean–Claude. "Règle d'interprétation idiomatique." *Journal of the Atlantic Provinces Linguistic Association*, 4 (1982), 36–53.
Foreign language / French / idiom / idiomaticity / interpretation / linguistics / semantics.

184. Christen, Barbara. *Die Rolle der rechten Hirnhälfte im Verständnis von Phraseolexemen mit und ohne Kontext.* Bern: Peter Lang, 1995. 236 pp.

Brain / cognition / comprehension / context / empiricism / informant / metaphor / phraseologism / proverbs test / psycholinguistics / psychology.

185. Chung, Chong–wha. "Identity of the Underprivileged and Reality of Poverty as Reflected in Korean Proverbs." *Memoirs of the '96 Tokyo International Proverb Forum*. Ed. Yoshikatsu Kitamura. Tokyo: The Japan Society for Proverb Studies, 1996. 31–42.
Class / content / culture / Korean / life / poverty / society / value / worldview.

186. Clark, Michael S., Beverley A. Dodd, Sandra A. Lowe, and Coralie B. Hayley. "The Use of Proverb Interpretation in the Detection of Cognitive Deficits." *Australian Journal of Human Communication Disorders*, 22, no. 2 (1994), 1–8.
Brain / cognition / disorder / interpretation / proverbs test / psychiatry / psycholinguistics / psychology.

187. Clark, Robert F. "The Proverbs of Evaluation: Perspectives from CSA's [Community Services Administration] Experience." *Public Administration Review*, 39 (1979), 562–566.
Administration / evaluation / maxim / principle / society / work.

188. Clements, Ronald E. "The Sources of Wisdom." *Understanding Wisdom: Sources, Science & Society*. Ed. Warren S. Brown. Philadelphia: Templeton Foundation Press, 2000. 15–34.
Bible / experience / God / life / morality / Old Testament / religion / wisdom.

189. Colman, Peter L. *Bambara/Jula Proverbs as Mediators in the Communication of Meaning: Toward a Conceptual, Hermeneutical Model for Increasing Intercultural Understanding*. Diss. Trinity Evangelical Divinity School, 1999. 382 pp.
African / Bambara / communication / culture / ethnolinguistics / field research / function / hermeneutics / Jula / meaning / missiology / religion / value / tradition.

190. Colombo, Lucia. "The Comprehension of Ambiguous Idioms in Context." *Idioms: Processing, Structure, and Interpretation*. Eds. Cristina Cacciari and Patrizia Tabossi. Hillsdale, New Jersey: Lawrence Erlbaum Associates, 1993. 163–200.
Ambiguity / comprehension / context / familiarity / idiom / psycholinguistics / psychology.

191. Colston, Herbert L. *Actions Speak Louder than Words: Understanding Figurative Proverbs*. Diss. University of California at Santa Cruz, 1995. 130 pp.
Abstraction / comprehension / figurativeness / literalness / metaphor / proverbs test / psycholinguistics / psychology.

192. Colston, Herbert L. "Richard Honeck, *A Proverb in Mind: The Cognitive Science of Proverbial Wit and Wisdom* (1997) – book review." *Journal of Pragmatics*, 32, no. 5 (2000), 627–638.
Brain / cognition / comprehension / definition / figurativeness / literalness / metaphor / proverbs test / psycholinguistics / psychology / wisdom.

193. Combet, Louis. "Los refranes: origen, función y futuro." *Paremia*, 5 (1996), 11–22.
Jean Baudrillard / Simone de Beauvoir / culture / education / French / function / history / morality / origin / philosophy / politics / religion / Jean Paul Sartre.

194. Cometa, Michael Stephen. *Logical Operations in Semantic Development: A Piagetian Model of Metaphor and Proverb Comprehension*. Diss. State University of New York at Albany, 1976. 146 pp.
Age / children / comprehension / development / figurativeness / interpretation / logic / metaphor / Jean Piaget / psycholinguistics / psychology.

195. Conca, Maria. "La fraseologia en l'ensenyament de la llengua catalana." *Communicacions i ponències Segon Simposi del professorat de valencià de l'ensenyament mitjà i de l'educació secundària obligatòria*. Eds. Vicent Sala i Bou and Vicent Satorres. València: Conselleria d'Educació i Ciència, 1994. 113–124.
Catalan / communication / context / education / grammar / language / pedagogy / phraseology / poetics / psycholinguistics / structure / teaching.

196. Conca, Maria. "La competència fraseològica en l'aprenentage de llengües." *Actes del I. Congrés Internacional de Didactica de la Llengua*. No editor given. Valencia: Universitat de Valencia, 1999. 325–332.
Communication / competence / discourse / foreign language / phraseology / pragmatics / teaching.

197. Conley, Janet E. "The Role of Idiomatic Expressions in the Reading of Deaf Children." *American Annals of the Deaf*, 121, no. 4 (1976), 381– 385.
Children / comprehension / deafness / idiom / idioms test / psychology / reading.

198. Cottino, Amedeo. "'Wine Is the Blood of the Earth': Popular Drinking Culture Through Proverbs." *Addiction Research*, 2, no. 3 (1995), 251–257.
Addiction / alcoholism / culture / psychology / society / tradition / value.

199. Coulmas, Florian. *Routine im Gespräch. Zur pragmatischen Fundierung der Idiomatik.* Wiesbaden: Athenaion, 1981. 262 pp.
Context / definition / discourse / ethnolinguistics / function / idiomaticity / linguistics / meaning / phraseologism / pragmatics / speech act / variation.

200. Cox, Heinrich L. "Beobachtungen zur standardsprachlichen Sprichwort–Kompetenz deutschsprachiger Universitätsstudent(inn)en." *Volkskunde im Spannungsfeld zwischen Universität und Museum. Festschrift für Hinrich Siuts.* Eds. Ruth–E. Mohrmann, Volker Rodekamp and Dietmar Sauermann. Münster: Waxmann, 1997. 43–65.
Competence / context / empiricism / familiarity / gender / German / informant / language / student.

201. Cox, Heinrich L. "'Morgenstund hat Gold im Mund': Sprichwörter mit einer Zeit–Komponente im Sprichwortschatz Bonner Student(inn)en. Ein Versuch zur begrifflichen Kategorisierung der Signifikate." *Rheinisches Jahrbuch für Volkskunde*, 33 (1999–2000), 81–95.
Empiricism / familiarity / meaning / psycholinguistics / student / time.

202. Cram, David. "The Linguistic Status of the Proverb." *Cahiers de lexicologie*, 43 (1983), 53–71. Also in *Wise Words: Essays on the Proverb*. Ed. Wolfgang Mieder. New York: Garland Publishing, 1994. 73–97.
Competence / lexicology / linguistics / logic / performance / proverbiality / quotation / speech act / structure / syntax.

203. Cram, David. "A Note on the Logic of Proverbs." *Proverbium*, 2 (1985), 271–272.

Contradiction / linguistics / logic / pragmatics / proverbiality / universality.

204. Cram, David. "Argumentum ad lunam: On the Folk Fallacy and the Nature of the Proverb." *Proverbium*, 3 (1986), 9–31.
Context / contradiction / definition / fallacy / folklore / speech act / truth / validity.

205. Crede, Claudia, and Udo Lakemper. "Empirische Untersuchungen zur Phraseologie im Ruhrgebiet." *"Das geht auf keine Kuhhaut": Arbeitsfelder der Phraseologie. Akten des Westfälischen Arbeitskreises Phraseologie/Parömiologie 1996.* Ed. Dietrich Hartmann. Bochum: Norbert Brockmeyer, 1998. 81–108.
Atlas / dialect / empiricism / familiarity / geography / German / informant / linguistics / phraseology.

206. Crida Álvarez, Carlos Alberto. "La mujer en los refraneros español y griego. Estudio sociocultural a través de paremias contrastadas." *Paremia*, 10 (2001), 99–110.
Anti–feminism / culture / gender / Greek / society / sociolinguistics / Spanish / women.

207. Cronk, Brian C., Susan D. Lima, and Wendy A. Schweigert. "Idioms in Sentences: Effects of Frequency, Literalness, and Familiarity." *Journal of Psycholinguistic Research*, 22, no. 1 (1993), 59–82.
Context / familiarity / figurativeness / frequency / idiom / literalness / psycholinguistics / sentence.

208. Crumpton, Evelyn. "Persistence of Maladaptive Responses in Schizophrenia." *Journal of Abnormal and Social Psychology*, 66 (1963), 615–618.
Abstraction / brain / concreteness / Donald R. Gorham / proverbs test / psychiatry / psychology / schizophrenia.

209. Cuenca, Maria Josep. "L'estudi de les construccions idiomàtiques des de la lingüística cognitiva i l'anàlisi contrastiva." *El discurs prefabricat: Estudis de fraseologia teòrica i aplicada.* Eds. Vicent Salvador and Adolf Piquer. Castelló de la Plana: Publicacions de la Universitat Jaume I, 2000. 33–48.
Cognition / English / idiom / idiomaticity / linguistics / semantics / Spanish / structure.

210. Cunning, Sandra A. *The Roles of Context and Familiarity in the Development of Proverb Comprehension in Children*, M.A. Thesis Laurentian University of Sudbury (Canada), 1995. 155 pp.
Age / children / comprehension / context / development / familiarity / figurativeness / meaning / psycholinguistics / psychology.

211. Cunningham, Dellena M. *Factors Affecting the Use of Proverb Interpretation as a Measure of Abstract Ability.* Diss. Howard University, 1986. 83 pp.
Abstraction / cognition / culture / familiarity / Donald R. Gorham / interpretation / proverbs test / psycholinguistics / psychology / value / vocabulary / worldview.

212. Cunningham, Dellena M., Stanley E. Ridley, and Alfonso Campbell. "Relationship between Proverb Familiarity and Proverb Interpretation: Implications for Clinical Practice." *Psychological Reports*, 60 (1987), 895–898.
Familiarity / interpretation / proverbs test / psycholinguistics / psychology / schizophrenia / student / validity.

D

213. Dagher, Joseph. "Parémiologie et village libanais: Étude sociolinguistique de quelques matériaux." *Arabica*, 41, no. 1 (1994), 1–29.
Classification / content / Lebanese / life / mentality / paremiology / sociolinguistics / village / worldview.

214. Dalfovo, Albert T. "African Proverbs and African Philosophy." *Embracing the Baobab Tree: The African Proverb in the 21st Century*. Ed. Willem Saayman. Pretoria: University of South Africa, 1997. 37–48.
African / culture / experience / life / message / philosophy / worldview.

215. Daniel, Jack L. "Towards an Ethnography of Afroamerican Proverbial Usage." *Black Lines*, 2, no. 4 (1973), 3–12.
African American / culture / development / ethnicity / ethnography / rhetoric / socialization / speech act / use.

216. Daniel, Jack L., Geneva Smitherman–Donaldson, and Milford A. Jeremiah. "Makin' a Way outa no Way: The Proverb Tradition in the Black Experience." *Journal of Black Studies*, 17, no. 4 (1987), 482–508.
African American / communication / culture / development / duel / function / rhetoric / socialization / speech act / tradition / use.

217. Daniels, Karlheinz. "Geschlechtsspezifische Stereotypen im Sprichwort. Ein interdisziplinärer Problemaufriß." *Sprache und Literatur in Wissenschaft und Unterricht*, 16, no. 56 (1985), 18–25.
Anti–proverb / content / emancipation / gender / graffiti / misogyny / sex / slogan / stereotype / women.

218. Das, R.C. "Psychology of Manpower Management in Proverbs." *Folklore* (Calcutta), 19 (1978), 245–253.
Administration / behavior / content / management / profession / psychology / work.

219. David, Anton. *Die Erziehung nach dem Sprichwort. Winke und Fingerzeige zur Erziehung der Kinder*. Paderborn: Bonifacius, 1889. 108 pp.
Children / development / didacticism / education / family / pedagogy / psychology.

220. Davis, Natalie Zemon. "Proverbial Wisdom and Popular Errors." In N.Z. Davis. *Society and Culture in Early Modern France*. Stanford, California: Stanford University Press, 1975. 227–267 and 336–346 (footnotes). Also in French translation as "Sagesse proverbiale et erreurs populaires." In N.Z. Davis. *Les cultures du peuple. Rituels, savoirs et résistances au XVIe siècle*. Paris: Aubier, 1979. 366–425. And in German translation as "Spruchweisheiten und populäre Irrlehren." *Volkskultur. Zur Wiederentdeckung des vergessenen Alltags (16.–20. Jahrhundert)*. Eds. Richard van Dülmen and Norbert Schindler. Frankfurt am Main: Fischer, 1984. 78–116 and 394–406 (notes).
Collection / culture / fallacy / French / function / literature / society / wisdom.

221. Dawes, Elizabeth. "Vestiges des bestiaires dans la phraséologie française." *Florilegium*, 15 (1998), 125–143.
Animal / French / linguistics / metaphor / origin / phraseology / semantics.

222. Dawes, Elizabeth. "Idioms: Variants, Modifications and Errors." *LACUS Forum XXVI. The Lexicon*. Eds. Alan K. Melby and Arle R. Lommel. Fullerton, California: The Linguistic Association of Canada and the United States, 2000. 503–512.
Error / idiom / linguistics / modification / morphology / semantics / syntax / variant.

223. de Caro, Francis (Frank) A. "Talk is Cheap: The Nature of Speech According to American Proverbs." *Proverbium*, 4 (1987), 17–37.
American / attitude / behavior / culture / life / psycholinguistics / speech / worldview.

224. Demorest, Amy, Lisa Silberstein, Howard Gardner, and Ellen Winner. "Telling It as It Isn't: Children's Understanding of Figurative Language." *British Journal of Developmental Psychology*, 1 (1983), 121–134.
Age / children / cognition / comprehension / figurativeness / language / psycho–linguistics / psychology.

225. Detje, Frank. "Über Fehler bei der Handlungsorganisation und die Sprichwörter, die uns davor warnen." *Mit Leib und Seele: Psychologie in Bamberg*. Eds. Lothar Laux and Hans Reinecker. Bamberg: Otto–Friedrich–Universität, 1994. 58–66. (= *Forschungsforum: Berichte aus der Otto–Friedrich–*

. (= *Forschungsforum: Berichte aus der Otto–Friedrich–Universität*, no. 6 [1994], 58–66).
Action / behavior / didacticism / life / performance / pragmatism / psycholinguistics / psychology.

226. Detje, Frank. "Die Bedeutung der Sprichwörter für das menschliche Handeln." *Proverbium*, 12 (1995), 97–118.
Action / behavior / comprehension / didacticism / life / meaning / performance / pragmatism / psycholinguistics / psychology.

227. Detje, Frank. *Sprichwörter und Handeln: Eine psychologische Untersuchung.* Bern: Peter Lang, 1996. 262 pp.
Action / behavior / definition / empiricism / life / performance / pragmatism / psycholinguistics / psychology / society / sociolinguistics.

228. Deutschmann, Peter, and Herwig Höller. "Vom Tratsch im globalen Dorf: Internet und Phrase." *Europhras 95: Europäische Phraseologie im Vergleich: Gemeinsames Erbe und kulturelle Vielfalt.* Ed. Wolfgang Eismann. Bochum: Norbert Brockmeyer, 1998. 137–150.
Communication / computer / frequency / idiom / internet / literacy / orality / phraseologism.

229. Díaz Pérez, Juan Carlos. "Desarrollo de la competencia paremiológica en estudiantes de enseñanza primaria y secundaria." *Paremia*, 6 (1997), 189–194.
Competence / education / empiricism / familiarity / frequency / student.

230. Dion, Kenneth L. "Psychology and Proverbs: Folk Psychology Revisited." *Canadian Psychology/Psychologie Canadienne*, 31, no. 3 (1990), 209–211.
Behavior / folklore / prediction / psychology / socialization / worldview.

231. Djap, Djam Dung. *Proverbial Understanding and the Development of Part–Whole Reasoning Skills.* Diss. University of Toronto, 1984. 238 pp.
Age / children / cognition / comprehension / development / literalness / metaphor / proverbs test / psycholinguistics / psychology / reasoning.

232. Dobrovol'skij, Dmitrij. *Phraseologie als Objekt der Universalienlinguistik.* Leipzig: VEB Verlag Enzyklopädie, 1988. 264 pp.
Linguistics / phraseology / semantics / structure / style / universal / variability.

233. Dobrovol'skij, Dmitrij. "Phraseologie und sprachliches Weltbild (Vorarbeiten zum Thesaurus der deutschen Idiomatik)." *Deutsche Phraseologie in Sprachsystem und Sprachverwendung.* Ed. Csaba Földes. Wien: Edition Praesens, 1992. 171–195.
Cognition / dictionary / German / idiom / lexicography / linguistics / phraseography / phraseology / worldview.

234. Dobrovol'skij, Dmitrij. "Die Theorie der sprachlichen Weltansicht Wilhelm von Humboldts im Spiegel der deutschen Idiomatik." *Sprachbilder zwischen Theorie und Praxis.* Eds. Christoph Chlosta, Peter Grzybek, and Elisabeth Piirainen. Bochum: Norbert Brockmeyer, 1994. 61–88.
German / Wilhelm von Humboldt / idiom / language / linguistics / number / semiotics / worldview.

235. Dobrovol'skij, Dmitrij. "Idiome in Text und mentalem Lexikon." *Von der Einwortmetapher zur Satzmetapher.* Eds. Rupprecht S. Baur and Christoph Chlosta. Bochum: Norbert Brockmeyer, 1995. 55–81.
Context / discourse / empiricism / function / German / idiom / linguistics / mentality.

236. Dobrovol'skij, Dmitrij. *Kognitive Aspekte der Idiom-Semantik: Studien zum Thesaurus deutscher Idiome.* Tübingen: Gunter Narr, 1995. 272 pp.
Classification / cognition / definition / dictionary / German / idiom / lexicography / linguistics / phraseography / semantics / structure.

237. Dobrovol'skij, Dmitrij. *Idiome im mentalen Lexikon: Ziele und Methoden der kognitivbezogenen Phraseologieforschung.* Trier: Wissenschaftlicher Verlag Trier, 1997. 288 pp.
Cognition / competence / function / idiom / lexicography / linguistics / mentality / metaphor / phraseology / pragmatics / semantics / semiotics / symbolism / typology / variation.

238. Dobrovol'skij, Dmitrij. "On Cultural Components in the Semantic Structure of Idioms." *Europhras 97: Phraseology and*

Paremiology. Ed. Peter Ďurčo. Bratislava: Akadémia PZ, 1998. 55–61.
Culture / equivalent / idiom / mentality / semantics / structure / worldview.

239. Dobrovol'skij, Dmitrij. "Ist die Semantik von Idiomen nichtkompositionell?" *Sprachspiel und Bedeutung. Festschrift für Franz Hundsnurscher.* Eds. Susanne Beckmann, Peter–Paul König, and Georg Wolf. Tübingen: Max Niemeyer, 2000. 113–124.
Competence / comprehension / idiom / linguistics / semantics / structure.

240. Dobrovol'skij, Dmitrij. "Zur Motivation in der Idiomatik." *Phraseologiae Amor: Aspekte europäischer Phraseologie. Festschrift für Gertrud Gréciano.* Eds. Annelies Häcki Buhofer, Harald Burger, and Laurent Gautier. Baltmannsweiler: Schneider Verlag Hohengehren, 2001. 89–98.
Cognition / culture / idiom / linguistics / metaphor / motivation / semantics.

241. Dobrovol'skij, Dmitrij, and Elisabeth Piirainen. *Symbole in Sprache und Kultur: Studien zur Phraseologie aus kultursemiotischer Perspektive.* Bochum: Norbert Brockmeyer, 1996. 485 pp.
Animal / color / culture / empiricism / language / metaphor / number / phraseology / semiotics / symbol / typology.

242. Dobrovol'skij, Dmitrij, and Elisabeth Piirainen. "On Symbols: Cognitive and Cultural Aspects of Figurative Language." *Lexicology: An International Journal on the Structure of Vocabulary,* 4, no. 1 (1998), 1–34.
Cognition / culture / equivalent / figurativeness / language / semiotics / symbol.

243. Dobrovol'skij, Dmitrij, and Elisabeth Piirainen. "'Keep the Wolf from the Door': Animal Symbolism in Language and Culture." *Proverbium,* 16 (1999), 61–93. With 5 illustrations.
Animal / bear / culture / horse / language / semiotics / symbolism / wolf.

244. Doerr, Karin. "'To Each His Own' (*Jedem das Seine*): The (Mis-)Use of German Proverbs in Concentration Camps and Beyond." *Proverbium,* 17 (2000), 71–90. With 3 illustrations.

Anti–Semitism / concentration camp / German / iconography / manipulation / National Socialism / politics / slogan / "Arbeit macht frei" / "Jedem das Seine."

245. Dogbeh, Lucia Isabelle. "Mutter, Besitz und Retterin: Zum Frauenbild in Fon–Sprichwörtern." *Proverbium*, 17 (2000), 91–99.
African / anti–feminism / culture / Fon / mother / stereotype / women / worldview.

246. Dolník, Juraj. "Language Economy and Phraseology." *Europhras 97: Phraseology and Paremiology*. Ed. Peter Ďurčo. Bratislava: Akadémia PZ, 1998. 62–65.
Frequency / idiomaticity / language / linguistics / phraseology / pragmatics / relevance.

247. Dorfmueller, Mark A., and Richard P. Honeck. "Centrality and Generativity Within a Linguistic Family: Toward a Conceptual Base Theory of Groups." *Psychological Record*, 30, no. 1 (1980), 95–109.
Centrality / cognition / context / generativity / interpretation / linguistics / memory / performance / psycholinguistics / psychology.

248. Dorn, Paméla J. "Gender and Personhood: Turkish Jewish Proverbs and the Politics of Reputation." *Women's Studies International Forum*, 9 (1986), 295–301.
Behavior / culture / gender / Jewish / men / personhood / reputation / society / Turkish / women / worldview.

249. Dörner, Dietrich, and Frank Detje. "Denksprüche und Sprichwörter des Planens." *Ja, mach nur einen Plan. Pannen und Fehlschläge: Ursachen, Beispiele, Lösungen*. Eds. Stefan Strohschneider and Rüdiger von der Weth. 2nd ed. Bern: Hans Huber, 2002. 255–271.
Action / behavior / life / maxim / planning / pragmatism / psycholinguistics / psychology / worldview.

250. Douglas, Joan Delahanty, and Bettina Peel. "The Development of Metaphor and Proverb Translation in Children Grades 1 through 7." *Journal of Educational Research*, 73, no. 2 (1979), 116–119.
Age / children / comprehension / development / figurativeness / metaphor / psycholinguistics / psychology.

251. Doyle, Charles Clay. "On 'New' Proverbs and the Conservativeness of Proverb Dictionaries." *Proverbium*, 13 (1996), 69–84.
Canonization / collection / dictionary / folklore / lexicography / modernity / neologism / origin / paremiography.

252. Doyle, Charles Clay. "Seeing Through Colored Glasses." *Western Folklore*, 60, no. 1 (2001), 67–91.
Color / diachronic / folklore / meaning / origin / phraseologism / variant / "To see through colored glasses."

253. Drew, Paul, and Elizabeth Holt. "Complainable Matters: The Use of Idiomatic Expressions in Making Complaints." *Social Problems*, 35, no. 4 (1988), 398–417.
Complaint / conversation / function / idiom / legitimacy / society / summary / use.

254. Drew, Paul, and Elizabeth Holt. "Idiomatic Expressions and Their Role in the Organization of Topic Transition in Conversation." *Idioma: Structural and Psychological Perspectives*. Eds. Martin Everaert, Erik–Jan van der Linden, André Schenk, and Rob Schreuder. Hillsdale, New Jersey: Lawrence Erlbaum Associates, 1995. 117–132.
Conversation / function / idiom / psycholinguistics / speech act / summary / topic / transition.

255. Drillon, Marie–Laurence. "Phraseme des Erfolges: Ein molekularer Beschreibungsansatz." *Phraseme in Kontext und Kontrast*. Eds. Gertrud Gréciano and Annely Rothkegel. Bochum: Norbert Brockmeyer, 1997. 61–79.
Dictionary / discourse / function / lexicography / phraseologism / success.

256. Dua, Hans Raj. "Ethnography of Proverbs and Folk–Lore." *Folklore* (Calcutta), 16 (1974), 300–313.
Behavior / communication / culture / ethnography / folklore / Indian / society.

257. Dugbartey, Anthony T. "Utility of Proverb Interpretation Measures with Cardiac Transplant Candidates." *Perceptual and Motor Skills*, 87, no. 3 (1998), 883–889.
Comprehension / heart / interpretation / literalness / medicine / neuropsychology / proverbs test.

258. Duncan, Hugh D. "Literature as Equipment for Action: Burke's Dramatistic Conception." *The Sociology of Art and Literature.* Eds. Milton C. Albrecht, James H. Barnett and Mason Griff. New York: Praeger Publishers, 1970. 713–723.
Kenneth Burke / dream / Sigmund Freud / language / literature / repetition / society / strategy / symbol.

259. Dundes, Alan. "Here I Sit – A Study of American Latrinalia." *The Kroeber Anthropological Society Papers*, no volume given, no. 34 (1966), 91– 105.
American / anality / content / culture / eroticism / folklore / form / graffiti / latrinalia / psychoanalysis / scatology / sex / structure / worldview.

260. Dundes, Alan. "Thinking Ahead: A Folkloristic Reflection of the Future Orientation in American Worldview." *Anthropological Quarterly*, 42, no. 2 (1969), 53–72.
American / anthropology / content / culture / divination / folklore / future / metaphor / myth / orality / prediction / science fiction / worldview.

261. Dundes, Alan. "Folk Ideas as Units of Worldview." *Towards New Perspectives in Folklore.* Eds. Américo Paredes and Richard Bauman. Austin, Texas: University of Texas Press, 1972. 93–103.
American / anthropology / content / culture / folk idea / folk value / folklore / genre / opposition / stereotype / tradition / worldview.

262. Dundes, Alan. "Seeing is Believing." *Natural History*, no volume given, no. 5 (May 1972), 8–14 and 86. Also published in A. Dundes. *Interpreting Folklore.* Bloomington, Indiana: Indiana University Press, 1980. 86–92.
American / cognition / culture / haptics / metaphor / perception / science / society / vision / worldview / "Seeing is believing, but feeling is the truth."

263. Dundes, Alan. "Slurs International: Folk Comparisons of Ethnicity and National Character." *Southern Folklore Quarterly*, 39 (1975), 15–38. Also in *Wise Words: Essays on the Proverb.* Ed. Wolfgang Mieder. New York: Garland Publishing, 1994. 183–209.
Blason populaire / ethnicity / ethnocentrism / folklore / national character / phraseology / prejudice / slur / stereotype / worldview.

264. Dundes, Alan. "The Crowing Hen and the Easter Bunny: Male Chauvinism in American Folklore." *Folklore Today. A Festschrift for Richard M. Dorson.* Eds. Linda Dégh, Henry Glassie and Felix J. Oinas. Bloomington, Indiana: Indiana University Press, 1976. 123–138.
American / chauvinism / culture / folk belief / folklore / gender / men / misogyny / women / "Whistling maids and crowing hens, Never come to no good end."

265. Dundes, Alan. "Life is Like a Chicken Coop Ladder: A Study of German National Character through Folklore." *Journal of Psychoanalytical Anthropology*, 4 (1981), 265–364. With some changes published in book form as: *Life is Like a Chicken Coop Ladder. A Portrait of German Culture through Folklore*. New York: Columbia University Press, 1984. 174 pp. Also in German translation as *Sie mich auch! Das Hinter–Gründige in der deutschen Psyche*. Weinheim: Beltz, 1985. 152 pp.
Anality / anthropology / anti–Semitism / Heinrich Böll / culture / folklore / Sigmund Freud / German / Günter Grass / history / language / literature / Martin Luther / Wolfgang Amadeus Mozart / national character / psychoanalysis / psychology / scatology / society / sociology / worldview.

266. Dundes, Alan. "Towards a Metaphorical Reading of 'Break a Leg': A Note on Folklore of the Stage." *Western Folklore*, 53, no. 1 (1994), 85–89.
Belief / benediction / custom / folklore / meaning / metaphor / origin / superstition / theatre / tradition / "Break a leg."

267. Dundes, Alan. "Much Ado About 'Sweet Bugger All': Getting to the Bottom of a Puzzle in British Folk Speech." *Folklore* (London), 113, no. 1 (2002), 35–49.
American / attitude / diachronic / English / folk speech / folklore / homosexuality / idiom / language / meaning / origin / psychoanalysis / sex / slang / worldview / "Sweet bugger all."

268. Dundes, Lauren, Michael B. Streiff, and Alan Dundes. "'When You Hear Hoofbeats, Think Horses, Not Zebras': A Folk Medical Diagnostic Proverb." *Proverbium*, 16 (1999), 95–103.
American / context / diagnostics / folklore / function / meaning / medicine / origin / "When you hear hoofbeats, think horses, not zebras."

269. Dunn, Anthony Charles. *The Development and Measurement of Analogic Thought*. Diss. University of Utah, 1981. 95 pp.
Abstraction / age / analogy / children / comprehension / concreteness / development / interpretation / metaphor / proverbs test / psycholinguistics / psychology.

270. Ďurčo, Peter. "Das Wort als phraseologische Konstituente. Zur Beziehung der linguistischen und psycholinguistischen Standpunkte." *Europhras 92: Tendenzen der Phraseologieforschung*. Ed. Barbara Sandig. Bochum: Norbert Brockmeyer, 1994. 67–79.
Empiricism / informant / linguistics / phraseologism / psycholinguistics / semantics / semiotics / word.

271. Ďurčo, Peter. "Acquisition of Idioms and Mind Mapping." *Europhras 97: Phraseology and Paremiology*. Ed. Peter Ďurčo. Bratislava: Akadémia PZ, 1998. 70–76.
Acquisition / empiricism / familiarity / foreign language / German / idiom / mentality / mind mapping / psycholinguistics / Slovakian / student / teaching.

272. Ďurčo, Peter. "Experimentelle Untersuchung der individuellen Bedeutung von Phraseologismen." *Europhras 95: Europäische Phraseologie im Vergleich: Gemeinsames Erbe und kulturelle Vielfalt*. Ed. Wolfgang Eismann. Bochum: Norbert Brockmeyer, 1998. 165–174.
Competence / empiricism / linguistics / memory / phraseologism / psycholinguistics / semantics.

273. Ďurčo, Peter. "Bekanntheit, Häufigkeit und lexikographische Erfassung von Sprichwörtern. Zu parömiologischen Minima für DaF." *Phraseologiae Amor: Aspekte europäischer Phraseologie. Festschrift für Gertrud Gréciano*. Eds. Annelies Häcki Buhofer, Harald Burger, and Laurent Gautier. Baltmannsweiler: Schneider Verlag Hohengehren, 2001. 99–106.
Familiarity / foreign language / frequency / lexicography / linguistics / paremiological minimum / pedagogy / teaching.

274. Dzobo, N.K. "The Indigenous African Theory of Knowledge and Truth: Example of the Ewe and Akan of Ghana." *Phenomenology in Modern African Studies*. Ed. Sunday O. Anozie. Owerri: Conch Magazine, 1982. 85–102.
African / Akan / attitude / culture / epistemology / Ewe / knowledge / truth / wisdom.

E

275. Eble, Connie C. *Slang and Sociability: In–Group Language among College Students*. Chapel Hill, North Carolina: University of North Carolina Press, 1996. 228 pp.
Allusion / American / culture / definition / form / language / meaning / slang / sociability / sociology / student / use.

276. Edwards, Peter. "Idioms and Reading Comprehension." *Journal of Reading Behavior*, 6 (1974), 287–293.
Children / comprehension / education / figurativeness / idiom / reading / teaching.

277. Egblewogbe, Eustace Yawo. "Apparent Fallacies in Some Ewe Proverbs." *Papers in Ghanaian Linguistics*. Eds. Kofi K. Saah and M.E. Kropp Dakubu. Legon: Institute of African Studies, University of Ghana, 1987. 51–58.
African / Ewe / fallacy / meaning / metaphor / morality / truth / wisdom.

278. Egudu, R.N. "Social Values and Thought in Traditional Literature: The Case of the Igbo Proverb and Poetry." *Nigerian Libraries*, 8 (1972), 63–84.
African / ethics / Igbo / literature / poetry / pragmatism / society / tradition / value / worldview.

279. Eismann, Wolfgang. "Psycholinguistische Voraussetzungen einer Definition der phraseologischen Einheit (phE)." *Phraseologie und ihre Aufgaben*. Ed. Josip Matešić. Heidelberg: Julius Groos, 1983. 59–95.
Abstraction / cognition / comprehension / definition / familiarity / frequency / memory / metaphor / neurolinguistics / phraseologism / psycholinguistics / psychology / schizophrenia / structure.

280. Eismann, Wolfgang. "Nationales Stereotyp und sprachliches Klischee. Deutsche und Slawen im Lichte ihrer Phraseologie und Parömiologie." *Europhras 92: Tendenzen der Phraseologieforschung*. Ed. Barbara Sandig. Bochum: Norbert Brockmeyer, 1994. 81–107.
Blason populaire / classification / cliché / ethnicity / German / national character / National Socialism / Polish / prejudice / Slavic / slur / stereotype.

281. Eismann, Wolfgang. "Einige Probleme und Perspektiven der kontrastiven Phraseologie." *Europhras 95: Europäische Phraseologie im Vergleich: Gemeinsames Erbe und kulturelle Vielfalt.* Ed. Wolfgang Eismann. Bochum: Norbert Brockmeyer, 1998. 1–30.
Diachronic / dictionary / empiricism / equivalent / linguistics / literature / phraseography / phraseology / psycholinguistics / semiotics / stereotype / universality / worldview.

282. Eismann, Wolfgang. "Der barbarische wilde Moskowit: Kontinuität und Wandel eines Stereotyps." *Europäischer Völkerspiegel: Imagologisch–ethnographische Studien zu den Völkertafeln des frühen 18. Jahrhunderts.* Ed. Franz K. Stanzel. Heidelberg: Carl Winter, 1999. 283–297.
Blason populaire / ethnicity / Muscovite / national character / prejudice / Russian / slur / stereotype.

283. Eismann, Wolfgang. "Korrelation und Klassifikation in der Phraseologie." *Die grammatischen Korrelationen.* Ed. Branko Tošović. Graz: Institut für Slawistik der Karl–Franzens–Universität, 1999. 97–116.
Classification / correlation / definition / form / mentality / phraseology / psycholinguistics / structure.

284. Eismann, Wolfgang. "Die Phraseologie, Sigmund Freud und Valerij Mokienko." *Slovo vo vremeni i prostranstve. K 60-letiiu professora V.M. Mokienko.* Eds. G.A. Lilich, A.K. Birikh, and E.K. Nikolaeva. Sankt–Peterburg: Folio–Press, 2000. 242–265.
Dream / Sigmund Freud / function / interpretation / meaning / Valerij Mokienko / neurolinguistics / phraseology / psychoanalysis / psycholinguistics / psychology / symbol.

285. Eismann, Wolfgang. "Jenseits der Weltbild–Phraseologie. Vergessene psychoanalytische Perspektiven in der Phraseologie." *Phraseologiae Amor: Aspekte europäischer Phraseologie. Festschrift für Gertrud Gréciano.* Eds. Annelies Häcki Buhofer, Harald Burger, and Laurent Gautier. Baltmannsweiler: Schneider Verlag Hohengehren, 2001. 107–121.
Culture / linguistics / national character / phraseology / psychoanalysis / psycholinguistics / psychology / women / worldview.

286. Eismann, Wolfgang. "Gibt es phraseologische Weltbilder? Nationales und Universales in der Phraseologie." *"Wer A sägt,*

muss auch B sägen": Beiträge zur Phraseologie und Sprichwortforschung aus dem Westfälischen Arbeitskreis. Eds. Dietrich Hartmann and Jan Wirrer. Baltmannsweiler: Schneider Verlag Hohengehren, 2002. 107–126.
Behavior / mentality / national character / phraseology / psycholinguistics / universality / worldview.

287. El–Sa'aty, Hassan. *The Wisdom of Lebanon. A Sociological Analysis of Its Proverbs.* Beirut: Beirut Arab University, 1971. 76 pp.
Arabic / behavior / content / culture / Lebanese / life / society / sociology / wisdom.

288. Elmore, Clyde M., and Donald R. Gorham. "Measuring the Impairment of the Abstracting Function with the Proverbs Test." *Journal of Clinical Psychology,* 13 (1957), 263–266.
Abstraction / brain / Donald R. Gorham / proverbs test / psychiatry / psychology / schizophrenia.

289. Elmquist, Russell A. "English Medical Proverbs." *Modern Philology,* 32 (1934–1935), 75–84.
Content / disease / English / health / meaning / medicine / physiology / science.

290. Elster, Jon. "A Plea for Mechanisms." In J. Elster. *Alchemies of the Mind: Rationality and the Emotions.* Cambridge: Cambridge University Press, 1999. 1–47 (proverbial mechanisms, pp. 10–13).
Behavior / contradiction / culture / generalization / meaning / mechanism.

291. Elster, Jon. "Sagesse et science: Le rôle des proverbes dans la connaissance de l'homme et de la société." *L'acteur et ses raisons. Mélanges en l'honneur de Raymond Boudon.* Eds. Jean Baechler, François Chazel, and Ramine Kamrane. Paris: Presses Universitaires de France, 2000. 351–362.
Behavior / belief / contradiction / definition / epistemology / generalization / knowledge / meaning / mechanism / psychology / science / sociology / wisdom.

292. England, Juliana Elizabeth. *Abstract Responding to a Proverbs Test by LCVA, RCVA, and Control Subjects.* Diss. State University of New York at Buffalo, 1986. 159 pp.
Abstraction / brain / cognition / interpretation / proverbs test / psychology.

293. Englisch, Paul. "Skatologische Sprichwörter." In P. Englisch. *Das skatologische Element in Literatur, Kunst und Volksleben.* Stuttgart: Julius Büttmann, 1928. 129–137.
Culture / eroticism / German / humor / misogyny / obscenity / scatology / sex.

294. Enright, Dennis J. (ed.). *Fair of Speech: The Uses of Euphemism.* Oxford: Oxford University Press, 1985. 219 pp.
Antiquity / children / discourse / euphemism / history / law / mass media / politics / profession / religion / sex / speech act.

295. Eret, Dylan. *Capitalizing on Self–Fulfilling Prophecies: The Vernacular Dimensions of Anthony Robbins' Self–Empowerment Enterprise.* Diss. University of Pennsylvania, 2001. 278 pp. (proverbs, pp. 43–71).
American / behavior / belief / maxim / psychology / Anthony Robbins / self–help book / therapy / wisdom.

296. Eret, Dylan. "'The Past Does Not Equal the Future': Anthony Robbins Self–Help Maxims as Therapeutic Forms of Proverbial Rhetoric." *Proverbium,* 18 (2001), 77–103.
American / behavior / belief / maxim / psychology / rhetoric / Anthony Robbins / self–help book / therapy / wisdom.

297. Essien, Patrick Paul. *The Use of Annang Proverbs as Tools of Education in Nigeria.* Diss. Saint Louis University, 1978. 232 pp.
African / Annang / culture / education / form / function / society / student / tradition / wisdom.

298. Esteban, José. *Refranero contra Europa.* Madrid: Ollero & Ramos, 1996. 78 pp.
Blason populaire / ethnicity / European / national character / prejudice / slur / stereotype.

299. Estill, Robert B., and Susan Kemper. "Interpreting Idioms." *Journal of Psycholinguistic Research,* 11 (1982), 559–568.
Comprehension / figurativeness / idiom / interpretation / literalness / meaning / proverbs test / psycholinguistics / psychology / student.

300. Everaert, Martin, Erik–Jan van der Linden, André Schenk, and Rob Schreuder (eds.). *Idioms: Structural and Psychological Perspectives.* Hillsdale, New Jersey: Lawrence Erlbaum Associates, 1995. 329 pp.

Figurativeness / fixididty / idiom / idiomaticity / linguistics / literalness / modification / phraseology / psycholinguistics / psychology / semantics / speech act / structure / syntax / variation.

301. Ewert, D. Merrill. "Proverbs, Parables and Metaphors: Applying Freire's Concept of Codification to Africa." *Convergence: An International Journal of Adult Education*, 14, no. 1 (1981), 32–43.
African / codification / context / culture / education / Paulo Freire / metaphor / parable / pedagogy / society / worldview.

302. Eybel, John. "Proverbs for Transformation: Working with Caregivers." *Wajibu: Journal of Social and Religious Concern*, 14, no. 1 (1999), 20–23.
African / behavior / caregiver / health / life / medicine / Swahili / transformation.

303. Eye, Alexander von. "Zur Lokalisation des Bildhaftigkeitseffekts beim Lernen verbalen Materials." *Zeitschrift für experimentelle und angewandte Psychologie*, 36, no. 3 (1989), 368–385.
Abstraction / concreteness / imagery / metaphor / proverbs test / psychology / reproducibility / statistics.

F

304. Fahd, T. "Psychologie animale et comportement humain dans les proverbes arabes." *Revue de synthèse*, no volume given, nos. 61–62 (1971), 5–43; nos. 65–66 (1972), 46–63; nos. 75–76 (1974), 233–256; no. 92 (1976), 307–356.
Animal / anthropology / Arabic / behavior / experience / life / psychology / worldview.

305. Falcone, Giuseppe. "La condizione femminile nella società agrario–contadina della Calabria attraverso i proverbi." *Proverbi locuzioni modi di dire nel dominio linguistico italiano.* Ed. Salvatore C. Trovato. Rome: Editrice "il Calamo," 1999. 289–304.
Anti–feminism / content / culture / dialect / Italian / society / stereotype / women.

306. Falk, Paul. "Le couvre–chef comme symbole du mari trompé. Etude sur trois mots galloromans." *Studia Neophilologica*, 33 (1961), 39–68.
Adultery / cuckoldry / culture / etymology / men / sex / symbol / "To bestow (plant) a pair of horns upon one's husband."

307. Fanany, Ismet and Rebecca. "Truth and Falsehood in the Imagery of Minangkabau Proverbs." *Jurnal Pengajian Melayu*, 9 (1999), 84–99.
Authority / falsehood / imagery / Indonesian / Minangkabau / tradition / truth / value.

308. Feichtl, Nancy G. *Using Proverbs to Facilitate Metaphorical Language Comprehension: A Curriculum Study.* Diss. University of Maryland, 1988. 263 pp.
Children / comprehension / curriculum / figurativeness / language / metaphor / proverbs test / psycholinguistics / student / teaching.

309. Fellbaum, Christiane. "The Determiner in English Idioms." *Idioms: Processing, Structure, and Interpretation.* Eds. Cristina Cacciari and Patrizia Tabossi. Hillsdale, New Jersey: Lawrence Erlbaum Associates, 1993. 271–295.
Definition / English / idiom / idiomaticity / lexicology / structure / variability.

310. Fernández Poncela, Anna M. "'La doncella, la boca muda, los ojos bajos y lista la aguja': Roles de genero en el refranero

popular." *La seduccion de la escritura: Los discursos de la cultura hoy.* Eds. Rosaura Hernandez Monroy and Manuel F. Medina. Mexico City: no publisher given, 1997. 91–113.
Anti–feminism / culture / gender / prejudice / society / Spanish / stereotype / women / worldview.

311. Fernández Sánchez, Eulalio. "El refranero desde una perspectiva cognitiva: convencionalización de las estructuras paremiológicas." *Paremia,* 8 (1999), 179–182.
Cognition / conventionalization / culture / linguistics / motivation / psycholinguistics / structure.

312. Feyaerts, Kurt. "Die Metonymie als konzeptuelles Strukturprinzip: eine kognitiv–semantische Analyse deutscher Dummheitsausdrücke." *Wörter in Bildern – Bilder in Wörtern: Beiträge zur Phraseologie und Sprichwortforschung aus dem Westfälischen Arbeitskreis.* Eds. Rupprecht S. Baur, Christoph Chlosta, and Elisabeth Piirainen. Baltmannsweiler: Schneider Verlag Hohengehren, 1999. 139–176.
Cognition / German / metaphor / metonymy / psycholinguistics / semantics / structure / stupidity.

313. Finckh, J. "Zur Frage der Intelligenzprüfung." *Centralblatt für Nervenheilkunde und Psychiatrie,* 17 (1906), 945–957.
Brain / cognition / intelligence / interpretation / proverbs test / psycholinguistics / psychology / psychiatry.

314. Firment, Michael Joseph. *Interpretation Components as a Measure of Learning Proverb–Based Conceptual Categories.* Diss. University of Cincinnati, 1990. 107 pp.
Analogy / comprehension / empiricism / meaning / performance / proverbs test / psycholinguistics / psychology / student.

315. Firth, Raymond. "Proverbs in Native Life, with Special Reference to those of the Maori." *Folklore* (London), 38 (1927), 134–153 and 245–270.
Anthropology / culture / definition / ethics / folklore / function / life / Maori / morality / transmission.

316. Fischer, J.L., and Teigo Yoshida. "The Nature of Speech According to Japanese Proverbs." *Journal of American Folklore,* 81 (1968), 34–43.
Belief / culture / custom / folklore / Japanese / language / speech / value / worldview.

317. Fisher, Elissa L., June Miller White, and James H. Fisher. "Teaching Figurative Language." *Academic Therapy*, 19, no. 4 (1984), 403–407.
Communication / figurativeness / language / literalness / psycholinguistics / psychology / teaching.

318. Fisher, Judith Tougas. *Adolescent Proverb Comprehension: Racial Similarities and Differences*. Diss. Florida State University, 1981. 78 pp.
Adolescence / children / comprehension / education / ethnicity / proverbs test / psycholinguistics / psychology / race / student.

319. Fogel, Max L. "The Proverbs Test in the Appraisal of Cerebral Disease." *Journal of General Psychology*, 72 (1965), 269–275.
Brain / disease / Donald R. Gorham / interpretation / proverbs test / psychology / psychiatry.

320. Folly, Dennis Wilson (Sw. Anand Prahlad). "'Getting the Butter from the Duck': Proverbs and Proverbial Expressions in an Afro–American Family." *A Celebration of American Family Folklore: Tales and Traditions from the Smithsonian Collection*. Eds. Steven J. Zeitlin, Amy J. Kotkin, and Holly Cutting Baker. New York: Pantheon, 1982. 232–241 and 290–291 (notes).
African American / American / authority / context / didacticism / discourse / ethnicity / family / field research / folklore / function / interview / meaning / speech act.

321. Folly, Dennis Wilson (Sw. Anand Prahlad). *The Poetry of African–American Proverb Usage: A Speech Act Analysis*. Diss. University of California at Los Angeles, 1991. 246 pp.
Aesthetics / African American / American / context / ethnicity / folklore / function / meaning / motto / narrative / poetics / slave / speech act / use / variability.

322. Forster, E.M. "The Ivory Tower." *The Atlantic Monthly*, 163 (January–June, 1939), 51–58.
Escapism / intellectualism / literature / religion / Charles Augusta Sainte–Beuve / society / symbol / "The Ivory Tower."

323. Forster, Eleanor Anne. *The Proverb and the Superstition Defined*. Diss. University of Pennsylvania, 1968. 169 pp.
Behavior / belief / context / definition / folklore / meaning / metaphor / superstition.

324. Fort, Denise C. *Parent–Child Effects on Performance, Thinking, and Communication in Families of Normal and Schizophrenic Sons and the Role of Attention in Communication.* Diss. The Catholic University of America, 1983. 351 pp.
Bibliography / children / cognition / communication / family / interpretation / parents / performance / proverbs test / psychology / psychiatry / schizophrenia.

325. Foster, George M. "Character and Personal Relationships Seen through Proverbs in Tzintzuntzan, Mexico." *Journal of American Folklore*, 83 (1970), 304–317.
Anthropology / behavior / character / children / community / folklore / life / Mexican / relationship / society.

326. Foulon, Jordanka Hristova. "Quand le proverbe se fait mémoire." *Cahiers de littérature orale*, no volume given, no. 13 (1983), 67–90.
Culture / dissemination / experience / language / Macedonian / memory / orality.

327. Franck, Jakob F. "'Blut ist dicker als Wasser'." *Preussische Jahrbücher*, 85 (1896), 584–594.
Belief / German / history / law / meaning / origin / variant / "Blut ist dicker als Wasser."

328. Frankenberg, Hartwig. "Sprichwort und Slogan: Zur Funktion des Sprichwortes in der Konsumwerbung." *Perspektive: textextern. Akten des 14. Linguistischen Kolloquiums Bochum 1979.* Eds. Edda Weigand and Gerhard Tschauder. Tübingen: Max Niemeyer, 1980. II, 73–84.
Advertising / consumer / function / language / manipulation / slogan / structure / worldview.

329. Freides, David, Burton J. Fredenthal, James L. Grisell and Bertram D. Cohen. "Changes in Two Dimensions of Cognition During Adolescence." *Child Development*, 34 (1963), 1047–1055.
Abstraction / adolescence / children / cognition / interpretation / meaning / psycholinguistics / psychology.

330. Freidhof, Gerd. "Russisches Sprichwort, Bibelzitat und semantische Distraktion. Zur Struktur und Semantik einer Einfachen Form." *Slavistische Beiträge*, 242 (1988), 35–64.
Bible / linguistics / loan translation / proverbiality / quotation / Russian / semantics / simple form / structure / variation.

331. Friedman, Thomas, and Guy J. Manaster. "Internal–External Control: Studied through the Use of Proverbs." *Psychological Reports*, 33 (1973), 611–615.
Attitude / internality / progress / proverbs test / psycholinguistics / psychology / student / use.

332. Friese, Heinz–Gerhard. *Zeiterfahrung im Alltagsbewußtsein. Am Beispiel des deutschen Sprichworts der Neuzeit.* Frankfurt am Main: Materialis, 1984. 212 pp.
Culture / didacticism / experience / German / life / society / time / worldview.

333. Fuchs, Sonja. *Die haitischen Tiersprichwörter und ihre Herkunft: Kulturelles Erbe afrikanischer Sklaven und europäischer Siedler in einer ehemaligen französischen Kolonie.* Diss. University of Bamberg, 1994. 549 pp.
African / animal / culture / European / French / Haitian / history / multilingualism / origin / slave / society / variant.

334. Funk, Gabriela. "Condiciones para el uso de paremias contradictorias. Estudio empírico." *Paremia*, 6 (1997), 245–250.
Context / contradiction / empiricism / linguistics / meaning / metaphor / use.

335. Funk, Gabriela. "A Contrastive Analysis of the Textual and Social Function of Proverbs in German and Portuguese." *Europhras 97: Phraseology and Paremiology.* Ed. Peter Ďurčo. Bratislava: Akadémia PZ, 1998. 110–116.
Collection / competence / context / culture / function / German / mass media / native speaker / Portuguese / society.

336. Furnham, Adrian. "The Proverbial Truth: Contextually Reconciling and the Truthfulness of Antonymous Proverbs." *Journal of Language and Social Psychology*, 6 (1987), 49–55.
Antonym / attitude / context / contradiction / culture / language / proverbs test / psycholinguistics / psychology / society / sociolinguistics / student / truth.

G

337. Gabriel, Gottfried. "Logik und Rhetorik der Sprichwörter." *Texte, Bilder, Kontexte: Interdisziplinäre Beiträge zu Literatur, Kunst und Ästhetik der Neuzeit.* Eds. Ernst Rohmer, Werner Wilhelm Schnabel, and Gunther Witting. Heidelberg: Carl Winter, 2000. 181–198.
Definition / form / function / logic / rhetoric / structure / validity.

338. Galef, David. "How to Gain Proverbial Wisdom, or It Takes One to Know One." *Verbatim: The Language Quarterly*, 19, no. 4 (1993), 5–7.
Advice / context / contradiction / life / truth / value / wisdom.

339. Gallacher, Stuart A. "'Stuff a Cold and Starve a Fever'." *Bulletin of the History of Medicine*, 11 (1942), 576–581. Also in *The Wisdom of Many. Essays on the Proverb.* Eds. Wolfgang Mieder and Alan Dundes. New York: Garland Publishing, 1981. 211–217.
Advice / disease / form / health / history / meaning / medicine / physiology / "Stuff a cold and starve a fever."

340. Gamoka, Pambu Wa. "Pour une épreuve d'abstraction mentale utilisant les proverbes africains." *Ethnopsychologie*, 32, no. 4 (1977), 303–311.
Abstraction / African / brain / interpretation / proverbs test / psychology.

341. Ganapol'skaya, Elena V. "Joint Study of Phraseological and Paremiological Fields as Basis for the Analysis of Their Metaphorical and Semantic Structures." *Europhras 97: Phraseology and Paremiology.* Ed. Peter Ďurčo. Bratislava: Akadémia PZ, 1998. 117–124.
Content / labor / metaphor / paremiology / phraseology / semantics / structure / work / worldview.

342. García de Mesa, Rafael. "El componente escatológico y sexual en refranes y dichos populares en un ambiente rural." *Paremia*, 8 (1999), 215–218.
Content / culture / meaning / metaphor / scatology / sex / society.

343. Garrard, Timothy F. "Erotic Akan Goldweights." *African Arts*, 15, no. 2 (1982), 60–62, and 88 (notes). With 3 illustrations.

Art / African / Akan / eroticism / gold weight / iconography / sex.

344. Garrison, F.H. "Medical Proverbs, Aphorisms and Epigrams." *Bulletin of the New York Academy of Medicine*, 4 (1928), 979–1005.
Aphorism / disease / epigram / health / history / medicine / physiology / psychology.

345. Gáspárné, Zauner Eva. *Mondásválasztás. Pedagógiai–pszichológiai módszer a személyiség értékrendszerének megismerésére.* Budapest: Akadémiai Kiadó, 1978. 213 pp.
Attitude / bibliography / character / Hungarian / proverbs test / psycholinguistics / psychology / quotation / worldview.

346. Gergen, Kenneth J. "Proverbs, Pragmatics, and Prediction." *Canadian Psychology/Psychologie Canadienne*, 31, no. 3 (1990), 212–213.
Behavior / culture / pragmatics / prediction / psychology / society.

347. Gerrig, Richard J., and Alice F. Healy. "Dual Processes in Metaphor Understanding: Comprehension and Appreciation." *Journal of Experimental Psychology: Learning, Memory, and Cognition*, 9, no. 4 (1983), 667–675.
Appreciation / cognition / comprehension / context / figurativeness / metaphor / psycholinguistics / psychology.

348. Gestel, Frank van. "En Bloc Insertion [of Idioms]." *Idioms: Structural and Psychological Perspectives*. Eds. Martin Everaert, Erik–Jan van der Linden, André Schenk, and Rob Schreuder. Hillsdale, New Jersey: Lawrence Erlbaum Associates, 1995. 75–96.
Fixidity / idiom / idiomatization / insertion / linguistics / structure / syntax.

349. Gheorghe, Manuela. "PROVERB–ul: pentru vorbire?" *Proverbium Dacoromania*, 4 (1989), 22–25.
Belief / communication / culture / language / Rumanian / speech / value / worldview.

350. Gibbs, Raymond W. "Spilling the Beans on Understanding and Memory for Idioms in Conversation." *Memory & Cognition*, 8, no. 2 (1980), 149–156.

Cognition / comprehension / context / conversation / figurativeness / idiom / literalness / meaning / memory / metaphor / psycholinguistics / psychology.

351. Gibbs, Raymond W. "A Critical Examination of the Contribution of Literal Meaning to Understanding Nonliteral Discourse." *Text*, 2 (1982), 9–27.
Cognition / comprehension / discourse / figurativeness / idiom / interpretation / literalness / meaning / metaphor / proverbs test / psycholinguistics / psychology.

352. Gibbs, Raymond W. "On the Process of Understanding Idioms." *Journal of Psycholinguistic Research*, 14, no. 5 (1985), 465–472.
Cognition / comprehension / empiricism / figurativeness / idiom / literalness / meaning / psycholinguistics / psychology.

353. Gibbs, Raymond W. "Skating on Thin Ice: Literal Meaning and Understanding Idioms in Conversation." *Discourse Processes*, 9 (1986), 17–30.
Cognition / comprehension / conversation / discourse / figurativeness / idiom / literalness / meaning / psycholinguistics / psychology.

354. Gibbs, Raymond W. "Linguistic Factors in Children's Understanding of Idioms." *Journal of Child Language*, 14 (1987), 569–586.
Children / cognition / comprehension / context / figurativeness / idiom / language / literalness / meaning / psycholinguistics / psychology.

355. Gibbs, Raymond W. "Why Idioms Are Not Dead Metaphors." *Idioms: Processing, Structure, and Interpretation*. Eds. Cristina Cacciari and Patrizia Tabossi. Hillsdale, New Jersey: Lawrence Erlbaum Associates, 1993. 57–77.
Cognition / comprehension / figurativeness / idiom / idiomaticity / meaning / metaphor / psycholinguistics / psychology.

356. Gibbs, Raymond W. "Idiomaticity." In R.W. Gibbs. *The Poetics of the Mind: Figurative Thought, Language, and Understanding*. Cambridge: Cambridge University Press, 1994. 265–318.
Cognition / competence / comprehension / context / idiomaticity / metaphor / motivation / poetics / psycholinguistics / semantics / syntax.

357. Gibbs, Raymond W. "Idiomaticity and Human Cognition." *Idioms: Structural and Psychological Perspectives*. Eds. Martin Everaert, Erik–Jan van der Linden, André Schenk, and Rob Schreuder. Hillsdale, New Jersey: Lawrence Erlbaum Associates, 1995. 97–116.
Cognition / comprehension / idiomaticity / meaning / metonymy / motivation / psycholinguistics / psychology.

358. Gibbs, Raymond W. "The Fight Over Metaphor in Thought and Language." In Albert N. Katz, Cristina Cacciari, Raymond W. Gibbs, and Mark Turner. *Figurative Language and Thought*. New York: Oxford University Press, 1998. 88–118.
Cognition / comprehension / figurativeness / language / linguistics / literalness / metaphor / motivation / psycholinguistics / psychology / thought.

359. Gibbs, Raymond W., and Dinara Beitel. "What Proverb Understanding Reveals About How People Think." *Psychological Bulletin*, 118, no. 1 (1995), 133–154.
Abstraction / bibliography / cognition / comprehension / figurativeness / literalness / meaning / psycholinguistics / psychology.

360. Gibbs, Raymond W., Herbert L. Colston, and Michael D. Johnson. "Proverbs and the Metaphorical Mind." *Metaphor and Symbol*, 11, no. 3 (1996), 207–216.
Cognition / comprehension / figurativeness / literalness / metaphor / psycholinguistics / psychology.

361. Gibbs, Raymond W., Michael D. Johnson, and Herbert L. Colston. "How to Study Proverb Understanding." *Metaphor and Symbol*, 11, no. 3 (1996), 233–239.
Cognition / comprehension / context / culture / metaphor / psycholinguistics / psychology.

362. Gibbs, Raymond W., and Nandini P. Nayak. "Psycholinguistic Studies on the Syntactic Behavior of Idioms." *Cognitive Psychology*, 21, no. 1 (1989), 100–138.
Cognition / comprehension / figurativeness / flexibility / idiom / literalness / metaphor / psycholinguistics / psychology / semantics / syntax.

363. Gibbs, Raymond W., Nandini P. Nayak, and Cooper Cutting. "How to Kick the Bucket and Not Decompose: Analyzability

and Idiom Processing." *Journal of Memory and Language*, 28 (1989), 576–593.
Cognition / comprehension / figurativeness / idiom / literalness / psycholinguistics / psychology / semantics / syntax.

364. Gibbs, Raymond W., and Jennifer E. O'Brien. "Idioms and Mental Imagery: The Metaphorical Motivation for Idiomatic Meaning." *Cognition*, 36 (1990), 35–68.
Brain / cognition / comprehension / figurativeness / idiom / imagery / literalness / meaning / metaphor / motivation / psycholinguistics / psychology.

365. Gibian, George. "How Russian Proverbs Present the Russian National Character." *Russianness: Studies on a Nation's Identity. In Honor of Rufus Mathewson, 1918–1978*. Ed. Robert L. Belknap. Ann Arbor/ Michigan: Ardis, 1990. 38–43.
Content / culture / life / national character / prejudice / Russian / stereotype / value / worldview.

366. Gillstrom, Brenda Jean. *Abstract Thinking in Criminal Psychopaths [Using Gorham's Proverbs Test]*. Diss. University of British Columbia, 1995. 113 pp.
Abstraction / cognition / criminality / Donald R. Gorham / proverbs test / psychology / psychopathy.

367. Giovannini, Maureen J. "A Structural Analysis of Proverbs in a Sicilian Village." *American Ethnologist*, 5 (1978), 322–333.
Anthropology / context / contradiction / culture / ethnography / field research / mediator / redundancy / Sicilian / society / structure / worldview.

368. Glass, Arnold L. "The Comprehension of Idioms." *Journal of Psycholinguistic Research*, 12 (1983), 429–442.
Cognition / comprehension / figurativeness / idiom / interpretation / literalness / meaning / proverbs test / psycholinguistics / psychology.

369. Glenk, Eva M.F. "Die Frau im Spiegel deutscher Sprichwörter." *Pandaemonium Germanicum*, 3, no. 1 (1999), 241–257.
Anti–feminism / German / mentality / misogyny / prejudice / stereotype / society / women.

370. Glovňa, Juraj. "Set Expressions in Jokes." *Europhras 97: Phraseology and Paremiology*. Ed. Peter Ďurčo. Bratislava: Akadémia PZ, 1998. 140–143.

Context / discourse / idiom / incongruence / joke / pun / semantics / wordplay.

371. Glucksberg, Sam. "Idiom Meanings and Allusional Content." *Idioms: Processing, Structure, and Interpretation.* Eds. Cristina Cacciari and Patrizia Tabossi. Hillsdale, New Jersey: Lawrence Erlbaum Associates, 1993. 3–26.
   Allusion / comprehension / content / flexibility / function / idiom / knowledge / lexicology / linguistics / meaning / psycholinguistics / variant.

372. Glucksberg, Sam. *Understanding Figurative Language: From Metaphors to Idioms.* New York: Oxford University Press, 2001. 134 pp.
   Cognition / comprehension / figurativeness / idiom / language / linguistics / literalness / metaphor / philosophy / psycholinguistics / psychology.

373. Glucksberg, Sam, Mary Brown, and Matthew S. McGlone. "Conceptual Metaphors are not Automatically Accessed during Idiom Comprehension." *Memory & Cognition,* 21, no. 5 (1993), 711–719.
   Analogy / cognition / comprehension / idiom / knowledge / metaphor / motivation / psycholinguistics / psychology.

374. Glucksberg, Sam, Patricia Gildea, and Howard B. Bookin. "On Understanding Nonliteral Speech: Can People Ignore Metaphors?" *Journal of Verbal Learning and Verbal Behavior,* 21 (1982), 85–98.
   Cognition / comprehension / context / figurativeness / literalness / meaning / metaphor / psycholinguistics / psychology / truth.

375. Goitein, S.D. "The Present–Day Arabic Proverb as a Testimony to the Social History of the Middle East." In S.D. Goitein. *Studies in Islamic History and Institutions.* Leiden: E.J. Brill, 1966. 361–379.
   Arabic / collection / culture / history / Islam / language / society.

376. Gökhan, Asli. "Speaking as Reflected in Turkish Proverbs." *Communication and Culture: Language Performance, Technology, and Media. Selected Proceedings from the Sixth International Conference on Culture and Communications, Temple*

University, 1986. Ed. Sari Thomas. Norwood, New Jersey: Ablex Publishing Corporation, 1990, 92–100.
Culture / discourse / elder / society / speech / Turkish / value / worldview.

377. Gökhan, Asli. *What Have the Ancestors Said: An Ethnography of Speaking Proverbs in a Turkish Community.* Diss. University of Pittsburgh, 1992. 173 pp.
Context / culture / discourse / elder / ethnography / field research / function / informant / society / speech / speech act / Turkish / wisdom / worldview.

378. Goldman, Deborah Sue. *Metaphorical Processes in Borderline, Schizophrenic and Normal Adults.* Diss. Adelphi University, 1984. 235 pp.
Brain / cognition / comprehension / figurativeness / metaphor / proverbs test / psycholinguistics / psychology / schizophrenia.

379. Goldstein, Robert H., and Leonard F. Salzman. "Proverb Word Counts as a Measure of Overinclusiveness in Delusional Schizophrenics." *Journal of Abnormal Psychology,* 70 (1965), 244–245.
Brain / cognition / comprehension / Donald R. Gorham / metaphor / psychology / schizophrenia / word.

380. Goldstein, Robert H., and Leonard F. Salzman. "Cognitive Functioning in Acute and Remitted Psychiatric Patients." *Psychological Reports,* 21 (1967), 24–26.
Abstraction / brain / cognition / comprehension / Donald R. Gorham / psychiatry / psychology / schizophrenia.

381. Golopentia–Eretescu, Sanda. "Paradoxical Proverbs, Paradoxical Words." *Proverbium,* 17 (1971), 626–629.
Linguistics / logic / paradox / semantics / society / structure / truth / word.

382. Golopentia–Eretescu, Sanda. "Paradoxical Words." *Revue roumaine de linguistique,* 16 (1971), 85–89.
Linguistics / logic / paradox / semantics / society / structure / truth.

383. Golopentia–Eretescu, Sanda. "What is Right is Right." *Semiotica,* 5 (1972), 118–161.
Analyticity / linguistics / logic / semantics / structure / syntax / tautology / truth.

384. Golopentia–Eretescu, Sanda. "Language Transmission and Language Explication." *Semiotica*, 7 (1973), 142–153.
Interpretation / language / tautology / transmission / semantics / semiotics / sign.

385. Goodwin, Paul D., and Joseph W. Wenzel. "Proverbs and Practical Reasoning: A Study in Socio–Logic." *The Quarterly Journal of Speech*, 65 (1979), 289–302. Also in *The Wisdom of Many. Essays on the Proverb.* Eds. Wolfgang Mieder and Alan Dundes. New York: Garland Publishing, 1981. 140–160.
Argument / convention / fallacy / inference / life / logic / reasoning / strategy / wisdom.

386. Gorham, Donald R. "A Proverbs Test for Clinical and Experimental Use." *Psychological Reports*, 2 (1956), 1–12 (= Monograph Supplement 1).
Abstraction / brain / cognition / comprehension / proverbs test / psychiatry / psychology / reliability / schizophrenia.

387. Gorham, Donald R. *Clinical Manual for the Proverbs Test.* Louisville: Psychological Test Specialists, 1956; rpt. Missoula: Psychological Test Specialists, 1965.
Abstraction / brain / cognition / comprehension / proverbs test / psychiatry / psychology / schizophrenia / therapy.

388. Gorham, Donald R. "Use of the Proverbs Test for Differentiating Schizophrenics from Normals." *Journal of Consulting Psychology*, 20 (1956), 435–440.
Abstraction / brain / cognition / comprehension / proverbs test / psychiatry / psychology / schizophrenia.

389. Gorham, Donald R. "Verbal Abstraction in Psychiatric Illness: Assay of Impairment Utilizing Proverbs." *Journal of Mental Science*, 107 (1961), 52–59.
Abstraction / bibliography / brain / children / intelligence / lobotomy / proverbs test / psychiatry / psychology / schizophrenia.

390. Gorham, Donald R. "Additional Norms and Scoring Suggestions for the Proverbs Test." *Psychological Reports*, 13 (1963), 487–492.
Abstraction / brain / cognition / comprehension / proverbs test / psychiatry / psychology / schizophrenia.

391. Gossen, Gary H. "Chamula Tzotzil Proverbs: Neither Fish nor Fowl." *Meaning in Mayan Languages. Ethnolinguistic Studies.* Ed. Munro S. Edmonson. The Hague: Mouton, 1973. 205–233. Also in *Wise Words: Essays on the Proverb.* Ed. Wolfgang Mieder. New York: Garland Publishing, 1994. 351–392.
Anthropology / Chamula / context / ethnicity / ethnolinguistics / field research / Mayan / Native American / orality / society / tradition.

392. Graber, Robert Bates, and Gregory C. Richter. "The Capon Theory of the Cuckold's Horns: Confirmation or Conjecture?" *Journal of American Folklore*, 100 (1987), 58–63.
Adultery / castration / cuckoldry / culture / custom / etymology / folklore / men / sex / symbol / "To bestow (plant) a pair of horns upon one's husband."

393. Grabner, Elfriede. "'Rotes Haar und roter Bart…': Redensart, Volksmedizin und Volksmeinung um die Rothaarigen." *Schweizer Volkskunde*, 53 (1963), 10–20.
Belief / color / folklore / medicine / prejudice / red hair / slur / somatism / stereotype / superstition / symbol.

394. Grauberg, Walter. "Proverbs and Idioms: Mirrors of National Experience?" *Lexicographers and Their Works.* Ed. Gregory James. Exeter/ United Kingdom: University of Exeter Press, 1989. 94–99.
Antiquity / Bible / dissemination / Erasmus of Rotterdam / idiom / nationality / semantics / somatism / worldview.

395. Gréciano, Gertrud. "Zur Semantik der deutschen Idiomatik." *Zeitschrift für Germanistische Linguistik*, 10, no. 3 (1982), 295–316.
Amassment / analogy / antonymy / comprehension / definition / German / idiom / idiomaticity / linguistics / phraseologism / semantics / synonymy.

396. Gréciano, Gertrud. *Signification et dénotation en allemand. La sémantique des expressions idiomatiques.* Paris: Librairie Klincksieck, 1983. 469 pp.
Antonymy / bibliography / cliché / comprehension / context / definition / denotation / epistemology / function / German / idiom / idiomaticity / lexicology / linguistics / phraseologism / phraseology / pragmatics / semantics / signification / stereotype / structure / synonymy.

397. Gréciano, Gertrud. "Das Idiom als Superzeichen. Pragmatische Erkenntnisse und ihre Konsequenzen." *Aktuelle Probleme der Phraseologie.* Eds. Harald Burger and Robert Zett. Bern: Peter Lang, 1987. 41–57.
Function / idiom / linguistics / metaphor / pragmatics / psycholinguistics / semiotics / sign / speech act.

398. Gréciano, Gertrud. "Das hintergründige Idiom: Über die Implikatur als theoretischen Erklärungsansatz für den Idiomgebrauch." *Wortbildung und Phraseologie.* Eds. Rainer Wimmer and Franz–Josef Berens. Tübingen: Gunter Narr, 1997. 45–64.
Idiom / indirection / linguistics / motivation / phraseologism / semantics / use.

399. Gréciano, Gertrud. "Zur Festigung von Phraseologie: Eine Merkmalanalyse." *Nominationsforschung im Deutschen: Festschrift für Wolfgang Fleischer.* Eds. Irmhild Barz and Marianne Schröder. Frankfurt am Main: Peter Lang, 1997. 167–175.
Fixity / lexicology / phraseology / semiotics / stability / variability.

400. Gréciano, Gertrud. "Phraseologie und medizinisches Wissen." *Phraseologismen in Text und Kontext. Phrasemata I.* Ed. Jan Wirrer. Bielefeld: Aisthesis Verlag, 1998. 197–208.
Context / disease / health / knowledge / lexicology / medicine / phraseology.

401. Gréciano, Gertrud. "Zur Phraseologie des Herzens." *Europhras 97: Phraseology and Paremiology.* Ed. Peter Ďurčo. Bratislava: Akadémia PZ, 1998. 144–150.
Cardiology / health / heart / medicine / metaphor / phraseology / somatism.

402. Gréciano, Gertrud. "Sprach-, Text- und Weltwissen als Erklärung von Phraseologie." *Phraseme und typisierte Rede.* Eds. Nicole Fernandez Bravo, Irmtraud Behr, and Claire Rozier. Tübingen: Stauffenburg, 1999. 1–14.
Competence / context / knowledge / language / literacy / meaning / orality / phraseology / use.

403. Green, Georgia M. "Nonsense and Reference; Or, the Conversational Use of Proverbs." *Papers from the Eleventh Regional Meeting of the Chicago Linguistic Society.* Eds. Robin E.

Grossman, L. James San, and Timothy J. Vance. Chicago: Linguistic Society, 1975. 226–239.
Context / conversation / discourse / function / grammar / meaning / nonsense / speech act / syntax.

404. Green, Jonathon. *Words Apart: The Language of Prejudice.* London: Kyle Cathie, 1996. 383 pp.
Animal / blason populaire / color / language / name / national character / onomastics / prejudice / sex / slur / somatism / stereotype / word / worldview.

405. Green, Thomas, and William Pepicello. "The Proverb and Riddle as Folk Enthymemes." *Proverbium*, 3 (1986), 33–45.
Ambiguity / analogy / Aristotle / context / enthymeme / familiarity / knowledge / logic / message / philosophy / reasoning / rhetoric / riddle / sign / strategy.

406. Gregg, Alan, and George H. Frank. "An Exploration of the Thought Disorder in Schizophrenia through the Use of Proverbs." *Journal of General Psychology*, 77 (1967), 177–182.
Brain / cognition / comprehension / proverbs test / psychiatry / psychology / schizophrenia.

407. Grésillon, Almuth, and Dominique Maingueneau. "Polyphonie, proverbe et détournement, ou un proverbe peut en cacher un autre." *Langages*, 19, no. 73 (1984), 112–125.
Anti–proverb / literature / meaning / message / parody / polyphony / variation / wordplay.

408. Grober–Glück, Gerda. *Motive und Motivationen in Redensarten und Meinungen.* 2 vols. (text and maps). Marburg: N.G. Elwert, 1974 (= Atlas der deutschen Volkskunde, Beiheft 3). I, 561 pp.; II, 49 maps.
Belief / currency / custom / distribution / empiricism / familiarity / field research / folklore / geography / German / motivation / phraseologism / red hair / somatism / superstition / variant.

409. Grobler, Gerhardus M.M. "The Right to Be Understood: Interpreting the Proverb in an African Society." *Proverbium*, 11 (1994), 93–102.
African / communication / context / interpretation / linguistics / meaning / society / Sotho.

410. Grobler, Gerhardus M.M. "The Power of the Mind: Metaphor and Nature in the Construction of Northern Sotho Proverbs." *Proverbium*, 18 (2001), 143–148.
African / analogy / animal / experience / life / metaphor / nature / perception / Sotho / structure.

411. Gross, Ruth V. "Rich Text / Poor Text: A Kafkan Confusion." *Publications of the Modern Language Association*, 95 (1980), 168–182.
Context / German / implication / indirection / Franz Kafka / literature.

412. Grotjahn, Rüdiger, and Peter Grzybek. "Methodological Remarks on Statistical Analyses in Empirical Paremiology." *Proverbium*, 17 (2000), 121–132.
Age / education / empiricism / familiarity / informant / knowledge / paremiology / statistics.

413. Grotjahn, Rüdiger, Anna Tóthné Litovkina, Peter Grzybek, Christoph Chlosta, and Undine Roos. "Statistical Methods in the Study of Proverb Knowledge: An Analysis of the Knowledge of Proverbs in Contemporary Hungarian Culture (Tolna County)." *Semiotische Berichte*, 17, nos. 3–4 (1993), 275–308.
Culture / empiricism / familiarity / field research / Hungarian / informant / knowledge / society / statistics.

414. Gruttmann, Felicitas. *Ein Beitrag zur Kenntnis der Volksmedizin in Sprichwörtern, Redensarten und Heilsegen des englischen Volkes, mit besonderer Berücksichtigung der Zahnheilkunde.* Greifswald: L. Bamberg, 1939. 34 pp.
Dentistry / disease / English / health / incantation / medicine.

415. Grzybek, Peter. "How to Do Things with Some Proverbs: Zur Frage eines parömischen Minimums." *Semiotische Studien zum Sprichwort. Simple Forms Reconsidered I.* Eds. P. Grzybek and Wolfgang Eismann. Tübingen: Gunter Narr, 1984. 351–358.
Currency / empiricism / familiarity / foreign language / frequency / paremiological minimum / Grigorii L'vovich Permiakov / teaching.

416. Grzybek, Peter. "Überlegungen zur semiotischen Sprichwortforschung." *Semiotische Studien zum Sprichwort. Simple Forms Reconsidered I.* Eds. P. Grzybek and Wolfgang Eis-

mann. Tübingen: Gunter Narr, 1984. 215–249 (English version no. 418 below).
Bibliography / context / Alan Dundes / function / André Jolles / linguistics / paremiology / Grigorii L'vovich Permiakov / semantics / semiotics / sign / simple form / structure / Archer Taylor.

417. Grzybek, Peter. "Zur Psychosemiotik des Sprichworts." *Semiotische Studien zum Sprichwort. Simple Forms Reconsidered I*. Eds. P. Grzybek and Wolfgang Eismann. Tübingen: Gunter Narr, 1984. 409–432.
John D. Benjamin / bibliography / cognition / comprehension / Donald R. Gorham / Richard P. Honeck / intelligence / proverbs test / psychiatry / psycholinguistics / psychology / psychosemiotics / schizophrenia.

418. Grzybek, Peter. "Foundations of Semiotic Proverb Study." *Proverbium*, 4 (1987), 39–85. Also in *Wise Words: Essays on the Proverb*. Ed. Wolfgang Mieder. New York: Garland Publishing, 1994. 31–71 (English version of no. 416 above).
Bibliography / context / Alan Dundes / function / André Jolles / linguistics / paremiology / Grigorii L'vovich Permiakov / semantics / semiotics / sign / simple form / structure / Archer Taylor.

419. Grzybek, Peter. "Kulturelle Stereotype und stereotype Texte." *Natürlichkeit der Sprache und Kultur*. Ed. Walter A. Koch. Bochum: Norbert Brockmeyer, 1990. 300–327.
Culture / definition / ethnicity / function / national character / prejudice / slur / stereotype / structure.

420. Grzybek, Peter. "Einfache Formen der Literatur als Paradigma der Kultursemiotik." *Cultural Semiotics: Facts and Facets / Fakten und Facetten der Kultursemiotik*. Ed. P. Grzybek. Bochum: Norbert Brockmeyer, 1991. 45–61.
Context / culture / function / André Jolles / Grigorii L'vovich Permiakov / semantics / semiotics / sign / simple form / structure.

421. Grzybek, Peter. "Sinkendes Kulturgut? Eine empirische Pilotstudie zur Bekanntheit deutscher Sprichwörter." *Wirkendes Wort*, 41, no. 2 (1991), 239–264.
Age / collection / culture / empiricism / familiarity / German / informant / paremiological minimum / Grigorii L'vovich Pemiakov / statistics.

422. Grzybek, Peter. "Blason Populaire." *Simple Forms: An Encyclopaedia of Simple Text–Types in Lore and Literature.* Ed. Walter A. Koch. Bochum: Norbert Brockmeyer, 1994. 19–25.
Blason populaire / collection / definition / ethnicity / genre / national character / prejudice / simple form / slur / stereotype.

423. Grzybek, Peter. "Proverb." *Simple Forms: An Encyclopaedia of Simple Text–Types in Lore and Literature.* Ed. Walter A. Koch. Bochum: Norbert Brockmeyer, 1994. 227–241.
Classification / collection / definition / dissemination / genre / history / origin / paremiography / paremiology / semantics / semiotics / simple form / structure.

424. Grzybek, Peter. "Prolegomena zur Bildhaftigkeit von Sprichwörtern." *Im Zeichen–Raum: Festschrift für Karl Eimermacher.* Eds. Anne Hartmann and Christoph Veldhues. Dortmund: Projekt Verlag, 1998. 133–152.
Context / figurativeness / imagery / metaphor / motivation / Grigorii L'vovich Permiakov / semantics / semiotics.

425. Grzybek, Peter. "Sprichwort – Wahrwort? Die 'Weisheit auf der Gasse' zwischen Norm und Denkmodell." *Kultur und Lebenswelt als Zeichenphänomene.* Eds. Jeff Bernard and Gloria Withalm. Wien: ÖGS/ISSS, 1998. 127–148.
Culture / definition / didacticism / empiricism / familiarity / informant / mentality / norm / rule / semiotics / society / truth / use.

426. Grzybek, Peter (ed.). *Die Grammatik der sprichwörtlichen Weisheit von G.L. Permjakov. Mit einer Analyse allgemein bekannter deutscher Sprichwörter.* Baltmannsweiler: Schneider Verlag Hohengehren, 2000. 199 pp.
Christoph Chlosta / classification / content / German / grammar / logic / paremiology / Grigorii L'vovich Permiakov / semantics / semiotics / structure / universality / wisdom.

427. Grzybek, Peter, and Christoph Chlosta. "Grundlagen der empirischen Sprichwortforschung." *Proverbium,* 10 (1993), 89–128.
Empiricism / familiarity / frequency / informant / mass media / paremiography / paremiological minimum / paremiology / Grigorii L'vovich Permiakov / statistics / variant.

428. Gülich, Elisabeth, and Käthe Henke. "Sprachliche Routine in der Alltagskommunikation. Überlegungen zu 'pragmatischen

Idiomen' am Beispiel des Englischen und des Französischen." *Die Neueren Sprachen*, 78 (1979), 513–530.
Behavior / communication / English / foreign language / French / idiom / routine formula / society / teaching.

429. Günthner, Susanne. "'A Language with Taste': Uses of Proverbial Sayings in Intercultural Communication." *Text*, 11, no. 3 (1991), 399–418.
Chinese / communication / culture / discourse / ethics / foreign language / German / introductory formula / norm / teaching.

430. Günthner, Susanne. "Chinesische Redensarten in interkulturellen Kommunikationssituationen." *Neue Fragen der Linguistik. Akten des 25. Linguistischen Kolloquiums, Paderborn 1990.* Eds. Elisabeth Feldbusch, Reiner Pogarell, and Cornelia Weiß. Tübingen: Max Niemeyer, 1991. II, 117–124.
Chinese / communication / context / culture / discourse / German / metaphor / rhetoric.

431. Günthner, Susanne. "Qi zui ba she (aus sieben Mündern mit acht Zungen): Verständigungsprobleme in der interkulturellen Kommunikation." *Europhras 92: Tendenzen der Phraseologieforschung.* Ed. Barbara Sandig. Bochum: Norbert Brockmeyer, 1994. 259–279.
Chinese / communication / culture / discourse / German / idiom / knowledge / routine formula.

432. Gustafson, Jerri L., and Charles A. Waehler. "Assessing Concrete and Abstract Thinking With the Draw–a–Person Technique." *Journal of Personality Assessment*, 59, no. 3 (1992), 439–447.
Abstraction / brain / concreteness / Donald R. Gorham / literalness / proverbs test / psychology / schizophrenia.

433. Guthke, Karl S. *Letzte Worte. Variationen über ein Thema der Kulturgeschichte des Westens.* München: C.H. Beck, 1990. 225 pp. Also in English translation as *Last Words: Variations on a Theme in Cultural History.* Princeton/New Jersey: Princeton University Press, 1992. 250 pp.
Authenticity / bibliography / biography / collection / convention / culture / Johann Wolfgang von Goethe / history / last word / life / literature / parody / quotation / "Mehr Licht."

434. Guthke, Karl S. "'Gipsabgüsse von Leichenmasken'? Goethe und der Kult des letzten Worts." *Jahrbuch der deutschen Schillergesellschaft*, 35 (1991), 73–95.
Authenticity / biography / German / Johann Wolfgang von Goethe / last word / literature / parody / variant / "Mehr Licht."

435. Guthke, Karl S. "Letzte Worte in der Medien–Kultur." *Zeitschrift für Volkskunde*, 95, no. 2 (1999), 197–219.
Advertising / cartoon / comics / culture / film / German / Johann Wolfgang von Goethe / last word / literature / mass media / obituary / "Mehr Licht."

H

436. Haas, Heather Andrine. *The Factor Structure of Proverb Endorsement: Implications for Personality Psychology.* Diss. University of Minnesota, 1999. 162 pp.
Attitude / character / endorsement / familiarity / frequency / personality / proverbs test / psycholinguistics / psychology / structure.

437. Haas, Heather Andrine. "Extending the Search for Folk Personality Constructs: The Dimensionality of the Personality–Relevant Proverb Domain." *Journal of Personality and Social Psychology,* 82, no. 4 (2002), 594–609.
Attitude / behavior / belief / character / familiarity / personality / proverbs test / psycholinguistics / psychology / student.

438. Häcki Buhofer, Annelies. "Psycholinguistische Aspekte in der Bildhaftigkeit von Phraseologismen." *Europhras 88. Phraséologie Contrastive. Actes du Colloque International Klingenthal–Strasbourg, 12–16 mai 1988.* Ed. Gertrud Gréciano. Strasbourg: Université des Sciences Humaines, 1989. 165–175.
Association / cognition / comprehension / figurativeness / German / imagery / meaning / metaphor / phraseologism / psycholinguistics / "Da liegt der Hase im Pfeffer" / "Jdm. einen Bären aufbinden."

439. Häcki Buhofer, Annelies. "Zur phraseologischen Bedeutung: Ein methodologischer Beitrag zu empirischen Bedeutungsbeschreibungen." *Sémantique et représentations. Contributions aux journées de linguistique Strasbourg–Bale, 1993. (= Acta romanica basiliensa* 5). Eds. Georges Lüdi and Simona Pekarek. Basel: Romanisches Seminar der Universität, 1995. 3–22.
Cognition / comprehension / empiricism / informant / meaning / paraphrase / phraseologism.

440. Häcki Buhofer, Annelies. "Phraseologismen im Spracherwerb." *Wortbildung und Phraseologie.* Eds. Rainer Wimmer and Franz–Josef Berens. Tübingen: Gunter Narr, 1997. 209–232.
Acquisition / children / codification / context / empiricism / idiom / informant / linguistics / metaphor / phraseologism / proverbs test / psycholinguistics.

441. Häcki Buhofer, Annelies. "Kenntnis- und Gebrauchsunterschiede bei Phraseologismen des Binnendeutschen, des Schweizerhochdeutschen und des Schweizerdeutschen." *Europhras 95: Europäische Phraseologie im Vergleich: Gemeinsames Erbe und kulturelle Vielfalt.* Ed. Wolfgang Eismann. Bochum: Norbert Brockmeyer, 1998. 295–313.
Collection / dialect / empiricism / equivalent / familiarity / German / informant / linguistics / phraseologism / semantics / student / Swiss German / use.

442. Häcki Buhofer, Annelies. "Processes of Idiomaticity: Idioms with Unique Components." *Europhras 97: Phraseology and Paremiology.* Ed. Peter Ďurčo. Bratislava: Akadémia PZ, 1998. 162–169.
Diachronic / idiom / idiomaticity / lexicology / phraseologism / synchronic.

443. Häcki Buhofer, Annelies. "Psycholinguistik der Phraseologie." *Phraseme und typisierte Rede.* Eds. Nicole Fernandez Bravo, Irmtraud Behr, and Claire Rozier. Tübingen: Stauffenburg, 1999. 63–75. With minor changes also in *Studia Germanica Universitatis Vesprimiensis,* 3, no. 2 (1999), 199–216.
Cognition / comprehension / familiarity / metaphor / paraphrase / phraseology / production / psycholinguistics / semantics / variant / variation.

444. Häcki Buhofer, Annelies, and Harald Burger. "Gehören Redewendungen zum heutigen Deutsch?" *Fremdsprachen Lehren und Lernen,* 21 (1992), 11–32.
Empiricism / familiarity / foreign language / German / informant / phraseologism / society / student / teaching.

445. Häcki Buhofer, Annelies, and Harald Burger. "Phraseologismen im Urteil von Sprecherinnen und Sprechern." *Europhras 92: Tendenzen der Phraseologieforschung.* Ed. Barbara Sandig. Bochum: Norbert Brockmeyer, 1994. 1–33.
Comprehension / dialect / empiricism / familiarity / informant / phraseologism / psycholinguistics / semantics / sociolinguistics / use.

446. Hackmann, Bärbel. *Diätetik und Physiologie im Spiegel des Sprichwortes.* Diss. Münster, 1964. 129 pp.
Advice / anatomy / diet / food / health / medicine / physiology / somatism.

447. Hadlich, Hedwig. "Schizophrene Denkstörung." *Psychologische Forschung*, 15 (1931), 359–373.
Abstraction / brain / disorder / fable / psychology / psychiatry / schizophrenia.

448. Hager, Philip E. "A Psychological Concept Embedded in Some Idiomatic and Metaphorical Expressions." *American Speech*, 40 (1965), 300–301.
Alienation / "Doppelgänger" / figurativeness / idiom / isolation / metaphor / psychology.

449. Hale, Janice. "The Transmission of Cultural Values [Proverb Tradition] to Young African Children." *Young Children*, 46, no. 6 (September 1991), 7–15.
African / African American / children / culture / orality / pedagogy / socialization / teaching / tradition / transmission / value.

450. Hallsteinsdóttir, Erla. *Das Verstehen idiomatischer Phraseologismen in der Fremdsprache Deutsch.* Hamburg: Kovač, 2001. 332 pp.
Competence / comprehension / context / equivalent / foreign language / German / Icelandic / idiom / meaning / metaphor / motivation / phraseologism / strategy.

451. Hallsteinsdóttir, Erla. "Das Verstehen unbekannter Phraseologismen in der Fremdsprache Deutsch." *"Wer A sägt, muss auch B sägen": Beiträge zur Phraseologie und Sprichwortforschung aus dem Westfälischen Arbeitskreis.* Eds. Dietrich Hartmann and Jan Wirrer. Baltmannsweiler: Schneider Verlag Hohengehren, 2002. 161–176.
Comprehension / context / equivalent / foreign language / German / Icelandic / meaning / motivation / phraseologism / semantics / strategy.

452. Hammer, Françoise. "Schimpf und Schande. Beschimpfung aus phraseologischer Sicht. Ein deutsch–französischer Vergleich." *Phraseologie in Raum und Zeit: Akten der 10. Tagung des Westfälischen Arbeitskreises "Phraseologie/Parömiologie" (Münster 2001).* Eds. Elisabeth and Ilpo Tapani Piirainen. Baltmannsweiler: Schneider Verlag Hohengehren, 2002. 239–254.
Curse / cursing / French / German / metaphor / phraseologism / shame / speech act / worldview.

453. Hand, Wayland D. "A Dictionary of Words and Idioms Associated with Judas Iscariot." *University of California Publications in Modern Philology*, 24, no. 3 (1942), 289–356.
Bible / culture / Judas Iscariot / meaning / red hair / religion / superstition.

454. Hanfmann, Eugenia. "Analysis of the Thinking Disorder in a Case of Schizophrenia." *Archives of Neurology and Psychiatry*, 41 (1939), 568–579.
Abstraction / brain / concreteness / disorder / fable / psychiatry / psychology / schizophrenia.

455. Harkey, Sharon M., and Robert J. Howell. "The Effect of Anxiety as Measured by the Taylor MAS Scale on Performance and the Gorham Proverb Tests [sic]." *Journal of Clinical Psychology*, 19 (1963), 106–108.
Abstraction / anxiety / Donald R. Gorham / proverbs test / psychology.

456. Harnish, Robert M. "Communicating with Proverbs." *Communication & Cognition*, 26, nos. 3–4 (1993), 265–290.
Cognition / communication / fixidity / idiom / indirection / metaphor / sentence.

457. Harris, Richard J. "Comprehension of Metaphors: A Test of the Two–Stage Model." *Bulletin of the Psychonomic Society*, 8 (1976), 312–314.
Comprehension / figurativeness / literalness / meaning / metaphor / psycholinguistics / psychology / quotation.

458. Harrison, Arthur W., Michael S. Spelman, and Graham W. Mellsop. "The Proverbs Test for Disorder of Thinking in Schizophrenia and Mania." *Australian and New Zealand Journal of Psychiatry*, 8 (1972), 52–56.
Brain / disorder / interpretation / mania / proverbs test / psychiatry / psychology / schizophrenia.

459. Harrow, Martin, Linda S. Grossman, Marshall Silverstein, and Herbert Meltzer. "Thought Pathology in Manic and Schizophrenic Patients: Its Occurrence at Hospital Admission and Seven Weeks Later." *Archives of General Psychiatry*, 39 (1982), 665–671.
Brain / disorder / Donald R. Gorham / mania / pathology / proverbs test / psychiatry / psychology / schizophrenia.

460. Harrow, Martin, Ilene Lanin–Kettering, Mel Prosen, and Joan G. Miller. "Disordered Thinking in Schizophrenia: Intermingling and Loss of Set." *Schizophrenia Bulletin*, 9 (1983), 354–367.
Brain / communication / disorder / Donald R. Gorham / intermingling / interpretation / proverbs test / psychiatry / psychology / schizophrenia / speech.

461. Harrow, Martin, and Joan G. Miller. "Schizophrenic Thought Disorders and Impaired Perspective." *Journal of Abnormal Psychology*, 89 (1980), 717–727.
Behavior / brain / disorder / perspective / proverbs test / psycholinguistics / psychology / schizophrenia.

462. Hartmann, Dietrich. "Zur Phraseologiebildung mittels metonymischer Prozesse aus der Sicht der kognitiven Linguistik." *Wörter in Bildern – Bilder in Wörtern: Beiträge zur Phraseologie und Sprichwortforschung aus dem Westfälischen Arbeitskreis*. Eds. Rupprecht S. Baur, Christoph Chlosta, and Elisabeth Piirainen. Baltmannsweiler: Schneider Verlag Hohengehren, 1999. 219–238.
Cognition / linguistics / metonymy / origin / phraseologism / psycholinguistics.

463. Hasan–Rokem, Galit. "The Pragmatics of Proverbs: How the Proverb Gets Its Meaning." *Exceptional Language and Linguistics*. Eds. Loraine K. Obler and Lise Menn. New York: Academic Press, 1982. 169–173.
Context / discourse / function / Jewish / lexicology / meaning / narrative / poetics / pragmatics / structure / syntax.

464. Hasan–Rokem, Galit. "Proverbs as Inter–Ethnic Dialogue in Israel." *Jewish Folklore and Ethnology Review*, 14, nos. 1–2 (1992), 52–55.
Arabic / conflict / context / dialogue / discourse / ethnicity / folklore / function / identity / Israel / Jewish / mass media / newspaper.

465. Hasan–Rokem, Galit. "Georgian Proverbs of Dialogue and Dialogue of Proverbs in Israel." *Proverbium*, 11 (1994), 103–116.
Context / culture / dialogue / discourse / ethnicity / field research / genre / Georgian / Israel / Jewish / narrative / rhetoric.

466. Hattemer, K., and E.K. Scheuch. *Sprichwörter. Einstellung und Verwendung*. Düsseldorf: Intermarket. Gesellschaft für internationale Markt- und Meinungsforschung, 1983. 197 pp.
Advertisement / age / empiricism / familiarity / frequency / gender / German / informant / society / statistics / use / validity / value / worldview.

467. Haverkamp, Anselm (ed.). *Theorie der Metapher*. Darmstadt: Wissenschaftliche Buchgesellschaft, 1983. 502 pp. 2nd edition 1996. 512 pp.
Bibliography / figurativeness / imagery / metaphor / metonymy / rhetoric / semantics / structure.

468. Haynes, Rita M., Phillip J. Resnick, Kathleen C. Dougherty, and Stanley E. Althof. "Proverb Familiarity and the Mental Status Examination." *Bulletin of the Menninger Clinic*, 57, no. 4 (1993), 523–528.
Abstraction / African American / brain / cognition / concreteness / ethnicity / familiarity / mentality / proverbs test / psycholinguistics / psychology / student.

469. Healey, Joseph G., and Donald Sybertz. *Towards an African Narrative Theology*. Maryknoll, New York: Orbis Books, 1996. 400 pp. (proverbs throughout, but especially pp. 34–43 and pp. 173–178).
African / Bible / context / culture / function / narrative / orality / religion / theology / value / worldview.

470. Henne, Helmut. "Sprüchekultur." In H. Henne. *Jugend und ihre Sprache. Darstellung, Materialien, Kritik*. Berlin: Walter de Gruyter, 1986. 115–129.
Age / anti–proverb / culture / empiricism / function / German / graffiti / language / linguistics / phraseologism / slogan / structure / teenager / worldview / youth.

471. Hentig, Hans von. "Physiognomik im Sprichwort." *Archiv für Kriminologie*, 80 (1927), 136–144.
Appearance / character / criminology / physiognomy / red hair / somatism / stereotype / superstition.

472. Hernadi, Paul, and Francis Steen. "The Tropical Landscapes of Proverbia: A Crossdisciplinary Travelogue." *Style*, 33, no. 1 (1999), 1–20.
Advice / behavior / definition / experience / memorability / poetics / syntax.

473. Hernandez, José Luis Alonso. "Interprétation psychoanalytique de l'utilisation des parémies dans la littérature espagnole." *Richesse du proverbe*. Eds. François Suard and Claude Buridant. Lille: Université de Lille, 1984. II, 213–225.
Context / culture / dream / folklore / Sigmund Freud / interpretation / literature / psychoanalysis / semantics / Spanish / worldview.

474. Herron, William G. "Abstract Ability in the Process–Reactive Classification of Schizophrenia." *Journal of General Psychology*, 67 (1962), 147–154.
Abstraction / Donald R. Gorham / proverbs test / psychiatry / psychology / schizophrenia.

475. Hertler, Chris A., Loren J. Chapman, and Jean P. Chapman. "A Scoring Manual for Literalness in Proverb Interpretation." *Journal of Consulting and Clinical Psychology*, 46 (1978), 551–555.
Abstraction / concretenss / Donald R. Gorham / intelligence / interpretation / literalness / proverbs test / psychiatry / psychology / schizophrenia.

476. Hertzler, Joyce O. "The Social Wisdom of the Primitives with Special Reference to Their Proverbs." *Social Forces*, 11 (1933), 313–325.
African / attitude / culture / experience / life / morality / society / sociology / value / wisdom.

477. Hertzler, Joyce O. "On Golden Rules." *International Journal of Ethics*, 44 (1933–1934), 418–436.
Bible / ethics / "Golden Rule" / Thomas Hobbes / Immanuel Kant / philosophy / society / variant / "Do unto others as you would have them do unto you."

478. Herzenstiel, Werner R. *Erziehungserfahrung im deutschen Sprichwort. Theorie einer freiheitlichen Erziehungspraxis*. Saarbrücken: Universitäts- und Schulbuchverlag, 1973. 178 pp.
Currency / definition / didacticism / education / form / German / metaphor / pedagogy / transmission / variant.

479. Hessky, Regina. "Zum kognitiven Ansatz in der Phraseologie: 'Aufgewärmter Kohl' oder 'eine neue Platte'?" *Die Ordnung der Wörter: Kognitive und lexikalische Strukturen*. Ed. Gisela Harras. Berlin: Walter de Gruyter, 1995. 289–302.

Cognition / linguistics / mentality / metaphor / phraseology / psycholinguistics / semiotics / structure.

480. Hessky, Regina. "Phraseologie: Vermittlungsinstanz zwischen Sprachsystem und Sprachverwendung." *Phraseme und typisierte Rede.* Eds. Nicole Fernandez Bravo, Irmtraud Behr, and Claire Rozier. Tübingen: Stauffenburg, 1999. 233–241.
Classification / competence / context / dictionary / phraseology / semantics / semiotics / use.

481. Hessky, Regina. "Das euphemistische Idiom – eine Problemskizze." *Phraseologiae Amor: Aspekte europäischer Phraseologie. Festschrift für Gertrud Gréciano.* Eds. Annelies Häcki Buhofer, Harald Burger, and Laurent Gautier. Baltmannsweiler: Schneider Verlag Hohengehren, 2001. 163–175.
Dictionary / euphemism / idiom / language / lexicographgy / linguistics / style.

482. Hier, Daniel B., and Joni Kaplan. "Verbal Comprehension Deficits after Right Hemisphere Damage." *Applied Psycholinguistics*, 1 (1980), 279–294.
Abstraction / brain / comprehension / Donald R. Gorham / interpretation / proverbs test / psycholinguistics / psychology.

483. Higbee, Kenneth L., and Richard J. Millard. "Visual Imagery and Familiarity Ratings for 203 Sayings." *American Journal of Psychology*, 96 (1983), 211–222.
Familiarity / imagery / memory / proverbs test / psycholinguistics / psychology / student.

484. Hiiemäe, Mall, and Arvo Krikmann. "On Stability and Variation on Type and Genre Level." *Folklore Processed in Honour of Lauri Honko on His 60th Birthday, 6th March 1992.* Ed. Reimund Kvideland. Helsinki: Suomalaisen kirjallisuuden seura, 1992. 127–140.
Walter Anderson / cliché / Estonian / folklore / genre / memorability / narrative / semantics / stability / structure / tradition / variation.

485. Hill, Robert R., Jane E. Budnek, and Linda K. Wise. "An Empirical Validation of an English Proverb." *The Journal of Irreproducible Results*, 29, no. 4 (1984), 2–4.
Empiricism / English / health / medicine / nutrition / validation / "An apple a day keeps the doctor away."

486. Hodara, Anne. "Sur quelques représentations de l'autre dans les proverbes espagnols." *Les représentations de l'autre dans l'espace ibérique et ibéro–américain*. Ed. Augustin Redondo. Paris: Presses de la Sorbonne Nouvelle, 1993. II, 249–258.
Content / culture / life / profession / religion / society / Spanish / women.

487. Hoffman, Robert R. "Recent Psycholinguistic Research on Figurative Language." *Discourses in Reading and Linguistics*. Eds. Sheila J. White and Virginia Teller. New York: New York Academy of Sciences, 1984. 137–166.
Bibliography / communication / figurativeness / imagery / language / memory / metaphor / proverbs test / psycholinguistcs / psychology.

488. Hoffman, Robert R., and Richard P. Honeck. "The Bidirectionality of Judgments of Synonymy." *Journal of Psycholinguistic Research*, 5 (1976), 173–184.
Interpretation / meaning / psycholinguistics / psychology / structure / synonymy.

489. Hoffman, Robert R., and Richard P. Honeck. "Proverbs, Pragmatics, and the Ecology of Abstract Categories." *Cognition and Symbolic Structures: The Psychology of Metaphoric Transformation*. Ed. Robert E. Haskell. Norwood, New Jersey: Ablex Publishing, 1987. 121–140.
Abstraction / comprehension / definition / empiricism / familiarity / imagery / meaning / metaphor / pragmatics / psycholinguistics / psychology / student.

490. Hoffmann, Fernand. "We Are What We Speak: The Psychology of the Luxemburger Seen through the Evolution of His Dialect, Speech Habits, Proverbs and Sayings." *Lore and Language*, 2, no. 1 (1974), 5–14.
Language / linguistics / Luxemburgish / meaning / metaphor / psychology / Michel Rodange / worldview.

491. Hofmeister, Wernfried. "Zur Wirkung des Sprichworts im verbalen Kontext: Skizze eines Modells der transgeneralisierenden parömischen Sinnentfaltung." *Europhras 95: Europäische Phraseologie im Vergleich: Gemeinsames Erbe und kulturelle Vielfalt*. Ed. Wolfgang Eismann. Bochum: Norbert Brockmeyer, 1998. 327–335.
Communication / context / meaning / pragmatics / semantics / speech act.

492. Holden, Marjorie H., and Mimi Warshaw. "A Bird in the Hand and a Bird in the Bush: Using Proverbs to Teach Skills and Comprehension." *English Journal*, 74, no. 2 (1985), 63–67.
Comprehension / ethnography / fable / grammar / morality / pedagogy / rhetoric / teaching.

493. Holland, Norman N. "The 'Unconscious' of Literature: The Psychoanalytical Approach [to Robert Frost's 'Mending Wall']." *Contemporary Criticism*. Eds. Malcolm Bradbury and David Palmer. New York: St. Martin's Press, 1970. 131–153.
American / Robert Frost / literature / poetry / psychoanalysis / "Good fences make good neighbors."

494. Holm–Hadulla, R.–M., and F. Haug. "Die Interpretation von Sprichwörtern als klinische Methode zur Erfassung schizophrener Denk-, Sprach- und Symbolisationsstörungen." *Nervenarzt*, 55, no. 9 (1984), 496–503.
Abstraction / brain / disorder / interpretation / meaning / metaphor / proverbs test / psychiatry / psychology / schizophrenia / speech / thought.

495. Holtzman, Wayne H., Donald R. Gorham, and Louis J. Moran. "A Factor–Analytic Study of Schizophrenic Thought Processes." *Journal of Abnormal and Social Psychology*, 69 (1964), 355–364.
Autism / communication / Donald R. Gorham / proverbs test / psychiatry / psychology / schizophrenia / thought.

496. Holzapfel, Otto. "Stereotype Redensarten über 'den Deutschen' in der neueren dänischen Literatur." *Proverbium*, 4 (1987), 87–110.
Blason populaire / Danish / German / literature / national character / National Socialism / phraseologism / prejudice / slur / stereotype / worldview.

497. Honeck, Richard P. "Interpretive Versus Structural Effects on Semantic Memory." *Journal of Verbal Learning and Verbal Behavior*, 12 (1973), 448–455.
Acquisition / memory / psycholinguistics / psychology / repetition / semantics.

498. Honeck, Richard P. *A Proverb in Mind: The Cognitive Science of Proverbial Wit and Wisdom*. Mahwah, New Jersey: Lawrence Erlbaum Associates, 1997. 308 pp.

Brain / cognition / communication / comprehension / definition / figurativeness / indirection / intelligence / language / literalness / memory / metaphor / motivation / proverbs test / psycholinguistics / psychology / symbolism.

499. Honeck, Richard P., and Clare T. Kibler. "The Role of Imagery, Analogy, and Instantiation in Proverb Comprehension." *Journal of Psycholinguistic Research*, 13, no. 6 (1984), 393–414.
Acquisition / analogy / comprehension / imagery / instantiation / metaphor / proverbs test / psycholinguistics / psychology.

500. Honeck, Richard P., Paul Riechmann, and Robert R. Hoffman. "Semantic Memory for Metaphor: The Conceptual Base Hypothesis." *Memory and Cognition*, 3 (1975), 409–415.
Abstraction / acquisition / context / imagery / interpretation / memory / metaphor / psycholinguistics / psychology / semantics.

501. Honeck, Richard P., Brenda M. Sowry, and Katherine Voegtle. "Proverbial Understanding in a Pictorial Context." *Child Development*, 49 (1978), 327–331.
Children / comprehension / context / metaphor / picture / proverbs test / psycho–linguistics / psychology.

502. Honeck, Richard P., Judith Sugar, and Clare T. Kibler. "Stories, Categories and Figurative Meaning." *Poetics: International Review for the Theory of Literature*, 11, no. 2 (1982), 127–144.
Abstraction / comprehension / figurativeness / meaning / metaphor / proverbs test / psycholinguistics / psychology / story.

503. Honeck, Richard P., and Jon G. Temple. "Proverbs: The Extended Conceptual Base and Great Chain Metaphor Theories." *Metaphor and Symbolic Activity*, 9, no. 2 (1994), 85–112.
Comprehension / context / creativity / metaphor / pragmatics / psycholinguistcs / psychology.

504. Honeck, Richard P., and Jon G. Temple. "Proverbs and the Complete Mind." *Metaphor and Symbol*, 11, no. 3 (1996), 217–232.
Cognition / comprehension / context / culture / figurativeness / memory / metaphor / psycholinguistics / psychology.

505. Honeck, Richard P., Katherine Voegtle, Mark A. Dorfmueller, and Robert R. Hoffman. "Proverbs, Meaning, and Group Structure." *Cognition and Figurative Language*. Eds. Richard Honeck and Robert Hoffman. Hillsdale/New Jersey: Lawrence Erlbaum Associates, 1980. 127–161.
Abstraction / behavior / bibliography / children / comprehension / context / figurativeness / imagery / instantiation / intelligence / literalness / meaning / memory / metaphor / psycholinguistics / psychology / structure / synonymy.

506. Honeck, Richard P., Katherine Voegtle, and Brenda M. Sowry. "Figurative Understanding of Pictures and Sentences." *Journal of Psycholinguistic Research*, 10 (1981), 135–154.
Abstraction / analogy / comprehension / figurativeness / instantiation / literalness / meaning / picture / psycholinguistics / psychology / student.

507. Honeck, Richard P., and Jeffrey Welge. "Creation of Proverbial Wisdom in the Laboratory." *Journal of Psycholinguistic Research*, 26, no. 6 (1997), 605–629.
Cognition / creation / culture / currency / moral / origin / production / proverbiality / psycholinguistics / psychology / traditionality / wisdom.

508. Honeck, Richard P., Jeffrey Welge, and Jon G. Temple. "The Symmetry Control in Tests of the Standard Pragmatic Model: The Case of Proverb Comprehension." *Metaphor and Symbol*, 13, no. 4 (1998), 257–273.
Comprehension / context / figurativeness / literalness / meaning / metaphor / psycholinguistics / psychology.

509. Horowitz, Leonard M., and Leon Manelis. "Recognition and Cued Recall of Idioms and Phrases." *Journal of Experimental Psychology*, 100 (1973), 291–296.
Idiom / phraseologism / proverbs test / psycholinguistics / psychology / recall / recognition.

510. Hose, Susanne. "Sprüche klopfen: Sprichwörter im Kommunikationsprozess." *Proverbium*, 17 (2000), 133–150.
Communication / culture / definition / diachronic / didacticism / folklore / function / genre / paremiology / phraseologism / value / wisdom.

511. Huber, Hugo. "Das Tier als Metapher: Zur Frage der semiotischen Logik westafrikanischer Sprichwörter." *Festschrift zum*

60. Geburtstag von P. Anton Vorbichler. Ed. Inge Hofmann. Wien: Afro–Pub., 1981. II, 85–126 (= *Beiträge zur Afrikanistik,* 12 [1981], 85–126).
African / animal / behavior / culture / field research / Krobo / logic / metaphor / semiotics / worldview.

512. Hudson, Catherine. "Traditional Proverbs as Perceived by Children from an Urban Environment." *Journal of the Folklore Society of Greater Washington, D.C.*, 3 (1972), 17–24.
Children / comprehension / folklore / perception / society / tradition / variant.

I

513. Iniobong Udoidem, Sylvanus. "The Epistemological Significance of Proverbs: An Africa[n] Perspective." *Présence africaine*, no. 132 (1984), 126–136.
African / communication / culture / epistemology / Ibibio / knowledge / memory / Nigerian / philosophy / worldview.

514. Irujo, Suzanne. *The Effects of Transfer on the Acquisition of Idioms in a Second Language*. Diss. Boston University, 1984. 209 pp.
Acquisition / competence / comprehension / English / equivalent / foreign language / idiom / informant / Spanish / teaching.

515. Irujo, Suzanne. "'A Piece of Cake': Learning and Teaching Idioms." *ELT [English Language Teaching] Journal*, 40, no. 3 (1986), 236–242.
Acquisition / competence / comprehension / foreign language / idiom / teaching.

516. Irujo, Suzanne. "'Don't Put Your Leg in Your Mouth': Transfer in the Acquisition of Idioms in a Second Language." *TESOL [Teachers of English to Speakers of Other Languages] Quarterly*, 20, no. 2 (1986), 287–304.
Acquisition / comprehension / English / foreign language / frequency / idiom / informant / Spanish / teaching.

517. Israelite, Neita, Patrick Schloss, and Maureen Smith. "Teaching Proverb Use through a Modified Table Game." *The Volta Review*, 88, no. 4 (1986), 195–207.
Comprehension / game / hearing–impaired / meaning / "Monopoly" / student / teaching.

J

518. Jackendoff, Ray. "The Boundaries of the Lexicon [Regarding Idioms and Fixed Expressions]." *Idioms: Structural and Psychological Perspectives*. Eds. Martin Everaert, Erik–Jan van der Linden, André Schenk, and Rob Schreuder. Hillsdale, New Jersey: Lawrence Erlbaum Associates, 1995. 133–165.
Fixidity / idiom / lexicology / linguistics / modularity / phraseologism / syntax.

519. Jackson–Lowman, Huberta. "Using Afrikan [*sic*] Proverbs to Provide for Afrikan–American Parental Values." *Language, Rhythm, and Sound: Black Popular Cultures into the Twenty–First Century*. Eds. Joseph K. Adjaye and Adrianne R. Andrews. Pittsburgh, Pennsylvania: University of Pittsburgh Press, 1997. 74–89.
African / African American / didacticism / ideology / morality / parents / value.

520. Jacob, Theodore. "Verbal Activity of Middle- and Lower–Class Parents when Teaching Their Child." *Psychological Reports*, 40 (1977), 575–578.
Children / class / parents / psycholinguistics / psychology / society / sociolinguistics / teaching.

521. Jacobson, Arland D. "Proverbs and Social Control: A New Paradigm for Wisdom Studies." *Gnosticism & the Early Christian World*. Eds. James E. Goehring, Charles W. Hedrick, Jack T. Sanders, and Hans Dieter Betz. Sonoma, California: Polebridge Press, 1990. 75–88.
Bible / collection / didacticism / function / morality / society / sociolinguistics / value / wisdom.

522. Jansen, William Hugh. "A Culture's Stereotypes and Their Expression in Folk Clichés." *Southwestern Journal of Anthropology*, 13 (1957), 184–200.
Anthropology / cliché / folklore / stereotype / Turkish / wisdom / worldview.

523. Januschek, Franz. "Redensarten und Sprüche der 'Jugendsprache': Was bedeuten sie wirklich?" *Sprachwissenschaft und Volkskunde. Perspektiven einer kulturanalytischen Sprachbetrachtung*. Eds. Herbert E. Brekle and Utz Maas. Opladen: Westdeutscher Verlag, 1986. 90–102.

Age / creativity / culture / language / meaning / metaphor / modernity / neologism / phraseologism / variant / variation / youth.

524. Jarosinska, E. "Deutsche und niederländische Phraseologismen mit Tierbezeichnungen zur Charakterisierung von menschlichen Eigenschaften." *Neerlandica Wratislaviensia* (= *Acta universitatis wratislaviensis*, no. 1299), 5 (1991), 249–258.
Animal / behavior / character / content / culture / Dutch / equivalent / German / phraseologism.

525. Jason, Heda. "Proverbs in Society: The Problem of Meaning and Function." *Proverbium*, 17 (1971), 617–623. Also in H. Jason. *Studies in Jewish Ethnopoetry*. Taipei: Chinese Association for Folklore, 1975. 178–191. A much shortened Russian summary appeared in *Paremiologicheskii Sbornik*. Ed. Grigorii L'vovich Permiakov. Moskva: "Nauka", 1978. 239–240.
Communication / context / culture / folklore / function / Jewish / meaning / message / society.

526. Jayne, Edward. "Up Against the 'Mending Wall': The Psychoanalysis of a Poem by Frost." *College English*, 34 (1973), 934–957.
American / Robert Frost / literature / poetry / psychoanalysis / "Good fences make good neighbors."

527. Jhering, Herbert. "Die kleinen Redensarten." *Berlinger Börsen–Courier*, no. 243 (May 27, 1932). Also in *Herbert Jhering. Der Kampf ums Theater und andere Streitschriften 1918 bis 1933*. Ed. Ludwig Hoffmann. Berlin: Henschelverlag, 1974. 58–64. Reprinted also in Wolfgang Mieder. *Deutsche Sprichwörter und Redensarten*. Stuttgart: Reclam, 1979. 134–140.
Attitude / culture / defeatism / German / National Socialism / society / worldview.

528. Johnston, Robert K. "It Takes Wisdom to Use Wisdom Wisely." *Understanding Wisdom: Sources, Science & Society*. Ed. Warren S. Brown. Philadelphia: Templeton Foundation Press, 2000. 135–150.
Bible / function / history / life / Abraham Lincoln / Wolfgang Mieder / politics / society / use / wisdom / "A house divided against itself cannot stand."

529. Jurika, Daina. "Teenagers' Sayings: A Rhetorical Device in the Family?" *The Family as the Tradition Carrier. Proceedings of the Nordic–Baltic–Finno–Ugric Conference.* Eds. Ingrid Rüütel and Kristin Kuutma. Tallinn: Institute of the Estonian Language, 1996. 56–63.
Age / communication / family / Latvian / modernity / modification / neologism / rhetoric / teenager / worldview / youth.

530. Jurjevich, R.M. "Intellectual Assessment with Gorham's Proverbs Test, Raven's Progressive Matrices, and WAIS." *Psychological Reports*, 20 (1967), 1285–1286.
Donald R. Gorham / intelligence / proverbs test / psycholinguistics / psychology.

K

531. Kahn, Charlotte. "Proverbs of Love and Marriage: A Psychological Perspective." *Psychoanalytic Review*, 70 (1983), 359–371.
Behavior / culture / experience / love / marriage / misogyny / psychoanalysis / psychology / sociology / "Marry in haste, repent at leisure."

532. Kalanidhi, M.S., and S. Gurudas. "Proverbs – A Study in the Folk Psychology of a Tribal Community." *Bulletin of the Institute of Traditional Cultures*, no volume given (1978), 39–44.
Anthropology / community / context / ethnography / field research / Indian / psychology / Pulayas / society / worldview.

533. Kalter, Marjorie Hope. "Oral Literature and Metaphorical Translation." *Language and Style*, 13 (1980), 55–63.
African / comprehension / literature / metaphor / orality / perception / translation.

534. Kamarah, Sheikh Umarr. "The Individual and Society: Political Philosophy in the Themne [Temne] Proverb." *International Journal of Sierra Leone Studies & Reviews*, 1, no. 1 (2000), 121–133.
African / culture / knowledge / philosophy / politics / society / sociology / Themne.

535. Kamwangamalu, Nkonko M. "*Ubuntu* in South Africa: A Sociolinguistic Perspective to a Pan–African Concept." *Critical Arts*, 13, no. 2 (1999), 24–41.
African / community / culture / interdependence / sociolinguistics / sociology / "Ubuntu" / value.

536. Kanyó, Zoltán. "Sprachlich–gedankliche Bedingungen der Abbildung der Sprichwortsstruktur." *Studia Poetica*, 3 (1980), 149–182.
Noam Chomsky / definition / Alan Dundes / grammar / linguistics / paremiology / Grigorii L'vovich Permiakov / proverbiality / semantics / semiotics / structure.

537. Kanyó, Zoltán. *Sprichwörter–Analyse einer Einfachen Form. Ein Beitrag zur generativen Poetik.* The Hague: Mouton, 1981. 310 pp.
Bibliography / form / grammar / linguistics / logic / poetics / pragmatics / semiotics / simple form / style / structure.

538. Katz, Albert N. "Figurative Language and Figurative Thought: A Review." In Albert N. Katz, Cristina Cacciari, Raymond W. Gibbs, and Mark Turner. *Figurative Language and Thought.* New York: Oxford University Press, 1998. 3–43.
Bibliography / cognition / figurativeness / function / grammar / language / linguistics / literalness / metaphor / pragmatics / psycholinguistics / semantics / speech.

539. Katz, Albert N., Cristina Cacciari, Raymond W. Gibbs, and Mark Turner. *Figurative Language and Thought.* New York: Oxford University Press, 1998. 195 pp.
Cognition / discourse / figurativeness / function / grammar / indirection / language / linguistics / literalness / metaphor / motivation / pragmatics / psycholinguistics / semantics.

540. Katz, Albert N., and Todd R. Ferretti. "Moment–By–Moment Reading of Proverbs in Literal and Nonliteral Contexts." *Metaphor and Symbol*, 16, nos. 3–4 (2001), 193–221.
Ambiguity / comprehension / context / figurativeness / interpretation / language / literalness / meaning / metaphor / psycholinguistics / reading.

541. Katz, Albert N., Mark Turner, Raymond W. Gibbs, and Cristina Cacciari. "Counterpoint Commentary." In Albert N. Katz, Cristina Cacciari, Raymond W. Gibbs, and Mark Turner. *Figurative Language and Thought.* New York: Oxford University Press, 1998. 158–192.
Cognition / figurativeness / language / literalness / metaphor / psycholinguistics.

542. Kauffman, Draper. "System Proverbs." *ETC.: A Review of General Semantics*, 47, no. 1 (1990), 20–29.
Context / contradiction / meaning / neologism / origin / quotation / rule.

543. Keene, H.G. "Conflicts of Experience." *Living Age*, 185 (May 24, 1890), 483–486.
Conflict / contradiction / culture / experience / life / society / truth / wisdom.

544. Kemper, Susan Jane. *Comprehension and the Interpretation of Proverbs.* Diss. Cornell University, 1978. 146 pp.
Comprehension / context / figurativeness / interpretation / literalness / meaning / metaphor / proverbs test / psycholinguistics / student.

545. Kemper, Susan Jane. "Comprehension and the Interpretation of Proverbs." *Journal of Psycholinguistic Research*, 10, no. 2 (1981), 179–198.
Comprehension / context / figurativeness / interpretation / literalness / meaning / metaphor / proverbs test / psycholinguistics / student.

546. Kempler, Daniel, and Diana Van Lancker. "Acquisition and Loss of Familiar Language: Idiom and Proverb Comprehension." *Confluence: Linguistics, L2 Acquisition and Speech Pathology*. Ed. Fred R. Eckman. Amsterdam: John Benjamins, 1993. 249–257.
Acquisition / brain / competence / comprehension / familiarity / foreign language / idiom / language / psycholinguistics / speech.

547. Kerschen, Lois. *American Proverbs about Women*. Diss. Columbia Pacific University, 1996. 284 pp. Also published as *American Proverbs about Women: A Reference Guide*. Westport, Connecticut: Greenwood Press, 1998. 200 pp.
American / anti–feminism / culture / meaning / misogyny / prejudice / stereotype / women / worldview.

548. Khayyat, Shimon L. "The Interrelationship Between Jews, Christians, Moslems, and Others as Reflected in Arabic Proverbs." *Essays on the Occasion of the Seventieth Anniversary of the Dropsie University (1909–1979)*. Eds. Abraham I. Katsh and Leon Nemoy. Philadelphia: Dropsie University, 1979. 237–263.
Arabic / Christian / collection / culture / ethnicity / Jewish / Moslem / religion / society / stereotype / variant.

549. Khayyat, Shimon L. "Relations between Muslims, Jews and Christians as Reflected in Arabic Proverbs." *Folklore* (London), 96, no. 2 (1985), 190–207.
Arabic / Christian / collection / culture / ethnicity / field research / folklore / Jewish / Muslim / religion / society / stereotype / variant.

550. Kibler, Clare T. *On the Structure of Conceptual Categories*. Diss. University of Cincinnati, 1984. 97 pp.
Abstraction / comprehension / figurativeness / literalness / meaning / metaphor / proverbs test / psycholinguistics / psychology / structure.

551. Kim, Kun Hwan. "Deutsche Sprichwörter im Spiegel der Gesellschaft: Analyse der von Deutschen am häufigsten genannten Sprichwörter." *Zeitschrift für deutsche Philologie*, 118, no. 1 (1999), 87–102.
Age / anti–proverb / culture / empiricism / frequency / German / informant / popularity / society / statistics / value / variation / worldview.

552. Kim, S. Peter, Gregory Siomopoulos, and Ronald Jay Cohen. "Verbal Abstraction and Culture: An Exploratory Study with Proverbs." *Psychological Reports*, 41 (1977), 967–972.
Abstraction / culture / interpretation / proverbs test / psycholinguistics / psychology / schizophrenia / value.

553. Kimmerle, Heinz. "Proverbs as a Source of African Philosophy: A Methodological Consideration." *Embracing the Baobab Tree: The African Proverb in the 21st Century.* Ed. Willem Saayman. Pretoria: University of South Africa, 1997. 58–71.
African / communication / culture / Jacques Derrida / experience / language / life / philosophy / wisdom / worldview.

554. Kindt, Walther. "Kommunikative Funktionen von Sprichwörtern: Ein Beispiel für die notwendige Verbindung von Phraseologie und Pragmatik." *Phraseologie in Raum und Zeit: Akten der 10. Tagung des Westfälischen Arbeitskreises "Phraseologie/Parömiologie" (Münster 2001).* Eds. Elisabeth and Ilpo Tapani Piirainen. Baltmannsweiler: Schneider Verlag Hohengehren, 2002. 273–286.
Argumentation / communication / culture / function / linguistics / phraseology / pragmatics / society.

555. Kirshenblatt–Gimblett, Barbara. "Toward a Theory of Proverb Meaning." *Proverbium*, 22 (1973), 821–827. A shortened Russian summary appeared in *Paremiologicheskii Sbornik.* Ed. G.L. Permiakov. Moskva: "Nauka", 1978. 241–244. Also in *The Wisdom of Many. Essays on the Proverb.* Eds. Wolfgang Mieder and Alan Dundes. New York: Garland Publishing, 1981. 111–121.
Context / English / life / meaning / performance / society / speech act / truth / use / "A friend in need is a friend indeed" / "A rolling stone gathers no moss."

556. Kleiber, Georges. "Les proverbes: Des dénominations d'un type 'très très spécial'." *Langue française*, 123 (1999), 52–69.
Collectivity / definition / denomination / introductory formula / judgment / mentality / proverbialization.

557. Kleiber, Georges. "Proverbe : sens et dénomination. Le proverbe, un pro...nom?" *Nouveaux Cahiers d'Allemand*, 17, no. 3 (1999), 515–531.
Collectivity / denomination / judgment / meaning / proverbialization / semantics / variation.

558. Kleiber, Georges. "Sur le sens des proverbes." *La parole proverbiale.* Ed. Jean–Claude Anscombre. Paris: Larousse, 2000. 39–58.
Context / denomination / experience / life / meaning / metaphor / semantics / structure.

559. Klimaszewska, Zofia. "De betekenis van de cognitieve semantiek voor het onderzoek van de idiomatiek." *Neerlandica Wratislaviensia*, 7 (1994), 183–188.
Cognition / culture / idiom / linguistics / mentality / psychology / semantics / worldview.

560. Klimkeit, Hans–J. "Ethical Issues in Indian Proverbial Wisdom." *Temenos: Studies in Comparative Religion*, 29 (1993), 73–100.
Didacticism / ethics / Indian / morality / religion / wisdom / worldview.

561. Knapp, Mark, Cynthia Stohl, and Kathleen K. Reardon. "'Memorable' Messages." *Journal of Communication*, 31, no. 4 (1981), 27–41.
Behavior / communication / experience / field research / life / memorable message / memory / personal proverb / reception / rule / transmission.

562. Koenig, Linda J., Ann B. Ragin, and Martin Harrow. "Accuracy and Bias in Depressives' Judgments for Self and Other [Using a Proverb Interpretation Task]." *Cognitive Theory and Research*, 19, no. 5 (1995), 505–517.
Brain / cognition / depression / interpretation / judgment / proverbs test / psycholinguistics / psychology.

563. Kohn, Alfie. "You Know What They Say... Are Proverbs Nuggets of Truth or Fool's Gold?" *Psychology Today*, 22, no. 4 (1988), 36–41.
Context / English / falsehood / truism / truth / universality / validity.

564. Koller, Werner. *Redensarten. Linguistische Aspekte, Vorkommensanalysen, Sprachspiel.* Tübingen: Max Niemeyer, 1977. 229 pp.
Advertisement / classification / currency / definition / empiricism / familiarity / frequency / German / lexicography / linguistics / literature / mass media / phraseologism / phraseology / semantics / structure / syntax / variant / wordplay.

565. Kone, Kassim. *Bamana Verbal Art: An Ethnographic Study of Proverbs.* Diss. Indiana University, 1996. 295 pp.
African / Bamana / discourse / ethnography / Mali / orality / philosophy / politics / rhetoric / song / speech act / theatre / verbal dueling / worldview.

566. Kordas, Bronislawa. "The Poetic Function and the Oral Transmission of Chinese Proverbs." *Chinoperl Papers*, no. 15 (1990), 85–94.
Chinese / function / linguistics / orality / phonetics / poetics / transmission.

567. Korhonen, Jarmo (ed.). *Untersuchungen zur Phraseologie des Deutschen und anderer Sprachen: einzelsprachspezifisch–kontrastiv–vergleichend.* Frankfurt am Main: Peter Lang, 1992. 219 pp.
Antonym / Bible / classification / dictionary / equivalent / idiom / lexicography / linguistics / mass media / modification / morphology / name / newspaper / onomastics / phraseology / somatism / youth.

568. Korhonen, Jarmo. "Verbidiome in Sportberichten deutscher und finnischer Tageszeitungen." *Osloer Beiträge zur Germanistik*, 16 (1994), 247–259.
Finnish / frequency / function / German / idiom / linguistics / mass media / modification / newspaper / semantics / sports / wordplay.

569. Korhonen, Jarmo. *Studien zur Phraseologie des Deutschen und Finnischen I.* Bochum: Norbert Brockmeyer, 1995. 410 pp.

Convergence / diachronic / dialect / dictionary / dissemination / divergence / equivalent / Finnish / German / idiom / lexicography / linguistics / literature / loan translation / mass media / morphology / negation / newspaper / phraseology / semantics / sports / syntax / translation.

570. Korhonen, Jarmo (ed.). *Studien zur Phraseologie des Deutschen und Finnischen II.* Bochum: Norbert Brockmeyer, 1996. 532 pp.
Austrian / dialect / equivalent / Finnish / German / idiom / lexicology / linguistics / modification / name / negation / onomastics / phraseology / semantics / Swiss German / syntax / valence / variability.

571. Kramp, Willy. "Sind Sprichwörter wahr?" *Die Furche*, 23 (1937), 135–140.
Context / contradiction / experience / life / truth / universality / validity.

572. Krauss, Friedrich S. "Erotische Sprichwörter bei den russischen Juden." *Zeitschrift für Sexualwissenschaft und Sexualpolitik*, 5 (1909), 452–466.
Ignaz (Ignace) Bernstein / culture / eroticism / Jewish / love / medicine / obscenity / psychology / Russian / scatology / sex / sexuality / Yiddish.

573. Krikmann, Arvo. *On Denotative Indefiniteness of Proverbs.* Tallinn: Academy of Sciences of the Estonian SSR, Institute of Language and Literature, 1974. 48 pp. Also in *Proverbium*, 1 (1984), 47–91.
Ambiguity / context / denotation / indefiniteness / interpretation / linguistics / logic / meaning / metaphor / pragmatics / semantics / syntax.

574. Krikmann, Arvo. *Some Additional Aspects of Semantic Indefiniteness of Proverbs.* Tallinn: Academy of Sciences of the Estonian SSR, Institute of Language and Literature, 1974. 35 pp. Also in *Proverbium*, 2 (1985), 58–85.
Function / indefiniteness / linguistics / pragmatics / semantics / structure.

575. Krikmann, Arvo. "The Great Chain Metaphor: An Open Sesame for Proverb Semantics?" *Proverbium*, 11 (1994), 117–124.

Cognition / comprehension / figurativeness / Mark Johnson / George Lakoff / linguistics / literalness / metaphor / psycholinguistics / semantics / semiotics / Mark Turner.

576. Krikmann, Arvo. "Proverbs on Animal Identity: Typological Memoirs." *Folklore* (Tartu), 17 (2001), 7–84.
Absurdity / animal / behavior / collection / folklore / frequency / identity / life / metaphor / people / structure / tautology.

577. Krueger, David W. "The Differential Diagnosis of Proverb Interpretation." *Phenomenology and Treatment of Schizophrenia.* Eds. William E. Fann, Ismet Karacan, Alex D. Pokorny, and Robert L. Williams. New York: Spectrum, 1978. 193–201.
Abstraction / concreteness / figurativeness / interpretation / literalness / proverbs test / psychiatry / psychology / schizophrenia.

578. Kudadjie, Joshua N. "Are African Proverbs an Ambiguous Source of Wisdom for Living? A Case Study of Ga and Dangme Proverbs." *Embracing the Baobab Tree: The African Proverb in the 21st Century.* Ed. Willem Saayman. Pretoria: University of South Africa, 1997. 176–191.
African / ambiguity / conflict / didacticism / Dangme / Ga / life / wisdom.

579. Kulah, Alfred Akki. *The Organization and Learning of Proverbs among the Kpelle of Liberia.* Diss. University of California at Irvine, 1973. 137 pp.
Acquisition / anthropology / comprehension / culture / Kpelle / Liberian / meaning / metaphor / society / value.

580. Kuusi, Matti. "Variations in the Popularity of Finnish Proverbs." In M. Kuusi, *Mind and Form in Folklore: Selected Articles.* Ed. Henni Ilomäki. Helsinki: Suomalaisen Kirjallisuuden Seura, 1994. 114–122. Translation of "Sananparsien suosionmuutoksista." *Virittäjä,* 57 (1953), 337–345.
Archaism / empiricism / Finnish / familiarity / frequency / popularity / statistics.

581. Kuusi, Matti. "Basic Images and Formulae." In M. Kuusi, *Mind and Form in Folklore: Selected Articles.* Ed. Henni Ilomäki. Helsinki: Suomalaisen Kirjallisuuden Seura, 1994. 142–144. Translated chapter from M. Kuusi, *Sanalaskut ja puheenparret.* Helsinki: Suomalaisen Kirjallisuuden Seura, 1954. 139–142 (chapter 40: "Perikuvat ja formulat").

Analogy / formula / imagery / origin / pattern / proverb type / structure / variant.

582. Kuusi, Matti. "On the Aptness of Proverbs." In M. Kuusi, *Mind and Form in Folklore: Selected Articles.* Ed. Henni Ilomäki. Helsinki: Suomalaisen Kirjallisuuden Seura, 1994. 105–113. Published lecture that Kuusi gave at the University of Helsinki on March 23, 1956.
Communication / computer / context / database / globality / proverb type / repertoire / speech act.

583. Kuusi, Matti. "Concerning Folk Paradoxes." In M. Kuusi, *Mind and Form in Folklore: Selected Articles.* Ed. Henni Ilomäki. Helsinki: Suomalaisen Kirjallisuuden Seura, 1994. 131–141. Translation of "Kansanparadokseista." *Kalevalaseuran vuosikirja,* 42 (1962), 56–68.
Antiquity / Bible / contradiction / Finnish / folklore / Jesus / Latin / law / New Testament / paradox / structure / "Summum ius, summa iniuria."

584. Kuusi, Matti. "Fatalistic Traits in Finnish Proverbs." *Fatalistic Beliefs in Religion, Folklore and Literature.* Ed. Helmer Ringgren. Stockholm: Almqvist & Wiksell, 1967. 89–96. Also in *The Wisdom of Many. Essays on the Proverb.* Eds. Wolfgang Mieder and Alan Dundes. New York: Garland Publishing, 1981. 275–283.
Culture / fatalism / Finnish / national character / pessimism / society / worldview.

585. Kuusi, Matti. "The Place of Women in the Proverbs of Finland and Ovamboland." In M. Kuusi, *Mind and Form in Folklore: Selected Articles.* Ed. Henni Ilomäki. Helsinki: Suomalaisen Kirjallisuuden Seura, 1994. 148–158. Translation of "Naisen arvo Suomen ja Ambomaan sananlaskustossa." *Suomen Akatemia,* 1 (1971), 99–107.
African / anti–feminism / empiricism / Finnish / misogyny / Ovambo / prejudice / society / statistics / stereotype / value / women / worldview.

L

586. Lafleche, Ginette, and Marilyn S. Albert. "Executive Function Deficits in Mild Alzheimer's Disease." *Neuropsychology*, 9, no. 3 (1995), 313–320.
Alzheimer's / brain / cognition / disease / neuropsychology / proverbs test / psychology.

587. Lakoff, George, and Mark Johnson. *Metaphors We Live By*. Chicago: University of Chicago Press, 1980. 242 pp.
Comprehension / conceptualization / culture / definition / experience / meaning / metaphor / metonymy / psycholinguistics / psychology / society / structure / truth.

588. Lakoff, George, and Mark Turner. "The Great Chain of Being." In G. Lakoff and M. Turner. *More than Cool Reason: A Field Guide to Poetic Metaphor*. Chicago: University of Chicago Press, 1989. 160–213.
Culture / literature / meaning / William Stanley Merwin / metaphor / modification / poetry / psycholinguistics / psychology / society / structure.

589. Lasky, Lawrence. "Alternate Forms of the Multiple Choice Version of the Proverbs Test." *Journal of Psychology*, 65 (1967), 59–60.
Donald R. Gorham / proverbs test / psychiatry / psychology / schizophrenia.

590. Latané, Bibb, Kipling Williams, and Stephen Harkins. "Many Hands Make Light the [*sic*] Work: The Causes and Consequences of Social Loafing." *Journal of Personality and Social Psychology*, 37 (1979), 822–832.
Attitude / collectivity / English / interpretation / loafing / personality / society / somatism / work / "Many hands make light work."

591. Lau, Kimberly J. "'It's about Time': The Ten Proverbs Most Frequently Used in Newspapers and Their Relation to American Values." *Proverbium*, 13 (1996), 135–159.
American / computer / database / empiricism / frequency / mass media / news–paper / time / value / worldview.

592. Layton, Monique J. "Le procédé métaphorique et l'énoncé proverbial." *Canadian Review of Sociology and Anthropology*, 13 (1976), 448–457.

African / anthropology / collectivity / context / function / Malagasy / metaphor / society / wisdom / Yoruba.

593. Lee, Davis Lin–Chuan. *Chinese Proverbs: A Pragmatic and Sociolinguistic Approach.* Diss. Georgetown University, 1979. 209 pp.
Chinese / culture / definition / language / origin / sociolinguistics / strategy / teaching / tradition.

594. Lehman, Edward. "The Monster Test." *Archives of General Psychiatry*, 3 (1960), 535–544. With 5 illustrations.
Abstraction / brain / disease / English / interpretation / proverbs test / psychiatry / psychology / somatism / "Two heads are better than one."

595. Lepicard, Etienne. "Talmudic Aphorisms on Diet." *Israel Journal of Medical Sciences*, 30, no. 7 (1994), 554–555.
Aphorism / diet / health / Hebrew / Jewish / medicine / religion / Talmud.

596. Lévi, Florence. "*Calar* ou *Falar*? Le silence et la parole à travers des proverbes portugais faisant référence à la bouche et à l'oreille." *Paremia*, 4 (1995), 133–139.
Ear / mouth / Portuguese / silence / somatism / speech / value / worldview.

597. Levin–Steinmann, Anke. "The Term *Metaphorisation* [sic] in its Usage on Words and Phraseologisms." *Europhras 97: Phraseology and Paremiology.* Ed. Peter „Ďurčo. Bratislava: Akadémia PZ, 1998. 211–215.
Classification / definition / linguistics / metaphorization / phraseologism / word.

598. Levorato, Maria Chiara. "The Acquisition of Idioms and the Development of Figurative Competence." *Idioms: Processing, Structure, and Interpretation.* Eds. Cristina Cacciari and Patrizia Tabossi. Hillsdale, New Jersey: Lawrence Erlbaum Associates, 1993. 101–128.
Acquisition / competence / comprehension / context / figurativeness / idiom / literalness / psycholinguistics.

599. Levorato, Maria Chiara, and Cristina Cacciari. "Children's Comprehension and Production of Idioms: The Role of Context and Familiarity." *Journal of Child Language*, 19 (1992), 415–433.

Acquisition / children / competence / comprehension / context / familiarity / frequency / idiom / production / psycholinguistics.

600. Lévy, Isaac Jack, and Rosemary Levy Zumwalt. "A Conversation in Proverbs: Judeo–Spanish Refranes in Context." *Proverbium*, 7 (1990), 117–132. Also published in *New Horizons in Sepharic [sic] Studies*. Eds. Yedida K. Stillman and George K. Zucker. Albany, New York: State University of New York Press, 1993. 269–283.
Belief / context / conversation / culture / discourse / field research / folklore / Jewish / Judeo–Spanish / religion / Sephardic / Spanish / speech act / tradition / worldview.

601. Lévy, Isaac Jack, and Rosemary Levy Zumwalt. "'Aun de lo suzio profita il mundo' (Even from the Dirty the World Profits): A Hidden Side of Sephardic Proverbs." *Proverbium*, 11 (1994), 143–158.
Culture / folklore / indirection / Jewish / Judeo–Spanish / meaning / obscenity / scatology / Sephardic / Spanish.

602. Lewandowska, Anna. "Das deutsche Sprichwort als mehrdimensionales Phänomen." *Zeszyty Naukowe Wyzszej Szkoly Pedagogicznej w Rzeszowie*, 26, no. 4 (1997), 153–167.
Context / definition / function / German / linguistics / semantics / semiotics / simple form / structure.

603. Lewandowska, Anna, and Gerd Antos. "Sprichwörter, metaphorische Konzepte und Alltagsrhetorik: Versuch einer kognitivistischen Begründung der Sprichwortforschung." *Proverbium*, 18 (2001), 167–183. With 2 illustrations.
Advertisement / anti–proverb / argumentation / cognition / context / culture / German / linguistics / mass media / metaphor / rhetoric / "Jeder ist seines Glückes Schmied."

604. Lewinsohn, Peter M., and Ann Riggs. "The Effect of Content upon the Thinking of Acute and Chronic Schizophrenics." *Journal of Abnormal and Social Psychology*, 65 (1962), 206–207.
Abstraction / brain / content / interpretation / orality / psychiatry / psychology / schizophrenia.

605. Lewis, George Cornewall. "The Value of Proverbs as the Expression of Popular Opinion." In G.C. Lewis. *An Essay on the Influence of Authority in Matters of Opinion*. London: Longmans, Green, and Company, 1849 (2nd ed., 1875). 122–124.

Behavior / contradiction / empiricism / experience / life / opinion / truth / value.

606. Lewis, Jerry M., E. Clay Griffith, Albert F. Riedel, and Belvin A. Simmons. "Studies in Abstraction: Schizophrenia and Orality: Preliminary Results." *Journal of Nervous and Mental Diseases*, 129 (1959), 564–567.
Abstraction / brain / content / meaning / orality / proverbs test / psychiatry / psychology / schizophrenia.

607. Lewis, Nona L. *Ego Boundaries and Comprehension of Metaphor in Schizophrenia: A Study of Symbolic Processes*. Diss. Adelphi University, 1983. 244 pp.
Abstraction / brain / comprehension / interpretation / metaphor / perception / proverbs test / psycholinguistics / psychology / schizophrenia / symbolism.

608. Lieber, Michael D. "Analogic Ambiguity: A Paradox of Proverb Usage." *Journal of American Folklore*, 97 (1984), 423–441. Also in *Wise Words: Essays on the Proverb*. Ed. Wolfgang Mieder. New York: Garland Publishing, 1994. 99–126.
Ambiguity / analogy / context / disambiguation / folklore / function / paradox / semantics / use.

609. Lienert, Gustav A., and Hans Zur Oeveste. "Configural Frequency Analysis as a Statistical Tool for Development Research." *Educational and Psychological Measurement*, 45, no. 2 (1985), 301–307.
Frequency / Donald R. Gorham / proverbs test / psychology / statistics.

610. Lipps, Hans. "Ausdrücke und Redensarten." In H. Lipps. *Untersuchungen zu einer hermeneutischen Logik*. Frankfurt am Main: Vittorio Klostermann, 1959 (3rd ed. 1968). 106–109.
Communication / context / hermeneutics / logic / meaning / metaphor / philosophy / phraseologism / sign / use.

611. Lipps, Hans. "Sprichwörter." In H. Lipps. *Untersuchungen zu einer hermeneutischen Logik*. Frankfurt am Main: Vittorio Klostermann, 1959 (3rd ed. 1968). 135–141.
Context / experience / hermeneutics / indirection / life / logic / meaning / metaphor / philosophy / recurrence.

612. Lodge, Donna Nemeth, and Edwin A. Leach. "Children's Acquisition of Idioms in the English Language." *Journal of Speech and Hearing Research*, 18 (1975), 506–520.
Acquisition / children / comprehension / English / figurativeness / idiom / literalness / meaning / psycholinguistics.

613. Loeb, Edwin. "The Function of Proverbs in the Intellectual Development of Primitive Peoples." *The Scientific Monthly*, 74 (1952), 100–104.
Abstraction / African / anthropology / ethics / Kuanyama Ambo / law / mentality / philosophy / religion.

614. Lombroso, Cesaro. "Il delitto nella coscienza popolare." *Minerva medicolegale; archivio di antropologia, criminale, psichiatria et medicina legale*, 3 (1882), 451–456.
Content / criminality / culture / law / medicine / psychology / society.

615. Long, James. "Oriental Proverbs and Their Uses, in Sociology, Ethnology, Philology, and Education." *Transactions of the Second Session of the International Congress of Orientalists*. Ed. Robert K. Douglas. London: Trübner, 1876. 380–395.
Education / ethnology / Indian / life / Oriental / philology / sociology / worldview.

616. Lopes, Ana Cristina Macário. "Texte proverbial et construction du sens." *Degrés: Revue de synthèse à orientation sémiologique*, 66 (1991), c1–c12.
Classification / collection / linguistics / Grigorii L'vovich Permiakov / semantics / semiotics / structure / syntax.

617. Lopes, Ana Cristina Macário. "Da ambivalência do texto proverbial." *Discursos*, 10 (1995), 77–94.
Ambivalence / culture / experience / linguistics / Grigorii L'vovich Permiakov / pragmatics / semantics / semiotics.

618. Lorén, José Maria de Jaime, and José de Jaime Gómez. "Las profesiones sanitarias a través del refranero español." *Proverbium*, 18 (2001), 205–217.
Content / health / medicine / pharmaceutics / physician / profession / veterinarian.

619. Louis, Cameron. "Proverbs and the Politics of Language." *Proverbium*, 17 (2000), 173–194.

Authority / Mikhail M. Bakhtin / communication / Jacques Derrida / Michel Foucault / ideology / language / linguistics / manipulation / politics / sociolinguistics.

620. Loukatos, Démétrios. "L'emploi du proverbe aux différents âges." *Proverbium*, 2 (1965), 17–26.
Age / children / elder / frequency / sociolinguistics / student / use.

621. Loukatos, Démétrios. "Sujets et éléments communs d'expérience et de sagesse populaires [sic] dans les proverbes grecs et bulgares." *Kulturni i literaturni otnosenija mezdu garci i balgari ot sredata ne XV do sredata ne XIX vek.* No editor given. Thessalonika: Hidryma Meleton Charsonesou tou Haimou, 1980. 39–45.
Bulgarian / commonality / content / experience / Greek / life / wisdom / world–view.

622. Loukatos, Démétrios. "Ordonnance médicale populaire, sortie des proverbes néohelléniques." *Laographia*, 38 (1995–1997), 113–121 (in Greek).
Content / disease / Greek / health / meaning / medicine / wisdom.

623. Loux, Françoise, and Philippe Richard. "Alimentation et maladie dans les proverbes français: un exemple d'analyse de contenu." *Ethnologie française*, 2, nos. 3–4 (1972), 267–286.
Content / disease / ethnology / French / medicine / nutrition / sociolinguistics.

624. Loux, Françoise, and Philippe Richard. *Sagesses du corps. La santé et la malade dans les proverbes français.* Paris: G.–P. Maisonneuve et Larose, 1978. 353 pp.
Age / bibliography / body / content / disease / French / health / medicine / nutrition / sexuality / sociolinguistics / wisdom.

625. Lüger, Heinz–Helmut. "Formen rituellen Sprachgebrauchs." *Deutsche Sprache*, 8 (1980), 21–39.
Context / definition / foreign language / form / idiom / language / linguistics / routine formula / speech act / stereotype / teaching.

626. Lüger, Heinz–Helmut. "Phraseologie und Argumentation." *Phraseologie und Phraseodidaktik.* Eds. Martine Lorenz–Bourjot and Heinz–Helmut Lüger. Wien: Edition Praesens,

jot and Heinz–Helmut Lüger. Wien: Edition Praesens, 2001. 65–83.
Argumentation / discourse / linguistics / phraseologism / phraseology / politics / rhetoric / semiotics / sign / speech act / variability.

627. Lutzer, Victoria D. "Comprehension of Proverbs by Average Children and Children with Learning Disorders." *Journal of Learning Disabilities*, 21 (1988), 104–108.
Brain / children / cognition / comprehension / disability / meaning / metaphor / psycholinguistics / psychology.

628. Lycaki, Helene, Gerald Rosenbaum, and Rue L. Cromwell. "The Effects of White Noise and Message Repetition on Proverb Interpretation in Good and Poor Premorbid Schizophrenia." *Journal of Nervous and Mental Diseases*, 157 (1973), 37–45.
Abstraction / brain / disease / interpretation / proverbs test / psychiatry / psychology / repetition / schizophrenia.

M

629. Majapuro, Anne. "Zum Frauenbild in deutschen und finnischen Sprichwörtern (Darstellung eines Forschungsvorhabens)." *LSP and Theory of Translation. 16th VAKKI Symposium. Vörå 10.–11.2.1996.* Eds. Rune Ingo, Christer Laurén, Henrik Nikula, and Patricia Poussa. Vaasa: University of Vaasa, Faculty of Humanities, 1996. 147–159.
Anti–feminism / Finnish / gender / German / misogyny / prejudice / society / stereotype / women / worldview.

630. Majapuro, Anne. "'Weinende Braut, lachende Frau': Geschlechtsspezifische Merkmale des Lachens und Weinens in deutschen und finnischen Sprichwörtern." *Laughter Down the Centuries.* Eds. Siegfried Jäkel, Asko Timonen, and Veli-Matti Rissanen. Turku: Turun Yliopisto, 1997. 233–248.
Anti–feminism / crying / emotion / Finnish / gender / German / laughter / men / misogyny / society / stereotype / women / worldview.

631. Majapuro, Anne. "'Kein Kleid steht den Weibern besser als Schweigen': Zum Thema 'Schweigen' im deutschen und finnischen Sprichwort aus der Sicht der Frauenforschung." *The Language of Silence.* Eds. Siegfried Jäkel and Asko Timonen. 2 vols. Turku: Turun Yliopisto, 2001. I, 281–296.
Anti–feminism / Finnish / gender / German / misogyny / silence / society / sociolinguistics / speech / stereotype / women / worldview.

632. Majapuro, Anne. "Zur Tradierung von Sprichwörtern zum Thema 'Frau': Einige deutsche und finnische Beispiele." *Zur Rolle der Sprache im Wandel der Gesellschaft.* Eds. Matti Luukkaianen and Riitta Pyykkö. Vantaa: Tummavuorem Kirjapaino Oy, 2002. 295–305.
Anti–feminism / Finnish / gender / German / misogyny / society / sociolinguistics / stereotype / traditionality / women / worldview.

633. Makkai, Adam. *Idiom Structure in English.* The Hague: Mouton, 1972. Esp. pp. 124–134.
English / figurativeness / idiom / linguistics / literalness / meaning / moral / paraphrase / structure / "Don't count your chickens before they're hatched."

634. Makkai, Adam. "Idiomaticity as a Language Universal." *Universals of Human Language*. Ed. Joseph H. Greenberg. Stanford, California: Stanford University Press, 1978. 401–448.
Ambiguity / definition / idiom / idiomaticity / language / linguistics / metaphor / origin / semantics / universality.

635. Makkai, Adam. "Idiomaticity and Phraseology in Post–Chomskian Linguistics: The Coming–of–Age of Semantics Beyond the Sentence." *Semiotica*, 64, nos. 1–2 (1987), 171–187.
Noam Chomsky / idiom / idiomaticity / language / linguistics / phraseology / pragmatics / semantics / sentence.

636. Makkai, Adam. "Idiomaticity as a Reaction to *L'Arbitraire du Signe* in the Universal Process of Semeio–Genesis." *Idioms: Processing, Structure, and Interpretation*. Eds. Cristina Cacciari and Patrizia Tabossi. Hillsdale, New Jersey: Lawrence Erlbaum Associates, 1993. 297–324.
Arbitrariness / Chinese / comprehension / idiom / idiomaticity / linguistics / metonymy / origin / pragmatics / semiotics / sign / universality.

637. Mandala, James Di Martini. *The Interpretation of Proverbs: A Cognitive Perspective*. Diss. California School of Professional Psychology at Berkeley, 1987. 235 pp.
Bibliography / children / cognition / comprehension / intelligence / interpretation / proverbs test / psycholinguistics / psychology / student.

638. Mansfeld de Agüero, Maria Eva, and Antonio Pamies Bertrán. "La relación hombre – mujer en los refranes paraguayos." *Trabajos de lexicografía y fraseología contrastivas*. Eds. Antonio Pamies Bertrán and Juan de Dios Luque Durán. Granada: Departamento de Lingüística General y Teoría de la Literatura de la Universidad de Granada, 2000. 193–208.
Anti–feminism / gender / men / misogyny / Paraguayan / stereotype / women / worldview.

639. Marcus, Mordecai. "Psychoanalytic Approaches to [Robert Frost's] 'Mending Wall'." *Robert Frost: Studies of the Poetry*. Ed. Kathryn Gibbs Harris. Boston, Massachusetts: G.K. Hall, 1979. 179–190.
American / Robert Frost / literature / poetry / psychoanalysis / "Good fences makes good neighbors."

640. Margolis, Joseph. "Notes on the Logic of Simile, Metaphor and Analogy." *American Speech*, 32, no. 3 (1957), 186–189.
Analogy / definition / figurativeness / literalness / logic / metaphor / simile.

641. Marian, Marin. "Adagiu folcloric la un concept psihanalitic." *Revista de etnografie si folclor*, 36, nos. 5–6 (1991), 241–247.
Adage / folklore / frustration / psychoanalysis / psychology / Rumanian / wedding.

642. Marton, Magda, and József Szirtes. "Saccade–Related Brain Potentials During Reading Correct and Incorrect Versions of Proverbs." *International Journal of Psychophysiology*, 6 (1988), 273–280.
Brain / comprehension / context / interpretation / meaning / perception / proverbs test / psychiatry / psychology.

643. Marzolf, Stanley S. "Common Sayings and 16PF Traits." *Journal of Clinical Psychology*, 30 (1974), 202–204.
Attitude / familiarity / frequency / personality / proverbs test / psycholinguistics / psychology / rationalization.

644. Matisoff, James A. *Blessings, Curses, Hopes, and Fears. Psycho–Ostensive Expressions in Yiddish.* Philadelphia: Institute for the Study of Human Issues, 1979. 140 pp.
Anxiety / blessing / culture / curse / emotion / ostentation / psycholinguistics / semantics / sociolinguistics / Yiddish / worldview.

645. Matta, Hilda. "Das Sprichwort: Versuch einer Definition." *Proverbium*, 5 (1988), 69–84.
Communication / content / context / definition / function / genre / introductory formula / linguistics / proverbiality / semiotics / speech act / structure / style / syntax / traditionality.

646. Maw, Wallace H., and Ethel W. Maw. "Contrasting Proverbs as a Measure of Attitudes of College Students Toward Curiosity–Related Behaviors." *Psychological Reports*, 37 (1975), 1085–1086.
Ambiguity / attitude / behavior / contradiction / proverbs test / psycholinguistics / psychology / student / worldview.

647. Maw, Wallace H., Ethel W. Maw, and Jane B. Laskaris. "Contrasting Proverbs as a Measure of Attitudes Toward Curiosity–

Related Behavior of Black and White College Students." *Psychological Reports*, 39 (1976), 1229–1230.
African American / attitude / behavior / contradiction / ethnicity / proverbs test / psycholinguistics / psychology / student / value / worldview.

648. Mazars Denys, Eliane, and Javier Jurado Merelo. "Les cris des animaux dans quelques expressions figées françaises en rapport avec le monde humain." *Paremia*, 8 (1999), 327–332.
Animal / behavior / French / life / meaning / people / phraseologism / sound / speech.

649. Mazzarella, Silvester. "Proverbs and Phrases in English Connected with Holding Candles, or Linking Cats with Candles." *Neuphilologische Mitteilungen*, 71 (1970), 683–689.
Animal / attitude / cat / English / folklore / meaning / narrative / phraseologism / "Nature passes (surpasses) nurture."

650. Mbuagbaw, Tanyi Eyong. "Apparent Fallacies in Some Kenyang Proverbs." *Notes on Sociolinguistics*, 5, no. 2 (2000), 69–75.
African / content / context / fallacy / Kenyang / moral / sociolinguistics / truth.

651. McAdoo, Harriette, and Margaret Rukuni. "A Prelimary Study of Family Values of the Women of Zimbabwe." *Journal of Black Psychology*, 19, no. 1 (1993), 48–62.
African / belief / children / family / psychology / Shona / value / women.

652. McGlone, Matthew S. "Concepts as Metaphors." In Sam Glucksberg. *Understanding Figurative Language: From Metaphors to Idioms*. New York: Oxford University Press, 2001. 90–107 and 115 (notes).
Comprehension / figurativeness / idiom / George Lakoff / linguistics / metaphor / psycholinguistics / structure.

653. McGlone, Matthew S., and Jessica Tofighbakhsh. "Birds of a Feather Flock Conjointly (?): Rhyme as Reason in Aphorisms." *Psychological Science*, 11, no. 5 (2000), 424–428.
Accuracy / aphorism / behavior / form / modification / perception / poetics / psycholinguistics / psychology / rhyme / semantics / truth / validity.

654. McKelvie, Donald. "Aspects of Oral Tradition and Belief in an Industrial Region." *Folk Life*, 1 (1963), 77–94.
Belief / field research / folklore / industry / orality / society / tradition.

655. McKelvie, Donald. "Proverbial Elements in the Oral Tradition of an English Urban Industrial Region." *Journal of the Folklore Institute*, 2 (1965), 244–261.
English / ethnicity / field research / folklore / industry / orality / society / tradition.

656. McKenzie, Alyce M. "The Preacher as Subversive Sage: Preaching on Biblical Proverbs." *Proverbium*, 12 (1995), 169–193.
Bible / didacticism / Jesus / New Testament / Old Testament / preaching / religion / sermon / subversion / wisdom.

657. McKenzie, Alyce M. "'Different Strokes for Different Folks': America's Quintessential Postmodern Proverb." *Theology Today*, 53 (July 1996), 201–212.
Advertisement / African American / American / Bible / Wolfgang Mieder / origin / postmodernism / society / variation / wisdom / "Different strokes for different folks."

658. McKenzie, Alyce M. *Preaching Proverbs: Wisdom for the Pulpit.* Louisville, Kentucky: Westminster John Knox Press, 1996. 170 pp.
Bible / didacticism / ethics / Jesus / morality / New Testament / Old Testament / preaching / religion / proverb duel / sermon / subversion / wisdom.

659. McKenzie, J. "Some Thoughts on Proverbs." *The Journal of the Anthropological Society of Bombay*, 14 (1929), 334–351.
Anthropology / experience / popularity / psychology / society / value / wisdom.

660. McLuhan, Marshall, and Wilfred Watson. *From Cliché to Archetype*. New York: The Viking Press, 1970. 213 pp.
American / archetype / cliché / English / literature / metaphor / paradox / parody / quotation / variation.

661. McNeil, William K. "The Nature of Speech According to Indian Proverbs." *Folklore Forum*, 4, nos. 1–2 (1971), 2–14.
Attitude / belief / culture / discourse / folklore / Indian / language / society / speech / worldview.

662. McWright, Linda Almond. *African–American Mothers' Perceptions of Grandparents' Use of Proverbs in Value Socialization of Grandchildren (Intergenerational)*. Diss. Michigan State University, 1998. 95 pp.
African American / belief / children / family / gender / grandparents / mother / parents / perception / socialization / society / transmission / use / value / wisdom.

663. Meadow, Arnold, Milton Greenblatt, and Harry C. Solomon. "'Looseness of Association' and Impairment in Abstraction in Schizophrenia." *Journal of Nervous and Mental Diseases*, 118 (1953), 27–35.
Abstraction / brain / proverbs test / psychiatry / psychology / schizophrenia.

664. Meisser, Ulrich M. "Tiersprichwörter und Verhaltensforschung. Zur gegenseitigen Erhellung von didaktischer Literatur und Naturwissenschaft." *Studium Generale*, 22 (1969), 861–889.
Animal / behavior / didacticism / epic / fable / meaning / psychology / science.

665. Meister, Charles W. "Franklin as a Proverb Stylist." *American Literature*, 24 (1952–1953), 157–166.
American / argumentation / didacticism / ethics / Benjamin Franklin / literature / moral / rhetoric / society / value / worldview.

666. Melerovič, Galina. "On Semantic Structure of the Proverbs." *Europhras 97: Phraseology and Paremiology*. Ed. Peter Ďurčo. Bratislava: Akadémia PZ, 1998. 225–229.
Behavior / culture / form / linguistics / metaphor / semantics / structure.

667. Mellado Blanco, Carmen. "Fraseologismos alemanes y españoles del campo de las emociones." *Paremia*, 6 (1997), 383–388.
Content / emotion / equivalent / German / phraseologism / psychology / Spanish.

668. Mellado Blanco, Carmen. "Acercamiento al fenómeno de la polisemia en la fraseología del alemán." *Paremia*, 7 (1998), 113–120.
Emotion / German / homonymy / phraseologism / semantics / somatism.

669. Meschonnic, Henri. "Les proverbes, actes de discours." *Revue des sciences humaines*, 41, no. 163 (1976), 419–430. Also in H. Meschonnic. *Pour la poétique V: Poésie sans répose*. Paris: Gallimard, 1978. 139–159.
Definition / discourse / form / function / meaning / popularity / structure.

670. Metzler, Franz Gebhard. *Die Erziehungsweisheit im Sprichwort*. Bregenz: Eugen Russ, 1953. 24 pp.
Children / content / education / ethics / morality / parents / pedagogy / psychology / religion / virtue / wisdom.

671. Meyer, Jürgen Bona. "Erziehungsweisheit im Sprichwort." In J.B. Meyer. *Probleme der Lebensweisheit*. Berlin: Allgemeiner Verein für deutsche Literatur, 1887. 1–33.
Children / content / education / ethics / parents / pedagogy / psychology / virtue / wisdom.

672. Michaux, Christine. *Le proverbe: Vers une théorie de la parole évocative*. Diss. Université Libre de Bruxelles, 1999. 352 pp.
Jean–Claude Anscombre / definition / discourse / Georges Kleiber / George Lakoff / linguistics / metaphor / nomination / proposition / semantics / Mark Turner.

673. Mieder, Barbara, Deborah Holmes, and Wolfgang Mieder. "'Morgenstunde hat Gold im Munde': A German Proverb and Young American School Children." *Proverbium*, 18 (2001), 231–246. With 12 illustrations.
American / children / education / foreign language / German / iconography / meaning / pedagogy / teaching / "Morgenstunde hat Gold im Munde."

674. Mieder, Wolfgang. "Das Wort 'Shit' und seine lexikographische Erfassung." *Sprachspiegel*, 34 (1978), 76–79.
Anality / linguistics / obscenity / phraseologism / psychoanalysis / scatology.

675. Mieder, Wolfgang. "The Use of Proverbs in Psychological Testing." *Journal of the Folklore Institute*, 15 (1978), 45–55.
John D. Benjamin / bibliography / context / Donald R. Gorham / intelligence / meaning / personality / proverbs test / psychiatry / psychology / schizophrenia.

676. Mieder, Wolfgang. *International Proverb Scholarship: An Annotated Bibliography*. 4 vols. New York: Garland Publishing, 1982, 1990, and 1993. New York: Peter Lang, 2001. I, 613 pp.; II, 436 pp.; III, 945 pp.; IV, 457 pp.
Bibliography / paremiography / paremiology / phraseography / phraseology.

677. Mieder, Wolfgang. "Proverbs in Nazi Germany. The Promulgation of Anti–Semitism and Stereotypes through Folklore." *Journal of American Folklore*, 95 (1982), 435–464. Also in W. Mieder. *Proverbs Are Never Out of Season: Popular Wisdom in the Modern Age*. New York: Oxford University Press, 1993. 225–255.
Anti–Semitism / collection / folklore / German / Adolf Hitler / Jewish / manipulation / National Socialism / politics / propaganda / race / rhetoric / stereotype.

678. Mieder, Wolfgang. "Sexual Content of German Wellerisms." *Maledicta*, 6 (1982), 215–223.
Content / German / graffiti / humor / mass media / obscenity / scatology / sex / sexuality / wellerism / wordplay.

679. Mieder, Wolfgang. "A Proverb a Day Keeps No Chauvinism Away." *Proverbium*, 2 (1985), 273–277.
Advertisement / anti–feminism / chauvinism / gender / misogyny / prejudice / slogan / stereotype / women.

680. Mieder, Wolfgang. "Neues zur demoskopischen Sprichwörterkunde." *Proverbium*, 2 (1985), 307–328.
Age / attitude / culture / empiricism / familiarity / field research / frequency / gender / German / Gerda Grober–Glück / K. Hattemer / Grigorii L'vovich Permiakov / paremiological minimum / E.K. Scheuch / society / sociology / statistics / use / value.

681. Mieder, Wolfgang. "Popular Views of the Proverb." *Proverbium*, 2 (1985), 109–143. Also in W. Mieder. *Proverbs Are Never Out of Season: Popular Wisdom in the Modern Age*. New York: Oxford University Press, 1993. 18–40.
tradition / truth / wisdom.

682. Mieder, Wolfgang. "History and Interpretation of a Proverb about Human Nature: 'Big Fish Eat Little Fish'." In W. Mieder. *Tradition and Innovation in Folk Literature*. Hanover,

New Hampshire: University Press of New England, 1987. 178–228 and 259–268 (notes). With 6 illustrations.
Advertisement / antiquity / behavior / Pieter Brueghel / context / culture / dissemination / folklore / history / iconography / literature / mass media / meaning / origin / society / "Big fish eat little fish."

683. Mieder, Wolfgang. "The Proverb in the Modern Age: Old Wisdom in New Clothing." In W. Mieder. *Tradition and Innovation in Folk Literature*. Hanover, New Hampshire: University Press of New England. 1987. 118–156 and 248–255 (notes). With 5 illustrations.
Anti–feminism / Pieter Brueghel / folklore / function / iconography / literature / Martin Luther / misogyny / modernity / poetry / society / tradition / wisdom / wordplay / "Wer nicht liebt Wein, Weib und Gesang, der bleibt ein Narr sein Leben lang."

684. Mieder, Wolfgang. *American Proverbs: A Study of Texts and Contexts*. Bern: Peter Lang, 1989. 394 pp. With 40 illustrations.
African American / American / anti–proverb / bibliography / context / culture / Ralph Waldo Emerson / ethnicity / folklore / Benjamin Franklin / iconography / literature / mass media / music / Native American / parody / poetry / society / wellerism / wordplay / "Different strokes for different folks."

685. Mieder, Wolfgang. "'It's Five Minutes to Twelve': Folklore and Saving Life on Earth." *International Folklore Review*, 7 (1989), 10–21. With 16 illustrations.
Cold War / environment / ethics / folklore / graffiti / iconography / literature / mass media / poetry / politics / society / war / "Hear no evil, see no evil, speak no evil."

686. Mieder, Wolfgang. "Consideraciones generales acerca de la naturaleza del proverbio." *Revista de Investigaciones Folkloricas*, 5 (1990), 7–16. Also in English as "General Thoughts on the Nature of the Proverb." *Revista de etnografie si folclor*, 36, nos. 3–4 (1991), 151–164. Translated into Russian by G.L. Kapchits as "O prirode poslovits." *Obraz mira v slove i rituale*. Eds. N.V. Zlydneva, V.N. Toporov, and T.V. Tsiv'ian. Moskva: Institut Slavianovedeniia Balkanistiki RAN, 1992. 188–201. Chinese translation by Hu Xinnian as "Yanyu Tezheng zhi Graishu." *Xiyu Wen–hua*, no volume given, no. 72 (February–March 1992), 12–18 and 26. Polish translation by

Stanisław Predota as "Ogólne uwagi o naturze przysłów." *Literatura Ludowa*, 37, no. 3 (1993), 49–63. Published again in Spanish as "Consideraciones generales acerca de la naturaleza del proverbio." *Paremia*, 3 (1994), 17–26. Japanese translation by Katsuaki Takeda as "Hitori no Kichi, Mannin no Chie." *Rekishiminzokugaku*, no volume given, no. 6 (1997), 234–261, based on Wolfgang Mieder's slightly longer version "'The Wit of One, and the Wisdom of Many': General Thoughts on the Nature of the Proverb." In W. Mieder. *Proverbs Are Never Out of Season: Popular Wisdom in the Modern Age*. New York: Oxford University Press, 1993. 3–17.
Context / currency / definition / marker / metaphor / origin / paremiology / poetics / semantics / structure / style / traditionality / variant.

687. Mieder, Wolfgang. "Paremiology and Psychology." *Canadian Psychology/Psychologie Canadienne*, 31, no. 3 (1990), 208 and 213–214.
Context / folklore / function / paremiology / proverbs test / psychology / Tim Rogers / semantics / truth / universality.

688. Mieder, Wolfgang. "'An Apple a Day Keeps the Doctor Away': Traditional and Modern Aspects of English Medical Proverbs." *Proverbium*, 8 (1991), 77–106. With 8 illustrations. Also in W. Mieder. *Proverbs Are Never Out of Season: Popular Wisdom in the Modern Age*. New York: Oxford University Press, 1993. 152–172. With 5 illustrations.
Diachronic / disease / English / health / iconography / medicine / "An apple a day keeps the doctor away" / "Early to bed and early to rise, makes a man healthy, wealthy and wise" / "Stuff a cold and starve a fever" / "Prevention is better than cure."

689. Mieder, Wolfgang. "'Good Proverbs Make Good Vermonters': A Study of Regional Proverbs in the United States." *Proverbium*, 9 (1992), 159–178. Also slightly shortened in *We Vermonters: Perspectives on the Past*. Eds. Michael Sherman and Jennie Versteeg. Montpelier, Vermont: Vermont Historical Society, 1992. 59–69. The longer version also in W. Mieder. *Proverbs Are Never Out of Season: Popular Wisdom in the Modern Age*. New York: Oxford University Press, 1993. 173–192. With 2 illustrations.
American / content / culture / distribution / folklore / iconography / meaning / origin / Vermont / society / worldview.

690. Mieder, Wolfgang. "Paremiological Minimum and Cultural Literacy." *Creativity and Tradition in Folklore: New Directions.* Ed. Simon J. Bronner. Logan, Utah: Utah State University Press, 1992. 185–203. Also in W. Mieder. *Proverbs Are Never Out of Season: Popular Wisdom in the Modern Age.* New York: Oxford University Press, 1993. 41–57. With 4 illustrations. Once again in *Wise Words: Essays on the Proverb.* Ed. W. Mieder. New York: Garland Publishing, 1994. 297–316.
American / cultural literacy / culture / English / familiarity / frequency / E.D. Hirsch / iconography / paremiological minimum / Grigorii L'vovich Permiakov / Bartlett Jere Whiting.

691. Mieder, Wolfgang. *Proverbs Are Never Out of Season: Popular Wisdom in the Modern Age.* New York: Oxford University Press, 1993. 302 pp. With 38 illustrations.
Advertising / American / anti–Semitism / cultural literacy / culture / definition / English / folklore / Benjamin Franklin / German / iconography / loan translation / mass media / medicine / metaphor / National Socialism / paremiological minmum / poetics / semantics / slogan / society / stereotype / structure / variation / Vermont / wisdom / "An apple a day keeps the doctor away" / "To throw the baby out with the bath water" / "Early to bed and early to rise, makes a man healthy, wealthy and wise" / "Stuff a cold and starve a fever" / "A picture is worth a thousand words" / "Prevention is better than cure."

692. Mieder, Wolfgang. "'The Apple Doesn't Fall Far From the Tree': A Historical and Contextual Proverb Study Based on Books, Archives, and Databases." *Midwestern Folklore*, 19, no. 2 (1993), 69–98. With 1 illustration. Also in W. Mieder. *Strategies of Wisdom: Anglo–American and German Proverb Studies.* Baltmannsweiler: Schneider Verlag Hohengehren, 2000. 109–144.
American / collection / computer / context / database / diachronic / dictionary / German / iconography / loan translation / mass media / "The apple doesn't fall far from the tree."

693. Mieder, Wolfgang. "'The Grass Is Always Greener on the Other Side of the Fence': An American Proverb of Discontent." *Proverbium*, 10 (1993), 151–184. With 10 illustrations. Also in *Wise Words: Essays on the Proverb.* Ed. W. Mieder. New York: Garland Publishing, 1994. 515–542.

American / iconography / literature / mass media / meaning / music / origin / worldview / "The grass is always greener on the other side of the fence."

694. Mieder, Wolfgang. "'The Only Good Indian Is a Dead Indian': History and Meaning of a Proverbial Stereotype." *Journal of American Folklore*, 106 (1993), 38–60. Also in *Folk Narrative and World View. Vorträge des 10. Kongresses der Internationalen Gesellschaft für Volkserzählungsforschung. Innsbruck 1992*. Ed. Leander Petzoldt. Frankfurt am Main: Peter Lang, 1996. 507–532; and in W. Mieder. *The Politics of Proverbs. From Traditional Wisdom to Proverbial Stereotypes*. Madison, Wisconsin: The University of Wisconsin Press, 1997. 138–159 and 221–227 (notes).
American / ethnicity / folklore / history / meaning / Native American / origin / prejudice / slur / stereotype / structure / variation / "The only good Indian is a dead Indian."

695. Mieder, Wolfgang (ed.). *Wise Words: Essays on the Proverb*. New York: Garland Publishing, 1994. 605 pp. With 2 illustrations.
Ambiguity / analogy / anthropology / Bible / bibliography / Pieter Brueghel / context / contradiction / cultural literacy / Emily Dickinson / ethnicity / fable / folklore / graffiti / history / iconography / linguistics / literature / metaphor / national character / paremiological minimum / paremiology / performance / perlocution / pragmatics / prejudice / proverb picture / proverbiality / psychology / semiotics / slur / society / structure / "When Adam delved and Eve span, who was then the gentleman?" / "The grass is always greener on the other side of the fence."

696. Mieder, Wolfgang. "'Make Hell While the Sun Shines': Proverbial Rhetoric in Winston Churchill's *The Second World War*." *Folklore* (London), 106 (1995), 57–69. Also in W. Mieder. *The Politics of Proverbs. From Traditional Wisdom to Proverbial Stereotypes*. Madison, Wisconsin: The University of Wisconsin Press, 1997. 39–66 and 200–206 (notes).
Winston S. Churchill / discourse / English / history / politics / rhetoric / speech / war / "Blood, sweat, and tears."

697. Mieder, Wolfgang. "Proverbial Manipulation in Adolf Hitler's *Mein Kampf*." *International Folklore Review*, 10 (1995), 35–53. Also in W. Mieder. *The Politics of Proverbs. From Traditional Wisdom to Proverbial Stereotypes*. Madison, Wiscon-

sin: The University of Wisconsin Press, 1997. 9–38 and 193–200 (notes).
Anti–Semitism / German / Adolf Hitler / Jewish / National Socialism / politics / propaganda / race / rhetoric / somatism / stereotype.

698. Mieder, Wolfgang. "Language and Folklore [including proverbs] of the Holocaust." *The Holocaust: Introductory Essays*. Eds. David Scrase and W. Mieder. Burlington, Vermont: The Center for Holocaust Studies at the University of Vermont, 1996. 93–106.
Anti–Semitism / folklore / German / Adolf Hitler / Holocaust / Jewish / language / National Socialism / prejudice / propaganda / race / stereotype.

699. Mieder, Wolfgang. "Modern Paremiology in Retrospect and Prospect." *Memoirs of the '96 Tokyo International Proverb Forum*. Ed. Yoshikatsu Kitamura. Tokyo: The Japan Society for Proverb Studies, 1996. 5–18. With slight modifications also in *Embracing the Baobab Tree: The African Proverb in the 21st Century*. Ed. Willem Saayman. Pretoria: University of South Africa, 1997. 3–36; and in *Paremia*, 6 (1997), 399–416. Also in W. Mieder. *Strategies of Wisdom: Anglo–American and German Proverb Studies*. Baltmannsweiler: Schneider Verlag Hohengehren, 2000. 7–36.
Anthropology / context / contradiction / culture / definition / empiricism / folklore / function / history / iconography / linguistics / literature / mass media / narrative / paremiology / pedagogy / philology / psychology / religion / semantics / semiotics / sociology / stereotype / Archer Taylor / teaching / use.

700. Mieder, Wolfgang. "'No Tickee, No Washee': Subtleties of a Proverbial Slur." *Western Folklore*, 55, no. 1 (1996), 1–40. Also in W. Mieder. *The Politics of Proverbs. From Traditional Wisdom to Proverbial Stereotypes*. Madison, Wisconsin: The University of Wisconsin Press, 1997. 160–189 and 227–235 (notes).
American / Chinese / Chinese American / dissemination / ethnicity / meaning / origin / prejudice / slur / stereotype / "No tickee, no washee."

701. Mieder, Wolfgang. "Raising the Iron Curtain: Proverbs and Political Rhetoric of the Cold War." *The Spoils of War: The Bright and Bitter Fruits of Human Conflict*. Eds. Jürgen Kleist

and Bruce A. Butterfield. New York: Peter Lang, 1997. 87–126. With 6 illustrations. Also in W. Mieder. *The Politics of Proverbs. From Traditional Wisdom to Proverbial Stereotypes*. Madison, Wisconsin: The University of Wisconsin Press, 1997. 99–137 and 214–221 (notes). With 20 illustrations. A much shorter version appeared in *Germany Reunified: A Five- and Fifty–Year Retrospective*. Eds. Peter M. Daly, Hans Walter Frischkopf, Trudis Goldsmith–Reber, and Horst Richter. New York: Peter Lang, 1997. 131–148. With 12 illustrations.
American / Cold War / discourse / German / iconography / Iron Curtain / mass media / politics / propaganda / rhetoric / Russian / war.

702. Mieder, Wolfgang. *The Politics of Proverbs. From Traditional Wisdom to Proverbial Stereotypes*. Madison, Wisconsin: The University of Wisconsin Press, 1997. 260 pp. With 20 illustrations.
Winston S. Churchill / communication / discourse / ethnicity / history / Adolf Hitler / iconography / mass media / metaphor / National Socialism / politics / propaganda / race / rhetoric / slur / stereotype / Harry S. Truman / wisdom / "The only good Indian is a dead Indian" / "No tickee, no washee."

703. Mieder, Wolfgang. *"A House Divided": From Biblical Proverb to Lincoln and Beyond*. Burlington, Vermont: The University of Vermont, 1998. 163 pp. With 10 illustrations.
American / Bible / Willy Brandt / German / history / iconography / Abraham Lincoln / literature / metaphor / politics / rhetoric / society / Daniel Webster / "A house divided against itself cannot stand."

704. Mieder, Wolfgang. *"'Alter schützt vor Torheit und Weisheit nicht': Sprichwörter über das Alter(n) aus Literatur und Massenmedien." Jura Soyfer: Internationale Zeitschrift für Kulturwissenschaften*, 8, no. 1 (1999), 5–16. With 14 illustrations.
Age / aging / content / culture / elder / German / gerontology / iconography / literature / mass media / society / worldview.

705. Mieder, Wolfgang. *Sprichwörter/Redensarten – Parömiologie*. Heidelberg: Julius Groos, 1999. 49 pp.
Anthropology / bibliography / folklore / genre / iconography / linguistics / paremiography / paremiology / poetics / psychology / semantics / semiotics.

706. Mieder, Wolfgang. "Sprichwörterkunde." *Einführung in die synchrone Sprachwissenschaft*. Ed. Peter Ernst. Wien: Edition Praesens, 1999. Chapter 17, 1–32.
Anthropology / bibliography / definition / folklore / genre / iconography / linguistics / literature / mass media / origin / paremiography / paremiology / psychology.

707. Mieder, Wolfgang. "'A House Divided Cannot Stand': From Bible Proverb to Abraham Lincoln and on to Willy Brandt." *Understanding Wisdom: Sources, Science, and Society*. Ed. Warren S. Brown. Radnor, Pennsylvania: Templeton Foundation Press, 2000. 57–102. Also in W. Mieder. *Strategies of Wisdom: Anglo–American and German Proverb Studies*. Baltmannsweiler: Schneider Verlag Hohengehren, 2000. 171–203.
American / Bible / Willy Brandt / folklore / German / history / Abraham Lincoln / literature / metaphor / politics / religion / rhetoric / society / "A house divided against itself cannot stand."

708. Mieder, Wolfgang. *Strategies of Wisdom: Anglo–American and German Proverb Studies*. Baltmannsweiler: Schneider Verlag Hohengehren, 2000. 372 pp.
African American / American / anti–Semitism / behavior / Willy Brandt / Bertolt Brecht / Lord Chesterfield / children / Civil War / culture / Charles Dickens / Frederick Douglass / education / English / ethnicity / folklore / Benjamin Franklin / German / Adolf Hitler / Victor Klemperer / language / Abraham Lincoln / literature / National Socialism / paremiology / politics / propaganda / race / rhetoric / society / stereotype / worldview.

709. Mieder, Wolfgang. *The Proverbial Abraham Lincoln: An Index to Proverbs in the Works of Abraham Lincoln*. New York: Peter Lang, 2000. 209 pp.
American / Bible / Civil War / collection / discourse / Abraham Lincoln / politics / rhetoric / slavery / war / "A house divided against itself cannot stand."

710. Mieder, Wolfgang. "'Do Unto Others as You Would Have Them Do Unto You': Frederick Douglass's Proverbial Struggle for Civil Rights." *Journal of American Folklore*, 114, no. 453 (2001), 331–357. Also in W. Mieder. *Strategies of Wisdom: Anglo–American and German Proverb Studies*. Baltmannsweiler: Schneider Verlag Hohengehren, 2000. 205–236.

African American / American / civil rights / Frederick Douglass / ethnicity / folklore / history / literature / politics / prejudice / race / rhetoric / slavery / society / stereotype.

711. Mieder, Wolfgang. *"No Struggle, No Progress": Frederick Douglass and His Proverbial Rhetoric for Civil Rights.* New York: Peter Lang, 2001. 532 pp.
African American / American / civil rights / collection / Frederick Douglass / ethnicity / folklore / history / literature / politics / prejudice / race / rhetoric / slavery / society / stereotype / "No struggle, no progress."

712. Mieder, Wolfgang. "'Paddle Your Own Canoe': Frederick Douglass's Proverbial Message in His 'Self–Made Men' Speech." *Midwestern Folklore*, 27, no. 2 (2001), 21–40.
African American / American / civil rights / Frederick Douglass / ethnicity / folklore / history / literature / politics / prejudice / race / slavery / slogan / society / stereotype / "Paddle your own canoe" / "Self–made men."

713. Mieder, Wolfgang. *"Call a Spade a Spade": From Classical Phrase to Racial Slur. A Case Study.* New York: Peter Lang, 2002. 251 pp. With 6 illustrations.
Advertisement / African American / American / antiquity / Aristophanes / empiricism / English / Erasmus of Rotterdam / ethnicity / folklore / history / iconography / literature / loan translation / mass media / meaning / origin / politics / prejudice / race / slur / society / sociology / stereotype.

714. Mieder, Wolfgang, and George B. Bryan. *The Proverbial Winston S. Churchill: An Index to Proverbs in the Works of Sir Winston Churchill.* Westport, Connecticut: Greenwood Press, 1995. 448 pp.
Winston S. Churchill / collection / discourse / English / history / politics / rhetoric / speech / war.

715. Mieder, Wolfgang, and George B. Bryan. *The Proverbial Harry S. Truman: An Index to Proverbs in the Works of Harry S. Truman.* New York: Peter Lang, 1997. 247 pp.
American / collection / discourse / politics / rhetoric / speech / Harry S. Truman.

716. Mieder, Wolfgang, and Alan Dundes (eds.). *The Wisdom of Many: Essays on the Proverb.* New York: Garland Publishing,

1981. Rpt. Madison, Wisconsin: The University of Wisconsin Press, 1994 (paperback edition). 352 pp.
Advertisement / African / Bible / Chinese / fatalism / Finnish / humor / Irish / literature / logic / mass media / medicine / metaphor / national character / New Testament / orality / politics / proverbs test / psychology / semantics / William Shakespeare / society / Spanish / structure / wisdom / Yiddish / "It is an ill bird that fouls its own nest" / "Stuff a cold and starve a fever."

717. Mieder, Wolfgang, and Deborah Holmes. *"Children and Proverbs Speak the Truth": Teaching Proverbial Wisdom to Fourth Graders.* Burlington, Vermont: The University of Vermont, 2000. 240 pp.
Abstraction / behavior / character / children / competence / comprehension / context / definition / empiricism / ethics / familiarity / frequency / iconography / meaning / morality / pedagogy / psychology / teaching / use / wisdom.

718. Mieder, Wolfgang, and Janet Sobieski. *Proverb Iconography: An International Bibliography.* New York: Peter Lang, 1999. 225 pp. With 25 illustrations.
Bibliography / Hieronymus Bosch / Pieter Brueghel / cloth / Francisco de Goya / graffiti / iconography / image / metaphor / misericord / "Netherlandic Proverbs" / proverb picture / textile / woodcut.

719. Mifsud–Chircop, George. "Proverbiality and Worldview in Maltese and Arabic Proverbs." *Proverbium*, 18 (2001), 247–255.
Arabic / culture / folklore / Maltese / proverbiality / society / worldview.

720. Mikulić, Gordana. "On Understanding Proverbs." *Studia ethnologica* (Zagreb), 3 (1991), 145–159.
American / comprehension / Croatian / empiricism / equivalent / foreign language / metaphor / statistics / structure / student / teaching.

721. Mine, Hisayo, Hiroshi Mine, and Haruyo Hama. "Affectional Expressions in Japanese Proverbs." *The Japanese Journal of Psychology*, 54 (1984), 382–385 (in Japanese with English abstract).
Affection / attitude / behavior / emotion / Japanese / psycholinguistics / psychology / student.

722. Mitschri, Elena. "Idiommodelle aus psycholinguistischer Sicht als Voraussetzung für das Erschließen des Gemeinsamen und des Besonderen in den einzelnen Sprachen." *Europhras 95: Europäische Phraseologie im Vergleich: Gemeinsames Erbe und kulturelle Vielfalt.* Ed. Wolfgang Eismann. Bochum: Norbert Brockmeyer, 1998. 523–534.
Anthropomorphism / behavior / cognition / culture / idiom / language / psycholinguistics / value / worldview.

723. Mkuchu, Jesca S. "Proverbs as Pillars of Social Structure: A Case Study of Kaguru Proverbs." *Embracing the Baobab Tree: The African Proverb in the 21st Century.* Ed. Willem Saayman. Pretoria: University of South Africa, 1997. 105–114.
African / context / enculturation / function / Kaguru / law / meaning / society.

724. Mohapatra, Kulamoni. "Social Context of Oriya Proverbs." *Folk Culture V: Folk Culture and the Great Tradition.* Ed. K. Mohapatra. Cuttack/Orissa: Institute of Oriental and Orissan Studies, 1984. 151–154.
Caste / content / context / culture / field research / folklore / Indian / Oriya / riddle / society.

725. Monteiro, George. "Robert Frost's 'Linked Analogies' [in 'Mending Wall']." *New England Quarterly*, 46 (1973), 463–468.
American / analogy / Robert Frost / literature / poetry / "Good fences make good neighbors."

726. Monye, Ambrose A. "Proverb Usage: Kinds of Relationships." *Proverbium*, 3 (1986), 85–99.
African / context / function / Igbo / meaning / metaphor / society / strategy / use.

727. Monye, Ambrose A. "Devices of Indirection in Aniocha Proverb Usage." *Proverbium*, 4 (1987), 111–126.
African / context / function / Igbo / indirection / metaphor / society / strategy / use.

728. Monye, Ambrose A. "On Why People Use Proverbs." *Africana Marburgensia*, 23, no. 1 (1990), 3–11.
African / argumentation / communication / context / didacticism / experience / Igbo / imagery / orality / speech act / tradition / wisdom.

729. Moon, W. Jay. "Builsa Proverbs and the Gospel." *Missiology: An International Review*, 30, no. 2 (2002), 171–186.
African / Bible / Builsa / culture / missionary / New Testament / religion / tradition / worldview.

730. Morawski, Stefan. "The Basic Functions of Quotation." *Sign, Language, Culture*. Ed. Algirdas–Julien Greimas et al. The Hague: Mouton, 1970. 690–705.
Amplification / authority / culture / function / literature / quotation / style.

731. Mouelle, E. Njoh. "Sagesse des proverbes et développement." *Abbia*, 27–28 (1974), 93–103; also published in *Zaïre–Afrique*, 92 (1974), 107–116.
African / economics / politics / proverbialization / society / sociology / truth / wisdom / worldview.

732. Mueller, Rachel A.G., and Raymond W. Gibbs. "Processing Idioms with Multiple Meanings." *Journal of Psycholinguistic Research*, 16, no. 1 (1987), 63–81.
Brain / comprehension / figurativeness / idiom / literalness / meaning / semantics / psycholinguistics / psychology.

733. Müller, Renate. *Phraseologismen in englischen Fachtexten der Humanmedizin: Eine empirische Untersuchung zur Fachphraseologie*. Frankfurt am Main: Peter Lang, 1993. 205 pp.
Communication / empiricism / English / function / idiom / linguistics / medicine / phraseologism / phraseology / profession / semantics / structure.

734. Müller, Siegfried. "Können Sprichwörter bei der Entwicklung psychologischer Theorien helfen?" *Gruppendynamik*, 29, no. 1 (1998), 75–105.
Abstraction / attitude / behavior / cognition / definition / psycholinguistics / psychology / sociology / therapy / validity / worldview.

735. Müller–Thurau, Claus Peter. *Laß uns mal 'ne Schnecke angraben. Sprache und Sprüche der Jugendszene*. Düsseldorf: Econ, 1983. 176 pp.
Antiproverb / attitude / collection / content / currency / German / graffiti / linguistics / meaning / phraseologism / slogan / society / sociolinguistics / structure / youth / worldview.

736. Munske, Horst Haider. "Wie entstehen Phraseologismen." *Vielfalt des Deutschen. Festschrift für Werner Besch.* Eds. Klaus J. Mattheier, Klaus–Peter Wegera, Walter Hoffmann, Jürgen Macha and Hans–Joachim Solms. Frankfurt am Main: Peter Lang, 1993. 481–516.
Definition / figurativeness / lexicology / linguistics / loan translation / metaphor / metonymy / modification / motivation / origin / phraseologism / poetics.

737. Münsterberg, Hugo. "Naive Psychology." In H. Münsterberg. *Psychology and Social Sanity.* Garden City, New York: Doubleday, Page & Co., 1914. 291–320.
Bible / Indian / mentality / psychology / science / truth / validity / wisdom.

738. Mutunga, Mutinda wa. *Akamba Theology and the Ecology of Marriage and Family in Cultural Context: A Proverb "Kalula Katune Katunivaw'a ni Kunengeleanilw'a".* Diss. Fuller Theological Seminary, 1996. 311 pp.
African / Akamba / Bible / context / culture / ethics / family / marriage / morality / religion / society.

N

739. Nahberger, Günter. "'Ende gut, alles gut': Anmerkungen zu einer sprechakttheoretischen Analyse von Sprichwörtern." *"Wer A sägt, muss auch B sägen": Beiträge zur Phraseologie und Sprichwortforschung aus dem Westfälischen Arbeitskreis.* Eds. Dietrich Hartmann and Jan Wirrer. Baltmannsweiler: Schneider Verlag Hohengehren, 2002. 255–272.
Communication / context / discourse / indirection / pragmatics / rhetoric / semantics / speech act.

740. Nahberger, Günter. "'Lügen haben kurze Beine': Welche Sprechhandlungen kann man mit Sprichwörtern vollziehen? Eine empirische Untersuchung." *"Wer A sägt, muss auch B sägen": Beiträge zur Phraseologie und Sprichwortforschung aus dem Westfälischen Arbeitskreis.* Eds. Dietrich Hartmann and Jan Wirrer. Baltmannsweiler: Schneider Verlag Hohengehren, 2002. 273–286.
Communication / context / discourse / empiricism / indirection / introductory formula / pragmatics / proverbs test / rhetoric / semantics / speech act.

741. Nakagawa, Y., H. Tanabe, M. Ikeda, H. Kazui, K. Ito, N. Inoue, Y. Hatakenaka, T. Sawada, H. Ikeda, and J. Shiraishi. "Completion Phenomenon [for Proverbs] in Transcortical Sensory Aphasia." *Behavioural Neurology*, 6, no. 3 (1993), 135–142.
Aphasia / brain / cognition / comprehension / meaning / memory / neurolinguistics / proverbs test / psychiatry / psychology.

742. Nakayama, Keiko. *Der menschliche Körper in den Sprichwörtern und sprichwörtlichen Redensarten im Deutschen und Japanischen.* M.A. Thesis University of Freiburg, 1992. 118 pp.
Behavior / equivalent / German / Japanese / metaphor / phraseologism / somatism / symbolism.

743. Nayak, Nandini P., and Raymond W. Gibbs. "Conceptual Knowledge in the Interpretation of Idioms." *Journal of Experimental Psychology: General*, 119, no. 3 (1990), 315–330.
Context / figurativeness / idiom / interpretation / knowledge / meaning / metaphor / psycholinguistics / psychology.

744. Ndzomo Malla, Jean–Marie. *Proverbes: Vrais ou faux? Crise et dangers du proverbe africain.* Bandundu, Zaire: Ceeba Publications, 1982. 86 pp.

African / classification / collection / context / definition / folklore / function / knowledge / life / orality / semantics / tradition / truth / wisdom / worldview.

745. Nel, Philip J. "Juxtaposition and Logic in the Wisdom Saying." *Journal of Northwest Semitic Languages*, 24, no. 1 (1998), 115–127.
Bible / experience / juxtaposition / logic / poetics / religion / structure / wisdom.

746. Newmeyer, Frederick J. "The Regularity of Idiom Behavior." *Lingua*, 34 (1974), 327–342.
Figurativeness / fixidity / idiom / linguistics / literalness / meaning / structure / syntax.

747. Nguyén, Nguyén, Edward F. Foules, and Kathleen Carlin. "Proverbs as Psychological Interpretations Among Vietnamese." *Asian Folklore Studies*, 50, no. 2 (1991), 311–318.
Behavior / communication / culture / folklore / indirection / interpretation / mentality / psychology / therapy / Vietnamese / worldview.

748. Niceforo, Alfredo. "Contributo dei proverbi alle 'autogiustificazioni' e alle 'autoconsolazioni.'" *Rivista di Etnografia*, 1, nos. 3–4 (1947), 23–29.
Attitude / behavior / consolation / experience / Italian / justification / life / rationalization / worldview.

749. Nichols, Ray. "Maxims, 'Practical Wisdom,' and the Language of Action: Beyond Grand Theory." *Political Theory*, 24, no. 4 (1996), 687–705.
Common sense / Francesco Guicciardini / François La Rochefoucauld / language / maxim / politics / Colin Powell / Henry Taylor / wisdom.

750. Nicolaisen, William F.H. "The Proverbial Scot." *Proverbium*, 11 (1994), 197–206.
Content / ethnicity / national character / prejudice / Scottish / stereotype / worldview.

751. Nicolas, Tim. "Semantics of Idiom Modification." *Idioms: Structural and Psychological Perspectives*. Eds. Martin Everaert, Erik–Jan van der Linden, André Schenk, and Rob Schreuder. Hillsdale, New Jersey: Lawrence Erlbaum Associates, 1995. 233–252.

Grammar / idiom / linguistics / modification / semantics / structure / syntax.

752. Niedermeier, Hans. "Die Rothaarigen in volkskundlicher Sicht." *Bayerisches Jahrbuch für Volkskunde*, no volume given (1963), 76–106.
Appearance / belief / character / folklore / German / phraseologism / red hair / somatism / superstition.

753. Nierenberg, Jess. "Proverbs in Graffiti: Taunting Traditional Wisdom." *Maledicta*, 7 (1983), 41–58. Also in *Wise Words: Essays on the Proverb*. Ed. Wolfgang Mieder. New York: Garland Publishing, 1994. 543–561.
American / anti–proverb / English / field research / German / graffiti / humor / morality / obscenity / parody / psychoanalysis / scatology / sex.

754. Nikolaeva, T.M. "Zagadka i poslovitsa: sotsial'nye funktsii i grammatika." *Issledovaniia v oblasti balto–slavianskoi dukhovnoi kul'tury: Zagadka kak tekst*. Ed. T. M. Nikolaeva. Moskva: Izdatel'stvo "Indrik", 1994. 143–177.
Communication / culture / function / grammar / linguistics / riddle / Russian / semantics / slogan / society.

755. Nippold, Marilyn A. "Comprehension of Figurative Language in Youth." *Topics in Language Disorders*, 5, no. 3 (1985), 1–20.
Adolescence / age / bibliography / children / cognition / comprehension / figurativeness / language / literalness / meaning / metaphor / psycholinguistics / psychology / youth.

756. Nippold, Marilyn A. "Figurative Language." *Later Language Development: Ages 9 Through 19*. Ed. Marilyn A. Nippold. Boston: College–Hill Press, 1988. 179–210.
Adolescence / age / children / cognition / comprehension / figurativeness / idiom / language / literalness / metaphor / proverbs test / psycholinguistics.

757. Nippold, Marilyn A., Melissa M. Allen, and Dixon I. Kirsch. "How Adolescents Comprehend Unfamiliar Proverbs: The Role of Top–Down and Bottom–Up Processes." *Journal of Speech, Language, and Hearing Research*, 43, no. 3 (2000), 621–630.

Adolescence / age / comprehension / concreteness / familiarity / figurativeness / language / literalness / psycholinguistics / semantics / student.

758. Nippold, Marilyn A., and Faridah Serajul Haq. "Proverb Comprehension in Youth: The Role of Concreteness and Familiarity." *Journal of Speech and Hearing Research*, 39, no. 1 (1996), 166–176.
Abstraction / adolescence / age / children / comprehension / concreteness / familiarity / figurativeness / literalness / psycholinguistics / youth.

759. Nippold, Marilyn A., Stephanie A. Martin, and Barbara J. Erskine. "Proverb Comprehension in Context: A Developmental Study with Children and Adolescents." *Journal of Speech and Hearing Research*, 31 (1988), 19–28.
Adolescence / age / analogy / children / comprehension / context / language / literalness / proverbs test / psycholinguistics.

760. Nippold, Marilyn A., and Michelle Rudzinski. "Familiarity and Transparency in Idiom Explanation: A Developmental Study of Children and Adolescents." *Journal of Speech and Hearing Research*, 36 (1993), 728–737.
Adolescence / age / children / comprehension / concreteness / familiarity / idiom / psycholinguistics.

761. Nippold, Marilyn A., and Catherine L. Taylor. "Idiom Understanding in Youth: Further Examination of Familiarity and Transparency." *Journal of Speech and Hearing Research*, 38 (1995), 426–433.
Adolescence / age / children / comprehension / concreteness / familiarity / idiom / psycholinguistics / youth.

762. Nippold, Marilyn A., Linda D. Uhden, and Ilsa E. Schwarz. "Proverb Explanation Through the Lifespan: A Developmental Study of Adolescents and Adults." *Journal of Speech, Language, and Hearing Research*, 40, no. 2 (1997), 245–253.
Abstraction / adolescence / adult / age / comprehension / concreteness / familiarity / figurativeness / life / proverbs test / psycholinguistics.

763. Nordland, Odd. "Ordtak, sosial funksjon og kultursamanheng." *Norveg*, 7 (1960), 49–92.
Behavior / culture / function / literature / poetry / society / sociology / wisdom.

764. Norrick, Neal R. "Proverbial Perlocutions: How to Do Things with Proverbs." *Grazer Linguistische Studien*, 17–18 (1982), 169–183. Also in *Wise Words: Essays on the Proverb*. Ed. Wolfgang Mieder. New York: Garland Publishing, 1994. 143–157.
Folklore / function / linguistics / performance / perlocution / speech act / tradition.

765. Norrick, Neal R. *How Proverbs Mean. Semantic Studies in English Proverbs*. Amsterdam: Mouton, 1985. 213 pp.
Ambiguity / bibliography / context / definition / didacticism / English / figurativeness / form / function / language / linguistics / literalness / literature / mass media / meaning / metaphor / paradox / semantics / William Shakespeare / speech act / structure / syntax / traditionality.

766. Norrick, Neal R. "How Paradox Means." *Poetics Today*, 10, no. 3 (1989), 551–562.
Contradiction / figurativeness / idiomaticity / language / linguistics / meaning / metaphor / paradox / phraseologism / speech act / structure.

767. Norrick, Neal R. "Proverbial Emotions: How Proverbs Encode and Evaluate Emotion." *Proverbium*, 11 (1994), 207–215.
Animal / emotion / ethics / hyperbole / image / linguistics / paradox / value / worldview.

768. Norrick, Neal R. "'Speech is Silver': On the Proverbial View of Language." *Proverbium*, 14 (1997), 277–287.
Content / ethics / language / linguistics / silence / speech / value / worldview.

769. Ntshinga, T.N. "How Proverbs Derive Their Meaning – Standard Proverbial Interpretation (SPI) vs. the Literal Reading of a Proverb." *South African Journal of African Languages*, 19, no. 2 (1999), 128–133.
African / culture / figurativeness / interpretation / literalness / meaning / metaphor / society.

770. Nuessel, Frank. "The Depiction of Older Adults and Aging in Italian Proverbs." *Proverbium*, 17 (2000), 299–314.
Adult / aging / behavior / content / elder / gender / gerontology / health / Italian / meaning / sexuality / society / wisdom.

771. Nuessel, Frank. "The Depiction of Women in Italian Proverbs." *Romance Languages Annual 1999*, 11 (2000), 235–241.
Behavior / character / content / culture / Italian / gender / women / misogyny / society / stereotype.

772. Nuessel, Frank, and Caterina Cicogna. "Proverbs and Metaphoric Language in Second–Language Acquisition." *Italiana*, 5 (1993), 259–273. With identical title under the sole authorship of Frank Nuessel also in *Studies in Applied Psychosemiotics*, 16 (1999), 157–178.
Discourse / foreign language / Italian / linguistics / metaphor / pedagogy / psycholinguistics / speech act / teaching.

773. Nussbaum, Stan. *The ABC of American Culture: First Steps toward Understanding the American People through Their Common Sayings and Proverbs.* Colorado Springs, Colorado: Global Mapping International, 1998. 55 pp.
American / collection / content / culture / ethics / life / national character / value / worldview.

774. Nwachukwu–Agbada, J.O.J. "Igbo 'Obscene' Proverbs: Context, Function and Annotation." *International Folklore Review*, 6 (1988), 42–52.
African / anthropology / context / ethics / folklore / function / humor / Igbo / meaning / obscenity / scatology / sex / sexuality / society / speech act.

775. Nwachukwu–Agbada, J.O.J. "An African Oral Literature and the Socialization of the Youth: The Case of Igbo Child–Proverbs." *Frankfurter Afrikanistische Blätter*, 2 (1990), 107–119.
African / children / ethics / Igbo / orality / parents / socialization / value / youth.

776. Nwachukwu–Agbada, J.O.J. "Wisdom in a Melting–Pot: Nigerian Urban Folk and Pidgin English Proverbs." *International Folklore Review*, 8 (1991), 124–129.
African / communication / ethnicity / folklore / language / linguistics / Nigerian / Pidgin English / society / wisdom.

777. Nwachukwu–Agbada, J.O.J. "Paradigms of Class Consciousness in the Igbo Past: Proverbs as Evidence." *Ihafa: A Journal of African Studies*, 1, no. 1 (1992–1993), 125–134.
African / class / culture / egalitarianism / history / Igbo / orality / society.

778. Nwasike, Dominic. "Complexity and Usage: Proverbs as Vehicle to African Philosophy." *Pan–African Journal*, 9 (1976), 55–71.
African / culture / history / Ibo / logic / morality / philosophy / religion / society.

779. Nze, Chukwuemeka. "The Concept of Contrariety in Igbo Proverbs." *The Nigerian Journal of Social Studies*, 2, no. 1 (1985), 12–17.
African / contradiction / Igbo / linguistics / logic / philosophy / wisdom.

780. Nze, Chukwuemeka. "The Ethicality of Igbo Contrary Proverbs." *Africana Marburgensia*, 23, no. 1 (1990), 12–22.
African / community / contradiction / ethics / Igbo / society / value.

O

781. Obelkevich, James. "Proverbs and Social History." *The Social History of Language*. Eds. Peter Burke and Roy Porter. Cambridge: Cambridge University Press, 1987. 43–72. Also in *Wise Words: Essays on the Proverb*. Ed. Wolfgang Mieder. New York: Garland Publishing, 1994. 211–252.
William Blake / Geoffrey Chaucer / class / collection / context / culture / diachronic / English / function / history / literature / meaning / mentality / William Shakespeare / society / sociology.

782. Obeng, Samuel Gyasi. "The Proverb as a Mitigating and Politeness Strategy in Akan Discourse." *Anthropological Linguistics*, 38, no. 3 (1996), 521–549.
African / Akan / anthropology / communication / discourse / field research / indirection / informant / interview / society / speech act / strategy.

783. Odlin, Terence. "Language Universals and Constraints on Proverbial Form." *Proverbium*, 3 (1986), 125–151.
Acquisition / comparison / form / linguistics / metaphor / proverbs test / structure / universality.

784. Oduyoye, Amba. "The Asante Woman: Socialization through Proverbs." *African Notes: Bulletin of the Institute of African Studies*, 8, no. 1 (1979), 5–11.
African / anthropology / Asante / Ashanti / behavior / children / gender / image / misogyny / sexuality / socialization / stereotype / worldview.

785. Ogishima, Takashi. "The Animals in the Finnish Proverbs." *Journal of Intercultural Studies*, extra series, no volume given, no. 2 (1992), 110–111.
Animal / behavior / cat / collection / culture / dog / Finnish / frequency / metaphor.

786. Ohaeto, Ezenwa. "The Context, Value, and Idea of Power in Igbo Proverbs." *Proverbium*, 11 (1994), 217–225.
African / behavior / community / context / culture / Igbo / power / society / value / worldview.

787. Oinas, Felix J. "The Foreigner as Devil, Thistle, and Gadfly." *Proverbium*, 15 (1970), 505–507.

Blason populaire / devil / ethnicity / foreigner / national character / prejudice / slur / stereotype.

788. Ojoade, J. Olowo. "African Sexual Proverbs: Some Yoruba Examples." *Folklore* (London), 94, no. 2 (1983), 201–213.
African / communication / ethics / folklore / narrative / obscenity / sex / sexuality / society / value / Yoruba.

789. Okenge, Osokonda, and Shomba Kinyamba. "Littérature orale tetela et éthique." *Africanistique*, 8 (1979), 107–121.
African / anthropology / ethics / function / literature / meaning / morality / orality / society / Tetela / use.

790. Olayinka, Bolaji Olukemi. "Proverbs: Issues of Yoruba Femininity from a Feminist Hermeneutical Perspective." *Embracing the Baobab Tree: The African Proverb in the 21st Century.* Ed. Willem Saayman. Pretoria: University of South Africa, 1997. 214–224.
African / anti–feminism / femininity / feminism / gender / hermeneutics / marriage / misogyny / prejudice / sexuality / stereotype / women / worldview / Yoruba.

791. Olejárová, Miriam. "Collocating Nature of Anomalies as a Basic Quality of Phraseological Units." *Europhras 97: Phraseology and Paremiology.* Ed. Peter Ďurčo. Bratislava: Akadémia PZ, 1998. 257–260.
Anomaly / collocation / figurativeness / idiomaticity / linguistics / phraseologism.

792. Olejárová, Miriam. "Einige Bemerkungen zu den Eigenschaften der Phraseologismen." *Proverbium*, 16 (1999), 279–285.
Anomaly / figurativeness / idiomaticity / linguistics / phraseologism / stability / syntax.

793. Olinick, Stanley L. "On Proverbs: Creativity, Communication, and Community." *Contemporary Psychoanalysis*, 23 (1987), 463–468.
Communication / community / creativity / experience / modernity / origin / psychoanalysis / psycholinguistics / repetition / society.

794. Oliver, Venita Sue. *Ideational Fluency and Proverb Comprehension: Comparisons Among and Between Bilingual and Monolingual College Students.* Diss. Northern Arizona University, 1991. 286 pp.

Bilingualism / cognition / comprehension / empiricism / figurativeness / informant / proverbs test / psychology / student.

795. Opata, Damian U. "The Nature of Speech in Igbo Proverbs." *Proverbium*, 9 (1992), 187–204.
African / behavior / ethics / Igbo / silence / speech / value / worldview.

796. Opata, Damian U. "Proverbs, Proverbial Idioms, and Intergroup Relations." *Proverbium*, 17 (2000), 315–328.
African / attitude / behavior / culture / ethnicity / folklore / generalization / idiom / Igbo / prejudice / society / sociology / worldview.

797. O'Reilly, P.O., and K. Harrison. "The Gorham Proverbs Test." *Diseases of the Nervous System*, 21 (1960), 382–385.
Abstraction / brain / Donald R. Gorham / proverbs test / psychiatry / psychology / schizophrenia.

798. Ortony, Andrew, Ralph E. Reynolds, and Judith A. Arter. "Metaphor: Theoretical and Empirical Research." *Psychological Bulletin*, 85 (1978), 919–943.
Analogy / bibliography / children / comprehension / context / empiricism / meaning / metaphor / psycholinguistics / psychology.

799. Ortony, Andrew, Diane L. Schallert, Ralph E. Reynolds, and Stephen J. Antos. "Interpreting Metaphors and Idioms: Some Effects of Context on Comprehension." *Journal of Verbal Learning and Verbal Behavior*, 17 (1978), 465–477.
Comprehension / context / figurativeness / idiom / interpretation / literalness / metaphor / psycholinguistics / psychology.

800. Ortony, Andrew, Terence J. Turner, and Nancy Larson–Shapiro. "Cultural and Instructional Influences on Figurative Language Comprehension by Inner City Children." *Research in the Teaching of English*, 19, no. 1 (1985), 25–36.
Children / cognition / comprehension / culture / education / figurativeness / pedagogy / teaching / verbal dueling.

801. Oschlies, Wolf. "'Der Deutsche hat den Affen erfunden...': Das Bild des Deutschen in slavischen Sprichwörtern." *Muttersprache*, 105 (1995), 324–346.

German / ethnicity / national character / prejudice / Russian / Slavic / slur / stereotype / "Der Deutsche hat den Affen erfunden."

802. Oshima, Tatehiko. "Proverbs in Japan." *Indian and Japanese Folklore: An Introductory Assessment.* Eds. Ramesh Mathur and Masahiro Manabe. Hirakata City, Japan: Kansai University of Foreign Studies Publication, 1984. 495–514.
Classification / content / culture / definition / genre / Japanese / life / meaning / mentality / paremiology / phraseologism / wordplay / worldview.

803. Ostrop, Gudula [sic]. *Die Wahl und Nutzung von Sprichwörtern in der Erforschung des Wissens über Selektion, Optimierung und Kompensation.* M.A. Thesis Freie Univ. Berlin, 1996. 94 pp.
Behavior / compensation / comprehension / culture / empiricism / informant / knowledge / optimization / psycholinguistics / selection / strategy / student.

804. Ostrop, Gudula, A.M. Freund, and Paul B. Baltes. "Selektion, Optimierung und Kompensation als Prozesse der erfolgreichen Entwicklung: Sprichwörter als Medium der Erfassung des kulturellen und individuellen Wissens." *40. Kongreß der Deutschen Gesellschaft für Psychologie, München, 22.–26. September 1996.* (unpublished handout at the congress). 11 pp.
Compensation / comprehension / culture / empiricism / informant / knowledge / optimization / psycholinguistics / selection / strategy / student.

805. Otakpor, Nkeonye. "A Note on the Logic of Proverbs: A Reply." *Proverbium,* 4 (1987), 263–269.
Analogy / argumentation / context / contradiction / David Cram / linguistics / logic / speech act / universality.

806. Owens, Christopher Charles. *Indexing and Retrieving Abstract Planning Knowledge.* Diss. Yale University, 1990. 203 pp.
Abstraction / cognition / context / intelligence / knowledge / memory / reasoning / retrieval / psycholinguistics / structure.

807. Owomoyela, Oyekan. "The Sociology of Sex and Crudity in Yoruba Proverbs." *Proverbium,* 20 (1972), 751–758.
African / context / metaphor / obscenity / sex / sexuality / sociology / Yoruba.

808. Owomoyela, Oyekan. "Proverbs: Exploration of an African Philosophy of Social Communication." *Ba Shiru: A Journal of African Languages and Literature*, 12, no. 1 (1984), 3–16.
African / attitude / communication / indirection / metaphor / philosophy / society / sociology / speech act / Yoruba.

P

809. Paczolay, Gyula. "Proverbs and Reality." *XIth Congress of the International Society for Folk–Narrative Research.* Ed. Jawaharlal Handoo. Mysore, India: Central Institute of Indian Languages, 1995. 223–241. Also published in *Proverbium*, 13 (1996), 281–297.
Ambiguity / contradiction / metaphor / reality / truth / universality / validity.

810. Paczolay, Gyula. "Reciprocity and Departures from it in Proverbs." *Folk Narrative and World View. Vorträge des 10. Kongresses der Internationalen Gesellschaft für Volkserzählungsforschung. Innsbruck 1992.* Ed. Leander Petzoldt. Frankfurt am Main: Peter Lang, 1996. 639–653.
Abstraction / linguistics / meaning / metaphor / reciprocity / structure.

811. Paczolay, Gyula. "Some Notes on the Theory of Proverbs." *Europhras 97: Phraseology and Paremiology.* Ed. Peter Ďurčo. Bratislava: Akadémia PZ, 1998. 261–266.
Behavior / definition / experience / meaning / metaphor / Wolfgang Mieder / poetics / Archer Taylor / variant / Bartlett Jere Whiting.

812. Page, Mary H., and Nancy D. Washington. "Family Proverbs and Value Transmission of Single Black Mothers." *The Journal of Social Psychology*, 127, no. 1 (1987), 49–58.
African American / behavior / children / collectivity / didacticism / experience / family / proverbs test / psychology / society / sociolinguistics / value / wisdom.

813. Palacios, Jesús. "Proverbs as Images of Children and Childrearing." *Images of Childhood.* Eds. C. Philip Hwang, Michael E. Lamb, and Irving E. Sigel. Hillsdale, New Jersey: Lawrence Erlbaum, 1996. 75–98.
Childrearing / children / didacticism / family / image / innovation / pedagogy / tradition / value / worldview.

814. Palm, Christine. "'Umgekehrt wird ein Schuh draus': Idiomatizität und Konnotation im Phrasem." *Deutsche Phraseologie in Sprachsystem und Sprachverwendung.* Ed. Csaba Földes. Wien: Edition Praesens, 1992. 89–106.
Connotation / emotion / history / idiomaticity / modality / phraseologism / semantics / style.

815. Palm, Christine. "'Habent sua fata idiomata': Beobachtungen zur Polysemie von Phraseologismen." *Europhras 92: Tendenzen der Phraseologieforschung.* Ed. Barbara Sandig. Bochum: Norbert Brockmeyer, 1994. 431–460.
Connotation / dictionary / lexicography / metaphor / phraseologism / semantics / style.

816. Palm, Christine. *Phraseologie: Eine Einführung.* Tübingen: Gunter Narr, 1995. 130 pp.
Classification / cognition / collection / competence / comprehension / definition / diachronic / equivalent / genre / idiomticity / phraseology / poetics / psycholinguistics / semantics / stability / structure / syntax / terminology.

817. Paredes, Américo. "Proverbs and Ethnic Stereotypes." *Proverbium*, 15 (1970), 511–513.
Culture / ethnicity / folklore / meaning / Mexican / prejudice / slur / stereotype / "No tiene la culpa el indio, sino el que lo hace compadre."

818. Park, Nancy. "Power in Imperial Chinese Proverbs." *Proverbium*, 15 (1998), 243–263.
Chinese / content / economics / politics / power / society / value / worldview.

819. Parker, Carolyn Ann. *Aspects of a Theory of Proverbs: Contexts and Messages of Proverbs in Swahili.* Diss. University of Washington, 1974. 193 pp.
African / behavior / context / function / message / society / Swahili / tradition.

820. Parker, Carolyn Ann. "Swahili Proverbs: The Nature and Value of Painful Experience." *Gar*, 32 (1978), 23 and 26–27.
African / behavior / experience / knowledge / life / Swahili / teaching / value.

821. Parker, Carolyn Ann. "Social Balance and the Threat of Revenge: The Message of Some Swahili Proverbs." *Greenfield Review*, 8, nos. 1–2 (1980), 163–175.
African / behavior / context / message / society / strategy / Swahili / value.

822. Pasamanick, Judith R. *The Proverb Moves the Mind: Abstraction and Metaphor in Children Six–Nine.* Diss. Yeshiva University, 1982. 395 pp.

Abstraction / analogy / children / cognition / competence / comprehension / context / interpretation / metaphor / psycholinguistics / sociolinguistics.

823. Pasamanick, Judith R. "Talk 'Does' Cook Rice: Proverb Abstraction through Social Interaction." *International Journal of the Sociology of Language*, 44 (1983), 5–25.
Abstraction / children / comprehension / interpretation / meaning / metaphor / psycholinguistics / society / sociolinguistics.

824. Pasamanick, Judith R. "Watched Pots Do Boil: Proverb Interpretation through Contextual Illustration." *Proverbium*, 2 (1985), 145–183.
Abstraction / children / comprehension / interpretation / meaning / metaphor / psycholinguistics / sociolinguistics.

825. Pasierbsky, Fritz. "'Wer lügt, der stiehlt': Deutsche Sprichwörter über Lügen und Gewalt." In F. Pasierbsky. *Lügensprecher, Ehebrecher, Mordstecher: Warum wir nicht lügen sollen und es doch nicht lassen können*. Frankfurt am Main: Peter Lang, 1996. 123–145 and 207–219.
Collection / content / German / lying / power / society / worldview / "Wer lügt, der stiehlt."

826. Paulhan, Jean. "L'expérience du proverbe." In J. Paulhan. *Oeuvres complètes*. Paris: Cercle du Livre Précieux, 1966. II, 101–124.
Acquisition / communication / culture / experience / foreign language / function / language / Malagasy.

827. Paulhan, Jean. "Sacred Language [of Proverbs]." *The College of Sociology (1937–39)*. Ed. Denis Hollier. Minneapolis, Minnesota: University of Minnesota Press, 1988. 304–321.
Ambiguity / communication / culture / experience / function / language / logic / Malagasy / value.

828. Payne, R.W., W.K. Caird, and S.G. Laverty. "Overinclusive Thinking and Delusions in Schizophrenic Patients." *Journal of Abnormal and Social Psychology*, 68 (1964), 562–566.
Abstraction / John D. Benjamin / brain / interpretation / proverbs test / psychiatry / psychology / schizophrenia.

829. Payne, R.W., and D. Friedlander. "A Short Battery of Simple Tests for Measuring Overinclusive Thinking." *Journal of Mental Science*, 108 (1962), 362–367.

Abstraction / John D. Benjamin / brain / interpretation / proverbs test / psychiatry / psychology / schizophrenia.

830. Payne, R.W., and J.H.G. Hewlett. "Thought Disorder in Psychotic Patients." *Experiments in Personality.* Ed. Hans Jürgen Eysenck. London: Routledge & Kegan Paul, 1960. II, 3–104.
Abstraction / John D. Benjamin / brain / disorder / interpretation / proverbs test / psychiatry / psychology / schizophrenia.

831. Payne, R.W., P. Mattussek, and E.I. George. "An Experimental Study of Schizophrenic Thought Disorder." *Journal of Mental Science*, 105 (1959), 627–652.
Abstraction / John D. Benjamin / brain / disorder / interpretation / proverbs test / psychiatry / psychology / schizophrenia.

832. Peacock, Martha Moffitt. "Proverbial Reframing – Rebuking and Revering Women in Trousers." *The Journal of the Walters Art Gallery*, 57 (1999), 13–34. With 21 illustrations.
Anti–feminism / Pieter Brueghel / gender / iconography / misogyny / prejudice / stereotype / women / world–upside–down / "To wear the pants."

833. Peek, Philip M. "The Roles of Sexual Expressions in African Insulting Language and Verbal Arts." *Folklore Interpreted: Essays in Honor of Alan Dundes.* Eds. Regina Bendix and Rosemary Lévy Zumwalt. New York: Garland Publishing, 1995. 401–414.
African / culture / folklore / informant / insult / language / metaphor / obscenity / sex / speech act.

834. Penfield, Joyce. "Quoting Behavior in Igbo Society." *Research in African Literatures*, 12 (1981), 309–337.
Advice / African / anthropology / authority / behavior / context / field research / folklore / function / Igbo / norm / society / speech act / value.

835. Penfield, Joyce. *Communicating with Quotes: The Igbo Case.* Westport, Connecticut: Greenwood Press, 1983. 138 pp.
Advice / African / anthropology / authority / communication / context / ethnography / field research / folklore / function / Igbo / Jan Mukarovsky / norm / society / speech act / value.

836. Penfield, Joyce. "The African Proverb: Sacred Text in Praxis." *Embracing the Baobab Tree: The African Proverb in the 21st*

Century. Ed. Willem Saayman. Pretoria: University of South Africa, 1997. 163–175.
African / behavior / belief / Igbo / morality / religion / sociolinguistics.

837. Penfield, Joyce, and Mary Dura. "Proverbs: Metaphors that Teach." *Anthropological Quarterly*, 61, no. 3 (1988), 119–128.
African / children / context / Igbo / morality / pedagogy / society / sociolinguistics / teaching / value / wisdom.

838. Peng, Kaiping. *Naive Dialecticism [in Proverbs] and Its Effects on Reasoning and Judgment about Contradiction.* Diss. University of Michigan, 1997. 119 pp.
American / argumentation / Chinese / cognition / contradiction / culture / dialectics / society / wisdom / worldview / Yiddish.

839. Penn, Nolan E., Teresa C. Jacob, and Malrie Brown. "Comparison Between Gorham's Proverbs Test and the Revised Shipley Institute of Living Scale for a Black Population." *Perceptual and Motor Skills*, 66 (1988), 839–845.
Abstraction / African American / ethnicity / Donald R. Gorham / proverbs test / psycholinguistics / psychology.

840. Penn, Nolan E., Teresa C. Jacob, and Malrie Brown. "Familiarity with Proverbs and Performance of a Black Population on Gorham's Proverbs Test." *Perceptual and Motor Skills*, 66 (1988), 847–854.
Abstraction / African American / ethnicity / familiarity / Donald R. Gorham / interpretation / proverbs test / psycholinguistics / psychology.

841. Perlinska, Agnieszka. "'Gdy sie baba rozpanoszy to i diabła wypłoszy': Images of Women in Polish Proverbial Folklore." *Proverbium*, 13 (1996), 299–312.
Anti–feminism / folklore / gender / image / metaphor / misogyny / Polish / prejudice / stereotype / women.

842. Permiakov, Grigorii L'vovich. *Ot pogovorki do skazki (Zametki po obschei teorii klishe).* Moskva: "Nauka", 1970. 239 pp. Also published in English translation by Y.N. Filippov with the title *From Proverb to Folk–Tale. Notes on the General Theory of Cliché.* Moscow: "Nauka" Publishing House, 1979. 287 pp.

Cliché / culture / fable / folklore / genre / linguistics / logic / metaphor / motivation / narrative / paremiology / phraseologism / Russian / semantics / semiotics / structure / syntax.

843. Permiakov, Grigorii L'vovich. "Grammatica poslovichnoi mudrosti." In G.L. Permiakov. *Poslovitsi i pogovorki narodov vostoka. Sistematizirovannoe sobranie izrechenii dvukhsot narodov.* Moskva: "Nauka", 1979. 7–57. Also in German translation by Peter Grzybek as "Die Grammatik der Sprichwörterweisheit." *Semiotische Studien zum Sprichwort. Simple Forms Reconsidered I.* Eds. Peter Grzybek and Wolfgang Eismann. Tübingen: Gunter Narr, 1984. 295–344; and in French translation by Victor Rosenzweig as "La grammaire de la sagesse proverbiale." *Tel grain tel pain. Poétique de la sagesse populaire.* Ed. G.L. Permiakov. Moscou: Éditions du Progrès, 1988. 11–81.
Classification / common sense / culture / grammar / linguistics / logic / paremiology / Russian / semantics / semiotics / structure.

844. Permiakov, Grigorii L'vovich. "K voprosu o russkom paremiologicheskom minimume." *Slovari i lingvostranovedenie.* Ed. E.M. Vereshchagina. Moskva: Russkii iazyk, 1982. 131–137. Also in shortened form in *Paremiologicheskie issledovaniia.* Ed. G.L. Permiakov. Moskva: "Nauka", 1984. 265–268. The original publication appeared in English translation by Kevin J. McKenna as "On the Question of a Russian Paremiological Minimum." *Proverbium,* 6 (1989), 91–102.
Acquisition / competence / dictionary / equivalent / familiarity / foreign language / frequency / paremiological minimum / Russian / student / teaching.

845. Perrin, Laurent. "Remarques sur la dimension générique et sur la dimension dénominative des proverbes." *La parole proverbiale.* Ed. Jean–Claude Anscombre. Paris: Larousse, 2000. 69–80.
Affirmation / context / denomination / idiom / metaphor / rhetoric / truth.

846. Perrin, Porter G. "'Pecking Order' 1927–54." *American Speech,* 30, no. 4 (1955), 265–268.
Animal / behavior / diachronic / English / metaphor / phraseologism / sociolinguistics / "Pecking order."

847. Peterson, Robert R., and Curt Burgess. "Syntactic and Semantic Processing During Idiom Comprehension: Neurolinguistic

and Psycholinguistic Dissociations." *Idioms: Processing, Structure, and Interpretation*. Eds. Cristina Cacciari and Patrizia Tabossi. Hillsdale, New Jersey: Lawrence Erlbaum Associates, 1993. 201–225.
Comprehension / idiom / neurolinguistics / psycholinguistics / semantics / syntax.

848. Petrova, Roumyana. "Language and Culture: One Step Further in the Search for Common Ground (A Study of Modern English Proverbs)." *Europe from East to West: Proceedings of the First International European Studies Conference, Varna, Bulgaria, June 1996*. Eds. Martin Dangerfield, Glyn Hambrook, and Ludmilla Kostova. Varna: PIC Publishers, 1996. 237–248.
Culture / English / folklore / language / message / tradition / validity / wisdom.

849. Piaget, Jean. "Some Peculiarities of Verbal Understanding in the Child Between the Ages of Nine and Eleven." In J. Piaget. *The Language and Thought of the Child*. 3rd ed. New York: The Humanities Press, 1959 (1st ed. 1926). 127–161.
Age / analogy / children / cognition / comprehension / figurativeness / literalness / meaning / psycholinguistics / psychology.

850. Piirainen, Elisabeth. "Phraseologie des Japanischen: Vorarbeiten zu einer interkulturellen Erforschung von Symbolen in der Sprache." *Von der Einwortmetapher zur Satzmetapher*. Eds. Rupprecht S. Baur and Christoph Chlosta. Bochum: Norbert Brockmeyer, 1995. 269–304.
Animal / color / culture / gender / Japanese / men / mentality / number / phraseology / semiotics / somatism / symbol / women / worldview.

851. Piirainen, Elisabeth. "Phraseologie und Symbolik." *Alte Welten – neue Welten. Akten des IX. Kongresses der Internationalen Vereinigung für germanische Sprach- und Literaturwissenschaft*. Ed. Michael S. Batts. Tübingen: Max Niemeyer, 1996. III, 84 (abstract).
Animal / color / mentality / number / phraseology / semiotics / symbolism / worldview.

852. Piirainen, Elisabeth. "Phraseologie und Symbolik." *Phraseologismen in Text und Kontext. Phrasemata I*. Ed. Jan Wirrer. Bielefeld: Aisthesis Verlag, 1998. 209–228.

Animal / color / culture / mentality / number / phraseology / semiotics / symbolism / worldview.

853. Piirainen, Elisabeth. "Phraseology and Research on Symbols." *Europhras 97: Phraseology and Paremiology.* Ed. Peter Ďurčo. Bratislava: Akadémia PZ, 1998. 280–287.
Culture / language / linguistics / number / phraseology / semiotics / symbol / worldview.

854. Piirainen, Elisabeth. "Symbole in Sprache und Kultur: Phraseologie als Gegenstand der Symbolforschung." *Weltuntergang und Erlösung. Opfer und Ritus.* Ed. Peter Gerlitz. Frankfurt am Main: Peter Lang, 1999. 9–26. (= *Symbolon: Jahrbuch für Symbolforschung*, 14 [1999], 9–26).
Culture / language / metaphor / number / phraseology / semiotics / symbol.

855. Piirainen, Elisabeth. "'Der hat aber Haare auf den Zähnen!' Geschlechtsspezifik in der deutschen Phraseologie." *Sprache – Erotik – Sexualität.* Ed. Rudolf Hoberg. Berlin: Erich Schmidt, 2001. 283–307.
Animal / culture / dialect / gender / German / linguistics / marker / men / metaphor / phraseology / society / women.

856. Piirainen, Ilpo Tapani. "Neue Phraseologismen für 'Sterben und Tod' in den deutschen Umgangssprachen." *Neue Phraseologie im neuen Europa.* Eds. Harry Walter, Walerij Mokijenko, and Michaił Aleksiejenki. Greifswald: Institut für Slawistik, Universität Greifswald, 2001. 50–52.
Culture / death / dying / euphemism / German / metaphor / modernity / phraseologism / worldview.

857. Pilz, Klaus Dieter. "Graffiti–Dialoge. Kommunikation im Intimbereich einer Universität." *Dialog. Festschrift für Siegfried Grosse.* Eds. Gert Rickheit and Sigurd Wichter, Tübingen: Max Niemeyer, 1990. 439–452.
Anti–proverb / content / graffiti / linguistics / message / parody / politics / quotation / scatology / sex / society / student / wordplay.

858. Pilz, Klaus Dieter. "'Frauensleute und Mannsleute sind die besten Menschen': Frau und Mann im Sprichwort (verschiedener Sprachen)." *Europhras 95: Europäische Phraseologie im Vergleich: Gemeinsames Erbe und kulturelle Vielfalt.* Ed. Wolfgang Eismann. Bochum: Norbert Brockmeyer, 1998. 693–708.

Anti–feminism / anti–proverb / culture / feminism / gender / language / men / misogyny / prejudice / stereotype / women.

859. Piñel López, Rosa María. "El mundo animal en las expresiones alemanas y españolas y sus connotaciones socioculturales." *Revista de Filologia Alemana*, no volume given, no. 5 (1997, published 1998), 259–274.
Animal / culture / equivalent / German / metaphor / phraseologism / semantics / society / Spanish.

860. Piñel López, Rosa María. "El animal en el refrán, reflejo de una cultura: Estudio contrastivo alemán–español." *Paremia*, 8 (1999), 411–416.
Animal / culture / equivalent / German / metaphor / semantics / Spanish.

861. Plekhanov, A. "Russian Folk Wisdom about Upbringing." *Russian Social Science Review*, 33, no. 3 (1992), 79–88.
Childrearing / children / culture / folklore / pedagogy / Russian / wisdom.

862. Poethe, Hannelore. "In Phraseologismen geronnene Alltagserfahrungen mit Sprache und Kommunikation." *Nominationsforschung im Deutschen: Festschrift für Wolfgang Fleischer*. Eds. Irmhild Barz and Marianne Schröder. Frankfurt am Main: Peter Lang, 1997. 177–190.
Communication / discourse / experience / language / phraseologism / semantics / structure / style / wisdom.

863. Pollio, Howard, Michael Fabrizi, Abigail Sills, and Michael Smith. "Need Metaphoric Comprehension Take Longer than Literal Comprehension?" *Journal of Psycholinguistic Research*, 13 (1984), 195–214.
Comprehension / context / figurativeness / idiom / literalness / metaphor / psycholinguistics / psychology / semantics.

864. Popiel, Stephen J., and Ken McRae. "The Figurative and Literal Senses of Idioms, or All Idioms Are Not Used Equally." *Journal of Psycholinguistic Research*, 17, no. 6 (1988), 475–487.
Empiricism / familiarity / figurativeness / frequency / idiom / informant / literalness / psycholinguistics / semantics / student / use.

865. Porsch, Peter. "Phraseologismen im interkulturellen Vergleich." *Nominationsforschung im Deutschen: Festschrift für Wolfgang Fleischer.* Eds. Irmhild Barz and Marianne Schröder. Frankfurt am Main: Peter Lang, 1997. 191–200.
Animal / Arabic / culture / equivalent / German / phraseologism / Polish / Portuguese / semiotics.

866. Pound, Louise. "American Euphemisms for Dying, Death, and Burial." *American Speech*, 11, no. 3 (1936), 195–202.
American / collection / death / dying / euphemism / metaphor / phraseologism.

867. Powell, J.C. "The Developmental Sequence of Cognition as Revealed by Wrong Answers." *Alberta Journal of Educational Research*, 23 (1977), 43–51.
Age / children / cognition / comprehension / Donald R. Gorham / metaphor / proverbs test / psycholinguistics / psychology.

868. Prahlad, Sw. Anand (Dennis Folly). "'No Guts, No Glory': Proverbs, Values and Image among Anglo–American University Students." *Southern Folklore*, 51 (1994), 285–298.
American / English / image / informant / meaning / student / value / worldview.

869. Prahlad, Sw. Anand (Dennis Folly). *African–American Proverbs in Context.* Jackson, Mississippi: University of Mississippi Press, 1996. 306 pp.
Aesthetics / African American / children / context / culture / didacticism / discourse / ethnicity / meaning / metaphor / music / society / speech act / value / worldview.

870. Prević, Fred H., and Shannon J. Murphy. "Vertical Eye Movements During Mental Tasks: Re–Examination and Hypothesis." *Perceptual and Motor Skills*, 84, no. 2 (1997), 835–847.
Brain / cognition / comprehension / eye / neurology / proverbs test / psychology.

871. Prinz, Philip M. "The Development of Idiomatic Meaning in Children." *Language and Speech*, 26, no. 3 (1983), 263–272.
Children / cognition / comprehension / idiom / idiomatization / literalization / meaning / psycholinguistics.

872. Profantová, Zuzana. "Ethnoidentification in Conversational Genres of Folklore alias Locus Standi." *Folklore in the Identi-*

fication Processes of Society. Eds. Gabriela Kiliánová and Eva Krekovicova. Bratislava: Ustav etnológie SAV, 1994. 75–81.
Blason populaire / ethnicity / folklore / genre / identity / national character / prejudice / Slovakian / slur / stereotype.

873. Profantová, Zuzana. "Worldview – Proverbs – Folk Narrative." *Folk Narrative and World View. Vorträge des 10. Kongresses der Internationalen Gesellschaft für Volkserzählungsforschung. Innsbruck 1992.* Ed. Leander Petzoldt. Frankfurt am Main: Peter Lang, 1996. 719–723.
Fable / fairy tale / folklore / metaphor / morality / narrative / semantics / semiotics / tradition / value / worldview.

874. Profantová, Zuzana. "Proverbial Tradition as a Cultural–Historical and Social Phenomenon." *Europhras 97: Phraseology and Paremiology.* Ed. Peter Ďurčo. Bratislava: Akadémia PZ, 1998. 302–307.
Culture / folklore / history / society / stability / tradition / transmission / universality / value / worldview.

875. Pulman, Stephen G. "The Recognition and Interpretation of Idioms." *Idioms: Processing, Structure, and Interpretation.* Eds. Cristina Cacciari and Patrizia Tabossi. Hillsdale, New Jersey: Lawrence Erlbaum Associates, 1993. 249–270.
Comprehension / form / function / idiom / interpretation / marker / structure / syntax / variation.

Q

876. Quasthoff, Uta. "The Uses of Stereotype in Everyday Argument." *Journal of Pragmatics*, 2 (1978), 1–48.
Argument / cliché / collectivity / function / linguistics / psychology / semantics / slogan / sociology / speech act / stereotype / use.

877. Quevedo Aparicio, Teresa. "La gerontología en los refraneros español y francés." *Paremia*, 3 (1994), 77–81.
Age / aging / content / culture / equivalent / French / gerontology / health / Spanish.

R

878. Rabin, Albert, and Daniel Broida. "Projection via Proverbs: Follow–up of a Suggestion." *Journal of Consulting Psychology*, 12 (1948), 246–250.
Attitude / family / gender / marriage / personality / projection / psychology.

879. Raders, Margit, and Denis Canellas de Castro Duarte. "La mujer en fraseologismos alemanes, españoles y portugueses: aportación a un análisis cultural contrastivo." *Paremia*, 6 (1997), 515–526.
Anti–feminism / culture / equivalent / gender / German / men / misogyny / phraseologism / Portuguese / prejudice / Spanish / stereotype / women.

880. Rattray, R. Sutherland. "The African Child in Proverb, Folklore, and Fact." *Africa*, 6, no. 4 (1933), 456–471.
African / childrearing / children / common sense / didacticism / folklore / society.

881. Raymond, Joseph. *Attitudes and Cultural Patterns in Spanish Proverbs*. Diss. Columbia University, 1951. 251 pp.
Attitude / Miguel de Cervantes Saavedra / collection / content / contradiction / culture / foreign language / national character / psychology / Spanish / teaching.

882. Raymond, Joseph. "Attitudes and Cultural Patterns in Spanish Proverbs." *The Americas*, 11 (1954–1955), 57–77.
Attitude / authority / content / culture / national character / society / Spanish.

883. Raymond, Joseph. "Tensions in Proverbs: More Light on International Understanding." *Western Folklore*, 15 (1956), 153–158. Also in *The Wisdom of Many. Essays on the Proverb*. Eds. Wolfgang Mieder and Alan Dundes. New York: Garland Publishing, 1981. 300–308.
Class / communication / national character / politics / rhetoric / slogan / society.

884. Reed, J.L. "The Proverbs Test in Schizophrenia." *British Journal of Psychiatry*, 111 (1968), 317–321.
Abstraction / brain / proverbs test / psychiatry / psychology / schizophrenia.

885. Reich, James H. "Proverbs and the Modern Mental Status Examination." *Comprehensive Psychiatry*, 22 (1981), 528–531.
Culture / Donald R. Gorham / intelligence / proverbs test / psychiatry / psychology / validity.

886. Reik, Theodor. "The Echo of the Proverb." *Life and Letters Today*, 21 (May 1939), 45–50 and 21 (June 1939), 43–49. Also in T. Reik. *From Thirty Years with Freud*. New York: Farrar & Rinehart, 1940. 228–241.
Children / Sigmund Freud / Jewish / joke / life / origin / psychoanalysis.

887. Reiman, Jeffrey, and Ernest Van den Haag. "On the Common Saying that 'It is Better that Ten Guilty Persons Escape than that One Innocent Suffer' – Pro and Con." *Social Philosophy and Policy*, 7, no. 2 (1990), 226–248.
Ethics / justice / law / morality / philosophy / society / "It is better that ten guilty persons escape than that one innocent suffer."

888. Reiner, Hans. "Die 'goldene Regel': Die Bedeutung einer sittlichen Grundformel der Menschheit." *Zeitschrift für philosophische Forschung*, 3 (1948), 74–105.
Bible / ethics / "Golden Rule" / morality / New Testament / Old Testament / philosophy / "Was du nicht willst, daß man dir tu, das füg auch keinem andern zu."

889. Reisner, Robert. *Graffiti. Two Thousand Years of Wall Writing*. New York: Cowles Book Company, 1971. 204 pp.
Anti–proverb / class / content / ethnicity / graffiti / history / language / politics / scatology / sex / structure.

890. Resnick, David A. *The Development of Children's Comprehension of Proverbs*. Diss. Columbia University, 1977. 169 pp.
Abstraction / age / analogy / children / cognition / comprehension / education / figurativeness / literalness / meaning / metaphor / psycholinguistcs / psychology.

891. Resnick, David A. "A Developmental Study of Proverb Comprehension." *Journal of Psycholinguistic Research*, 11 (1982), 521–538.
Abstraction / children / cognition / comprehension / experience / intelligence / metaphor / psycholinguistics / psychology / society.

892. Reveal, Robert. *The Development and Validation of a Proverbs Test for the Selection of Supervisors.* Diss. University of Southern California, 1960. 129 pp.
Attitude / behavior / life / profession / proverbs test / psycholinguistics / socio–linguistics / supervisor / value.

893. Reyne, Claude. "Remarques sur le phénomène de la redondance dans les *refranes*." *Paremia*, 2 (1993), 27–31.
Form / memorability / redundancy / repetition / semantics / structure / syntax.

894. Rezus, Petru. "Arhetipuri paremiologice." *Proverbium Dacoromania*, 4 (1989), 31–34.
Antiquity / archetype / behavior / Bible / culture / experience / language / life / Rumanian / universality.

895. Rezvanian, Mohamed Hassan. "Quelques aspects de la psychologie des Iraniens à traves leurs proverbes." *Revue de psychologie des peuples*, 24 (1969), 47–63.
Content / gender / humor / Iranian / misogyny / psychology / women / worldview.

896. Rezvanian, Mohamed Hassan. "Recherches parémiologiques comparées." *Ethnopsychologie*, 32 (1977), 349–363.
Advice / content / French / Iranian / national character / paremiology / universality / worldview.

897. Richard, Phillippe. "Mesurer le non–mesurable: Le cas des proverbes." *Ethnologie française*, 20, no. 3 (1990), 341–349.
Context / metaphor / semantics / simple form / structure / style / variant.

898. Richards, Dickinson W. "The First Aphorism of Hippocrates." *Perspectives in Biology and Medicine*, 5 (1961), 61–64.
Aphorism / Greek / Hippocrates / meaning / medicine / profession / "Life is short, and the art long."

899. Richardson, Claudia, and Joseph Church. "A Developmental Analysis of Proverb Interpretations." *Journal of Genetic Psychology*, 94 (1959), 169–179.
Adult / age / children / cognition / comprehension / interpretation / maturity / proverbs test / psychiatry / psychology / schizophrenia.

900. Riechmann, Paul F. *Does Imagery Facilitate Memory for Conceptual Information?* Diss. University of Cincinnati, 1974. 67 pp.
Acquisition / comprehension / imagery / interpretation / memory / metaphor / proverbs test / psycholinguistics / psychology.

901. Riechmann, Paul F., and Ellen L. Coste. "Mental Imagery and the Comprehension of Figurative Language: Is there a Relationship?" *Cognition and Figurative Language*. Eds. Richard P. Honeck and Robert R. Hoffman. Hillsdale/New Jersey: Lawrence Erlbaum, 1980. 183–200.
Comprehension / figurativeness / imagery / memory / metaphor / proverbs test / psycholinguistics / psychology.

902. Riegel, Martin. "'Qui dort dîne' ou le pivot implicatif dans les énoncés parémiques." *Travaux de linguistique et de littérature*, 24, no. 1 (1986), 85–99.
Zoltán Kanyó / language / linguistics / logic / semantics / semiotics / structure.

903. Risley, Sir Herbert. "Caste in Proverbs and Popular Sayings." In H. Risley. *The People of India*. Calcutta: Thacker, Spink & Co., 1908 (2nd edition, 1915). 128–153.
Caste / collection / content / culture / ethnicity / Indian / profession / society.

904. Rittersbacher, Christa. *Frau und Mann im Sprichwort. Einblicke in die sprichwörtliche Weltanschaung Großbritanniens und Amerikas*. Heidelberg: Das Wunderhorn, 2002. 332 pp.
American / anti–feminism / collection / content / culture / English / gender / meaning / men / misogyny / prejudice / society / stereotype / women / worldview.

905. Rivard, Adjutor. "A propos de proverbes." *Le Canada français*, 4 (1920), 400–407.
Content / culture / English / French / national character / society / worldview.

906. Roback, Abraham Aaron. "The Yiddish Proverb – A Study in Folk Psychology." *The Jewish Forum*, 1 (1918), 331–338 and 418–426.
Culture / dream / folklore / Hebrew / humor / Jewish / psychoanalysis / psychology / religion / worldview / Yiddish.

907. Roback, Abraham Aaron. *Psychological Aspects of Jewish Protective Phrases.* New York: Jewish Academy of Arts and Sciences, 1938 (= *Bulletin of the Jewish Academy of Arts and Sciences*, no. 4). 16 pp.
Belief / death / folklore / Sigmund Freud / Jewish / phylacterism / psychoanalysis / psychology / superstition.

908. Roberts, John M., and Jeffrey C. Hayes. "Young Adult Male Categorizations of Fifty Arabic Proverbs." *Anthropological Linguistics*, 29, no. 1 (1987), 35–48.
Anthropology / Arabic / context / culture / ethnography / gender / informant / meaning / men / worldview.

909. Roberts, John W. "Slave Proverbs: A Perspective." *Callaloo*, 1, no. 4 (1978), 129–140.
African American / behavior / ethics / folklore / indirection / morality / slavery.

910. Roberts, Murat H. "The Science of Idiom: A Method of Inquiry into the Cognitive Design of Language." *Publications of the Modern Language Association*, 59 (1944), 291–306.
Cognition / discourse / grammar / idiom / language / linguistics / literature.

911. Roberts, Sydney Gordon. "Tamil Proverbs: A Key to the Language and to the Mind of the People." *The Asiatic Review*, 16 (1920), 448–478.
Collection / culture / Indian / language / meaning / mentality / Tamil / worldview.

912. Robinson, F.N. "Irish Proverbs and Irish National Character." *Modern Philology*, 43 (1945), 1–10. Also in *The Wisdom of Many. Essays on the Proverb.* Eds. Wolfgang Mieder and Alan Dundes. New York: Garland Publishing, 1981. 284–299.
Culture / experience / Irish / national character / society / stereotype / worldview.

913. Robinson, Herbert. "Family Sayings from Family Stories: Some Louisiana Examples." *Louisiana Folklore Miscellany*, 6, no. 4 (1991), 17–24.
American / family / folklore / narrative / phraseologism / worldview.

914. Rodegem, Francis M. "La parole proverbiale." *Richesse du proverbe*. Eds. François Suard and Claude Buridant. Lille: Université de Lille, 1984. II, 121–135.
Analogy / definition / function / genre / norm / paremiology / semantics / style.

915. Rodegem, Francis M. "Proverbes et pseudo–proverbes." *Annales Aequatoria*, 6 (1985), 67–83.
Analogy / currency / function / genre / memorability / orality / pseudo–proverb / structure.

916. Rodegem, Francis M., and P. Van Brussel. "Proverbes et pseudo–proverbes. La logique des parémies." *Europhras 88. Phraséologie Contrastive. Actes du Colloque International Klingenthal–Strasbourg, 12–16 mai 1988.* Ed. Gertrud Gréciano. Strasbourg: Université des Sciences Humaines, 1989. 349–356.
Analogy / definition / form / function / genre / language / norm / pseudo–proverb / structure / style.

917. Rogers, Alan D. "Human Prudence and Implied Divine Sanctions in Malagasy Proverbial Wisdom." *Journal of Religion in Africa*, 15 (1985), 216–226.
African / anthropology / culture / Malagasy / prudence / religion / society / wisdom / worldview.

918. Rogers, Rex Stainton. "Normative Prescriptions in Ordinary Language: A Notation for Approaching the Mechanisms of Response Generation." *Functional Studies in Language and Literature*. Eds. Frank Coppieters and Didier L. Goyvaerts. Ghent: Story–Scientia, 1978. 119–131.
Attitude / behavior / cognition / culture / language / norm / prescription / psycholinguistics / wisdom.

919. Rogers, Tim B. "Psychological Approaches to Proverbs: A Treatise on the Import of Context." *Canadian Folklore Canadien*, 8, nos. 1–2 (1986), 87–104. Also in *Wise Words: Essays on the Proverb*. Ed. Wolfgang Mieder. New York: Garland Publishing, 1994. 159–181.
Addiction / attitude / behavior / brain / children / cognition / communication / comprehension / context / disease / drug / folklore / intelligence / metaphor / personality / proverbs test / psychiatry / psycholinguistics / psychology / schizophrenia / society / therapy.

920. Rogers, Tim B. "The Use of Slogans, Colloquialisms, and Proverbs in the Treatment of Substance Addiction: A Psychological Application of Proverbs." *Proverbium*, 6 (1989), 103–112.
Addiction / alcoholism / colloquialism / context / drug / psychology / slogan / sociology / therapy / value.

921. Rogers, Tim B. "Proverbs as Psychological Theories… Or Is It the Other Way Around?" *Canadian Psychology/Psychologie Canadienne*, 31, no. 3 (1990), 195–207 and 215–217 (comments).
Bibliography / communication / context / contradiction / empiricism / metaphor / psycholinguistics / psychology / semantics / society / truth / value.

922. Rogow, Arnold, Gloria Carey, and Calista Farrell. "The Significance of Aphorisms in American Culture." *Sociology and Social Research*, 41 (1957), 417–420.
American / aphorism / culture / society / sociology / value / wisdom.

923. Röhrich, Lutz, and Wolfgang Mieder. *Sprichwort*. Stuttgart: Metzler, 1977.
Bibliography / collection / content / definition / distribution / folklore / form / genre / German / language / literature / mass media / metaphor / narrative / origin / paremiology / semantics / society / structure / tradition / worldview.

924. Ronesi, Lynne. "'Mightier than the Sword': A Look at Proverbial Prejudice." *Proverbium*, 17 (2000), 329–347.
Arabic / attitude / blason populaire / caste / ethnicity / ethnophaulism / Indian / national character / Native American / prejudice / slur / stereotype.

925. Rooth, Anna Birgitta. "Domestic Animals and Wild Animals as Symbols and Referents in the Proverbs." *Proverbium*, 11 (1968), 286–288.
Animal / behavior / culture / meaning / metaphor / society / Swedish.

926. Rose, James H. "Types of Idioms." *Linguistics*, 203 (1978), 55–62.
Classification / definition / idiom / linguistics / metaphor / semantics.

927. Rossman, Jeffrey Michael. *Metaphor and Affect: A Study of Metaphorical Thinking and Affective Responsibility in Schizophrenia.* Diss. Adelphi University, 1985. 177 pp.
Abstraction / bibliography / brain / cognition / comprehension / figurativeness / literalness / metaphor / proverbs test / psychiatry / psychology / schizophrenia.

928. Rotan, Leo William. *An Investigation of Male Myocardial Infarction Victims' Reported Behavior and Attitudes in Relation to Selected Proverbs.* Diss. Florida State University, 1981. 91 pp.
Attitude / behavior / disease / proverbs test / psycholinguistics / psychology.

929. Rothstein, Robert A. "Jews in Slavic Eyes – The Paremiological Evidence." *Proceedings of the Ninth World Congress of Jewish Studies.* No editor given. Jerusalem: World Union of Jewish Studies, 1986. II, 181–188.
Anti–Semitism / belief / custom / ethnicity / folklore / Gypsies / Jewish / prejudice / Slavic / slur / stereotype.

930. Roventa–Frumusani, Daniela. "Le proverbe e(s)t énonciation éconcée." *Revue Roumaine de Linguistique,* 30, no. 2 (1985), 159–167.
Argument / context / definition / semiotics / speech act / strategy / wisdom.

931. Ruduri, Kwezi. "Les thèmes de la 'jeunesse' et de la 'vieillesse' dans quelques proverbes Rwanda: Considerations socio–culturelles." *Proverbium,* 10 (1993), 281–295.
African / age / content / culture / life / Rwandan / society / worldview / youth.

932. Ruediger, Edgar. "Unser Leben in gesunden und kranken Tagen: Ein medizinischer Streifzug in das Gebiet von Sprichwort, Redewendung und Sprache." *Münchener Medizinische Wochenschrift,* 77, no. 40 (October 3, 1930), 1714–1716.
Content / culture / disease / folklore / health / medicine / somatism / validity.

933. Ruef, Hans. "Understanding Proverbs: Scene Development as a Process of Motivation." *Linguistic Agency University of Trier,* series A, no. 111 (1983), 1–14.
Cognition / comprehension / context / image / linguistics / meaning / motivation / truth / wisdom.

934. Ruef, Hans. *Sprichwort und Sprache: Am Beispiel des Sprichworts im Schweizerdeutschen*. Berlin: Walter de Gruyter, 1995. 303 pp.
Collection / context / contradiction / dialect / language / paradox / paremiological minimum / semantics / structure / Swiss German / syntax / wordplay.

935. Ruiz Gurillo, Leonor. "Relevancia y fraseología: La desautomatización en la conversación coloquial." *Español Actual*, 68 (1997), 21–30.
Context / deautomatization / discourse / language / phraseologism / phraseology / speech act.

936. Ruiz Gurillo, Leonor. *La fraseología des español coloquial*. Barcelona: Editorial Ariel, 1998. 126 pp.
Classification / context / discourse / form / function / lexicology / phraseologism / phraseology / pragmatics / Spanish / speech act / structure / syntax / worldview.

937. Russell, Melissa Anne. "'Kill 'em All and Let God Sort 'em Out': The Proverb as an Expression of Verbal Aggression." *Proverbium*, 16 (1999), 287–302. With 2 illustrations.
Aggression / American / Bible / culture / origin / society / variant / worldview / "Kill 'em all and let God sort 'em out."

938. Ruwet, Nicolas. "Du bon usage des expressions idiomatiques dans l'argumentation en syntaxe générative." *Revue québécoise de linguistique*, 13, no. 1 (1983), 9–145 [*sic*].
Argumentation / Noam Chomsky / discourse / grammar / idiom / linguistics / structure / syntax.

939. Ruxāndoiu, Pavel. "Functia socialǎ a proverbelor." *Analele Universitǎtii Bucureşti. Seria Limbǎ şi Literaturǎ Romȃnǎ*, 22 (1973), 81–87.
Attitude / experience / function / norm / prescription / Rumanian / society / value.

S

940. Sacks, Harvey. "On Proverbs." In H. Sacks. *Lectures on Conversation*. Ed. Gail Jefferson. Oxford: Blackwell, 1992. I, 104–112.
Collection / context / English / meaning / proposition / phraseologism / society / truth.

941. Salami, Yunusa Kehinde. "Yoruba Proverbs as Mechanism for Social Regulation." *Afrikanistische Arbeitspapiere*, 56 (1998), 147–161.
African / behavior / culture / life / rule / society / value / Yoruba.

942. Salamon, Hagar. "Metaphors as Corrective Exegesis: Three Proverbs of the Beta–Israel." *Proverbium*, 12 (1995), 295–313.
Anthroplogy / Beta–Israel / Ethiopian / experience / field research / informant / meaning / metaphor / religion / society / worldview.

943. Salamone, Frank A. "The Arrow and the Bird: Proverbs in the Solution of Hausa Conjugal–Conflicts." *Journal of Anthropological Research*, 32 (1976), 358–371.
African / anthropology / context / culture / gender / Hausa / marriage / society.

944. Salvador, Vicent. "Idiomaticitat i discurs prefabricat." *El discurs prefabricat: Estudis de fraseologia teòrica i aplicada*. Eds. Vicent Salvador and Adolf Piquer. Castelló de la Plana: Publicacions de la Universitat Jaume I, 2000. 19–31.
Discourse / idiomaticity / linguistics / metaphor / phraseologism / phraseology.

945. Samper, David A. "Woman as *Gallina* – Man as *Gallo*: An Interpretation of a Metaphor in Latin American Proverbs and Proverbial Expressions." *Proverbium*, 14 (1997), 347–366.
Animal / anti–feminism / gender / Latin American / men / metaphor / misogyny / obscenity / phraseologism / prejudice / sex / sexuality / Spanish / stereotype / women.

946. Sánchez García, Jesús. "Lexical and Cultural Semantics of the Idioms of Change." *Paremia*, 8 (1999), 475–480.
Change / culture / idiom / lexicology / linguistics / metaphor / semantics / verb.

947. Sánchez Sánchez, Ana Leonor. "Valoración de la no–actividad comunicativa en el refranero." *Paremia*, 5 (1996), 147–152.
Communication / culture / discourse / silence / speech / value / worldview.

948. Sander, Fred M., and Harvey R. Greenberg. "A Proverbial Excursion: On the Hazards of Administering Proverbs to Test the Capacity to Abstract." *Psychiatric Quarterly*, 42 (1968), 696–697.
Abstraction / brain / context / interpretation / proverbs test / psychiatry / psychology / student / "The tongue is the enemy of the neck."

949. Sandig, Barbara. "Formeln des Bewertens." *Europhras 90. Akten der internationalen Tagung zur germanistischen Phraseologieforschung, Aske/Schweden 12.–15. Juni 1990.* Ed. Christine Palm. Uppsala: Acta Universitatis Upsaliensis, 1991. 225–252.
Behavior / emotion / evaluation / formula / linguistics / negation / phraseologism.

950. Sandig, Barbara. "Zu Konzeptualisierungen des Bewertens, anhand phraseologischer Einheiten." *Europhras 92: Tendenzen der Phraseologieforschung*. Ed. Barbara Sandig. Bochum: Norbert Brockmeyer, 1994. 549–596.
Analogy / behavior / emotion / evaluation / formula / linguistics / metaphor / phraseologism.

951. Santorum, Aldo. *Differences in Formal Thinking Disorders Between Process and Reactive Schizophrenics as Measured by Proverbs.* Diss. University of Ottawa, 1954. 76 pp.
Abstraction / brain / disorder / proverbs test / psychiatry / psychology / schizophrenia.

952. Satz, Paul, and L.T. Carroll. "Utilization of the Proverbs Test as a Projective Instrument: An Objective Approach Through Language Behavior." *Journal of General Psychology*, 67 (1962), 205–213.
Behavior / brain / Donald R. Gorham / language / personality / projection / proverbs test / psycholinguistics / psychology / schizophrenia.

953. Sawadogo, Gérémie. "Proverbs and Philosophy of Education in the Mossi Culture: Some Implications." *Embracing the Baobab Tree: The African Proverb in the 21st Century*. Ed.

Willem Saayman. Pretoria: University of South Africa, 1997. 115–124.
African / culture / education / experience / Mossi / pedagogy / philosophy.

954. Scarcella, Robin C. "'Watch up!': A Study of Verbal Routines in Adult Second Language Performance." *Working Papers on Bilingualism*, 19 (1979), 79–88.
Acquisition / competence / foreign language / idiom / memorization / routine formula.

955. Schapira, Charlotte. *Les stéréotypes en français: Proverbes et autres formules.* Paris: Editions Ophrys, 1999. 172 pp.
Classification / definition / fixidity / French / genre / idiom / metaphor / poetics / phraseologism / proverbialization / routine formula / semantics / simple form / stereotype / structure / style.

956. Schapira, Charlotte. "Proverbe, proverbialisation et déproverbialisation." *La parole proverbiale.* Ed. Jean–Claude Anscombre. Paris: Larousse, 2000. 81–97.
Deproverbialization / context / discourse / fixidity / formula / linguistics / origin / proverbialization.

957. Schellbach–Kopra, Ingrid. "Das Alter im Sprichwort der Deutschen und Finnen – eine kontrastive Betrachtung." *Jahrbuch für finnisch–deutsche Literaturbeziehungen*, 20 (1988), 95–106.
Age / aging / culture / Finnish / German / gerontology / society / worldview.

958. Schellbach–Kopra, Ingrid. "Zu Ethnonym und Ethnostereotyp in der finnischen Phraseologie." *Europhras 95: Europäische Phraseologie im Vergleich: Gemeinsames Erbe und kulturelle Vielfalt.* Ed. Wolfgang Eismann. Bochum: Norbert Brockmeyer, 1998. 743–754.
Blason populaire / ethnicity / ethnonym / Finnish / folklore / phraseology / prejudice / Russian / slur / stereotype / structure.

959. Schemann, Hans. *Das idiomatische Sprachzeichen: Untersuchung der Idiomatizitätsfaktoren anhand der Analyse portugiesischer Idioms und ihrer deutschen Entsprechungen.* Tübingen: Max Niemeyer, 1981. 412 pp.

Context / equivalent / function / German / idiom / idiomaticity / lexicology / linguistics / Portuguese / pragmatics / semiotics / style.

960. Schemann, Hans. *Idiomatik und Anthropologie: "Bild" und "Bedeutung" in linguistischer, sprachgenetischer und philosophischer Perspektive.* Hildesheim: Georg Olms, 2000. 207 pp.
Anthropology / culture / idiomaticity / image / linguistics / meaning / philosophy / semiotics / somatism.

961. Schenk, André. "The Syntactic Behavior of Idioms." *Idioms: Structural and Psychological Perspectives.* Eds. Martin Everaert, Erik–Jan van der Linden, André Schenk, and Rob Schreuder. Hillsdale, New Jersey: Lawrence Erlbaum Associates, 1995. 253–271.
Collocation / definition / dialect / idiom / linguistics / syntax / variation.

962. Scherer, Thomas. *Phraseologie im Schulalter. Untersuchung zur Phraseologie deutschschweizerischer Schüler und ihrer Sprachbücher.* Bern: Peter Lang, 1982. 167 pp.
Age / children / comprehension / context / dialect / education / familiarity / field research / German / language / pedagogy / phraseologism / phraseology / psycholinguistics / student / Swiss German / teaching.

963. Schiepek, Joseph. *Bemerkungen zur psychologischen Grundlage des Sprichwortes.* Saaz: Verlag des K.K. Ober–Gymnasiums, 1890 (= Programm des Kaiserlich–Königlichen Staats–Ober–Gymnasiums zu Saaz 1890, pp. 1–16). Also in *Deutsche Sprichwörterforschung des 19. Jahrhunderts.* Ed. Wolfgang Mieder. Bern: Peter Lang, 1984. 173–199.
Content / experience / form / imagery / life / psychology / structure / variant.

964. Schievella, Daniel Francis. *Comparison of Cognitive Deficits in Paranoid Schizophrenia and Manic Affective Disorders.* Diss. St. John's University, 1984. 112 pp.
Abstraction / brain / cognition / disorder / Donald R. Gorham / mania / proverbs test / psychiatry / psychology / schizophrenia.

965. Schindler, Franz. "Sociolingvistické, paremiologické a paremiografické výsledky empirického výzkumu znalosti přísloví:

Na základě anket 316 informátorů z Čech a Moravy." *Slovo a slovesnost*, 57, no. 4 (1996), 264–282.
Czech / empiricism / familiarity / informant / Moravian / paremiological minimum / sociolinguistics / statistics.

966. Schindler, Franz. "Ergebnisse einer empirischen Untersuchung zur Kenntnis tschechischer Sprichwörter (im Vergleich zur Simrock–Untersuchung von Chlosta et al.)." *"Das geht auf keine Kuhhaut": Arbeitsfelder der Phraseologie. Akten des Westfälischen Arbeitskreises Phraseologie/Parömiologie 1996.* Ed. Dietrich Hartmann. Bochum: Norbert Brockmeyer, 1998. 279–309.
František Ladislav Čelakovský / Christoph Chlosta / collection / Czech / empiricism / familiarity / German / paremiological minimum / Karl Simrock.

967. Schlutz, Erhard. "Sprachliche Defizite oder Verdinglichung von Sprache?" *Sprache und Beruf. Zeitschrift für deutsche Sprache und Literatur in Schule, Weiterbildung und Betrieb*, no volume given, no. 1 (1985), 2–13.
Acquisition / communication / context / education / inadequacy / language / metaphor / phraseologism / sociolinguistics / "Angriff ist die beste Verteidigung."

968. Schmidlin, Regula. "Idiomatic Expressions in Oral and Written Narratives Produced by German and Swiss Primary School Children." *Europhras 97: Phraseology and Paremiology.* Ed. Peter Ďurčo. Bratislava: Akadémia PZ, 1998. 321–326.
Acquisition / age / children / dialect / empiricism / German / idiom / literacy / narrative / orality / statistics / Swiss German.

969. Schmidlin, Regula. "Standardsprachliche Phraseologismen in mündlichen und schriftlichen Erzählungen von deutschschweizerischen und deutschen Grundschulkindern." *Wörter in Bildern – Bilder in Wörtern: Beiträge zur Phraseologie und Sprichwortforschung aus dem Westfälischen Arbeitskreis.* Eds. Rupprecht S. Baur, Christoph Chlosta, and Elisabeth Piirainen. Baltmannsweiler: Schneider Verlag Hohengehren, 1999. 309–326.
Acquisition / age / children / classification / dialect / empiricism / German / literacy / narrative / orality / phraseologism / statistics / Swiss German.

970. Schmidt–Radefeldt, Jürgen. "Structure argumentative, reference et contextualité du proverbe." *Stylistique, rhétorique et*

poétique dans les langues romanes. Ed. Jean–Claude Bouvier. Aix–en–Provence: Université de Provence, 1986. 87–102.
Argument / communication / context / grammar / linguistics / meaning / semantics / speech act / structure / syntax / use.

971. Schneider, Klaus P. "Stereotype und Sprachbewußtsein: Beispiel 'small talk'." *Sprachwissenschaft und Volkskunde. Perspektiven einer kulturanalytischen Sprachbetrachtung.* Eds. Herbert F. Brekle and Utz Maas. Opladen: Westdeutscher Verlag, 1986. 140–154.
Attitude / communication / context / field research / folklore / linguistics / phraseologism / society / stereotype / value / worldview / "Small talk."

972. Schoeps, Hans–Joachim. "Völkerpsychologie im Sprichwort." In H.–J. Schoeps. *Ungeflügelte Worte. Was nicht im Büchmann stehen kann.* Berlin: Haude & Spener, 1971. 162–171.
Blason populaire / ethnicity / folklore / national character / prejudice / psychology / slur / stereotype.

973. Schönau, Walter. "Die gnomischen Formen [bei Sigmund Freud]." In W. Schönau. *Sigmund Freuds Prosa: Literarische Elemente seines Stils.* Stuttgart: Metzler, 1968. 122–129.
Aphorism / Sigmund Freud / gnome / language / literature / psychoanalysis / quotation / style.

974. Schubert, Gabriella. "Aspekte des Lachens in den Sprichwörtern der Südslaven." *Zeitschrift für Balkanologie*, 31, no. 1 (1995), 83–94.
Content / culture / emotion / humor / laughter / Slavic / stereotype / worldview.

975. Schumacher, Meinolf. "'…ist menschlich'." Mittelalterliche Variationen einer antiken Sentenz." *Zeitschrift für deutsches Altertum und deutsche Literatur*, 119 (1990), 163–170.
Antiquity / context / literature / loan translation / origin / Alexander Pope / variation / "Errare humanum est" / "To err is human, to forgive divine."

976. Schumacher, Robert M. *Factors Affecting Memorial Access to Analogical Similarity.* Diss. University of Illinois at Urbana–Champaign, 1989. 128 pp.
Analogy / memorization / memory / proverbs test / psycholinguistics / psychology / repetition / structure.

977. Schwartz, Gerald B. *Thought Disturbances in Mania and Schizophrenia*. Diss. Yeshiva University, 1982. 205 pp.
Abstraction / John D. Benjamin / brain / concreteness / interpretation / mania / proverbs test / psychiatry / psychology / schizophrenia.

978. Schweigert, Wendy A. "The Comprehension of Familiar and Less Familiar Idioms." *Journal of Psycholinguistic Research*, 15, no. 1 (1986), 33–45.
Comprehension / empiricism / familiarity / figurativeness / idiom / informant / literalness / meaning / psycholinguistics / statistics / student.

979. Schweigert, Wendy A., and Danny R. Moates. "Familiar Idiom Comprehension." *Journal of Psycholinguistic Research*, 17, no. 4 (1988), 281–296.
Comprehension / familiarity / figurativeness / literalness / idiom / meaning / psycholinguistics.

980. Schwer, Wilhelm. "Zur Soziologie des Sprichworts." *Bonner Mitteilungen*, 5 (1931), 8–14.
Class / conservativeness / culture / function / modernity / obsoleteness / society / sociology / tradition / validity.

981. Scott, R.B.Y. "Precepts and Proverbs." In R. Scott. *The Way of Wisdom in the Old Testament*. New York: Macmillan, 1971. 48–70.
Authority / behavior / Bible / experience / generalization / Old Testament / precept / religion / rule / wisdom.

982. Scott, W.T. "Proverbs, Postmodernity, and Unacknowledged Legislation." *Law and Literature Perspectives*. Eds. Bruce L. Rockwood and Roberta Kevelson. New York: Peter Lang, 1996. 341–352.
Allusion / anti–proverb / Bible / context / culture / function / law / modification / postmodernity / reduction / rule / tradition / wisdom.

983. Seidl, Helmut A. "Health Proverbs in Britain and Bavaria. A Sampling of Parallels." *Bavarica Anglica. A Cross–Cultural Miscellany Presented to Tom Fletcher*. Ed. Otto Hietsch. Bern: Peter Lang, 1979. 71–97.
Culture / disease / English / equivalent / folklore / German / health / meaning / medicine / metaphor / origin / structure.

984. Seidl, Helmut A. *Medizinische Sprichwörter im Englischen und Deutschen. Eine diachrone Untersuchung zur vergleichenden Parömiologie*. Bern: Peter Lang, 1982. 406 pp.
Culture / diachronic / disease / English / equivalent / folklore / German / health / history / meaning / medicine / metaphor / nutrition / origin / paremiology / somatism / structure.

985. Seitel, Peter. "Proverbs: A Social Use of Metaphor." *Genre*, 2 (1969), 143–161. Also in *The Wisdom of Many. Essays on the Proverb*. Eds. Wolfgang Mieder and Alan Dundes. New York: Garland Publishing, 1981. 122–139.
African / anthropology / context / definition / folklore / function / genre / Ibo / metaphor / society / strategy / use.

986. Seitel, Peter. *Proverbs and the Structure of Metaphor Among the Haya of Tanzania*. Diss. University of Pennsylvania, 1972. 258 pp.
African / anthropology / context / figurativeness / folklore / function / Haya / metaphor / society / speech act / structure / Swahili / use / variant.

987. Seitel, Peter. "Saying Haya Sayings: Two Categories of Proverb Use." *The Social Use of Metaphor: Essays on the Anthropology of Rhetoric*. Eds. J. David Sapir and J. Christopher Crocker. Philadelphia: University of Pennsylvania Press, 1977. 75–99.
African / anthropology / context / culture / folklore / Haya / meaning / society / speech act / use / value.

988. Serrano Vivero, Fuensanta. "Estereotipo social y refrán." *Paremia*, 5 (1996), 175–181.
Anti-feminism / family / gender / men / misogyny / prejudice / profession / society / stereotype / women.

989. Sevilla Muñoz, Julia. *Hacia una aproximación conceptual de las paremias francesas y españolas*. Madrid: Editorial Complutense, 1988. 245 pp.
Adage / aphorism / classification / definition / equivalent / French / genre / linguistics / metaphor / paremiology / poetics / semantics / Spanish / structure / wellerism.

990. Sevilla Muñoz, Julia, and Juan Carlos Diaz. "La competencia paremiologica: Los refranes." *Proverbium*, 14 (1997), 367–381.

Competence / empiricism / frequency / genre / informant / paremiological minimum / Spanish / statistics / student.

991. Shalimova, D.V. "Transformatsiia smyslov i znachenii slov pri ponimanii poslovits." *Voprosy psikhologii*, no. 4 (1990), 42–47.
Cognition / comprehension / figurativeness / meaning / metaphor / psychology.

992. Sheba, J. Olaide. "'Different Strokes for Different Folks': An Assessment of Yoruba Worldview in Proverbs." *Proverbium*, 18 (2001), 299–305.
African / attitude / content / culture / differentiation / society / worldview / Yoruba.

993. Shelton, Austin J. "Proverbs and Education in West Africa." *Oversea Education*, 34 (1963), 181–186.
African / culture / education / knowledge / orality / pedagogy / student / teaching / value / wisdom.

994. Shelton, Austin J. "Relativism, Pragmatism and Reciprocity in Igbo Proverbs." *The Conch*, 3, no. 2 (1971), 46–62.
African / behavior / content / culture / Igbo / meaning / pragmatism / reciprocity / relativism / worldview.

995. Shimkin, D.B., and Pedro Sanjuan. "Culture and World View: A Method of Analysis Applied to Rural Russia." *American Anthropologist*, 55 (1953), 329–348.
Anthropology / attitude / content / culture / ethnicity / psychology / Russian / society / sociology / value / worldview.

996. Shimkunas, Algimantas M., Malcolm D. Gynther, and Kathleen Smith. "Abstracting Ability of Schizophrenics Before and During Phenothiazine Therapy." *Archives of General Psychiatry*, 14 (1966), 79–83.
Abstraction / brain / concreteness / intelligence / interpretation / proverbs test / psychiatry / psychology / schizophrenia / therapy.

997. Shimkunas, Algimantas M., Malcolm D. Gynther, and Kathleen Smith. "Schizophrenic Responses to the Proverbs Test: Abstract, Concrete, or Autistic?" *Journal of Abnormal Psychology*, 72 (1967), 128–133.
Abstraction / autism / brain / concreteness / interpretation / proverbs test / psychiatry / psychology / schizophrenia.

998. Shinjo, Mahiko, and Jerome L. Myers. "The Role of Context in Metaphor Comprehension." *Journal of Memory and Language*, 26 (1987), 226–241.
Comprehension / context / informant / metaphor / psycholinguistics / psychology / student.

999. Shivtiel, Avihai. "Customs, Manners and Beliefs as Reflected by Some Arabic Proverbs and Idioms." *Proceedings of the Colloquium on Logos, Ethos, Mythos in the Middle East and North Africa. II. Popular Religion, Popular Culture and History*. Eds. Kinga Dévényi, Tamás Iványi, Alexander Fodor, and A. Shivtiel. Budapest: Eötvös Loránd University, 1996. II, 113–121.
Arabic / belief / content / culture / custom / experience / idiom / life / manners.

1000. Shivtiel, Avihai. "Women in Arabic Proverbs from Yemen." *New Arabian Studies*, 3 (1996), 164–175.
Anti–feminism / Arabic / attitude / culture / gender / male / marriage / misogyny / prejudice / society / stereotype / women.

1001. Sialm, Ambros. *Semiotik und Phraseologie. Zur Theorie fester Wortverbindungen im Russischen*. Bern: Peter Lang, 1987. 185 pp.
Bibliography / classification / definition / fixidity / idiomaticity / linguistics / phraseologism / phraseology / Russian / semantics / semiotics.

1002. Sigal, Georges. "Dictons et proverbes russes: Reflets d'une psychologie collective toute différente de celle des français." *Revue de psychologie des peuples*, 25 (1970), 308–324.
Collectivity / content / culture / French / phraseologism / psychology / Russian / worldview.

1003. Sigelman, Lee. "Is Ignorance Bliss? A Reconsideration of the Folk Wisdom." *Human Relations*, 34, no. 11 (1981), 965–974.
Anomia / folklore / intelligence / interview / psycholinguistics / validity / "Ignorance is bliss."

1004. Simon, Herbert. "Proverbs of Administration." *Public Administration Review*, 6 (1946), 53–67.
Administration / contradiction / principle / pseudo–proverb / rule / society.

1005. Simon, John. "The Wit and Wisdom of Catch Phrases." In J. Simon. *Paradigms Lost. Reflections on Literacy and Its Decline*. New York: Clarkson N. Potter, 1980. 75–80.
Catch phrase / content / definition / humor / Eric Partridge / phraseologism / psychology / wit / wisdom / worldview.

1006. Simon, Michael J. "Use of the Proverbs Test in the Assessment of Competency to Stand Trial." *Psychological Reports*, 60 (1987), 1166.
Comprehension / criminality / Donald R. Gorham / intelligence / interpretation / law / proverbs test / psychology.

1007. Šipoš, Ivan, Gabriel Horkovič, and Zdena Droppová. "Systems Approach to Memory: Psychology, Neurophysiology, Modelling." *Studia Psychologica*, 19 (1977), 178–190.
Meaning / memory / neurophysiology / proverbs test / psycholinguistics / psychology / recognition / semantics.

1008. Šipoš, Ivan, Luba Palúchová, and Gabriel Farkaš. "Continuous Short–Term Recognition of Proverbs." *Studia Psychologica*, 18 (1976), 278–285.
Memory / proverbs test / psycholinguistics / psychology / recognition / semantics.

1009. Šipoš, Ivan, and Otília Škarbová. "Kurzzeit–Reproduktion der Sprichwörter." *Studia Psychologica*, 20 (1978), 58–62.
Meaning / memory / proverbs test / psycholinguistics / psychology / recognition / semantics.

1010. Šipoš, Ivan, and L'ubica Stupavská. "Experimental Verification of Miller's Limit in Short–Term Memory." *Studia Psychologica*, 20 (1978), 184–193.
Meaning / memory / poetics / proverbs test / psycholinguistics / psychology / recognition / semantics.

1011. Siran, Jean–Louis. "Rhetoric, Tradition and Communication: The Dialectics of Meaning in Proverb Use." *Man: The Journal of the Royal Anthropological Institute*, 28, no. 1 (1993), 225–242.
African / anthropology / communication / definition / dialectics / meaning / rhetoric / speech act / tradition / use / Vute.

1012. Škara, Danica. "Linguistic Stereotypes: Crosscultural Analysis of Proverbs." *Radovi*, 22–23 (1992–1994), 127–134.

Croatian / culture / English / equivalent / Italian / linguistics / marker / semantics / stereotype / structure / value / universality.

1013. Škara, Danica. "On the Structure of the Proverb: The Search for Associative Links." *Europhras 95: Europäische Phraseologie im Vergleich: Gemeinsames Erbe und kulturelle Vielfalt.* Ed. Wolfgang Eismann. Bochum: Norbert Brockmeyer, 1998. 755–764.
Association / Croatian / English / equivalent / Italian / linguistics / marker / parallelism / structure / symmetry / syntax.

1014. Slovenko, Ralph. "Mixed Messages in Proverbs." *The Journal of Psychiatry & Law*, 21, no. 3 (1993), 405–409.
Abstraction / antithesis / behavior / collection / contradiction / law / message / psychiatry / rule / truth.

1015. Smith, Barbara Herrnstein. "Saying and Sayings." In B.H. Smith. *On the Margins of Discourse: The Relation of Literature to Language.* Chicago: University of Chicago Press, 1978. 69–75.
Context / language / literature / meaning / metaphor / origin / poetry / structure / universality / truth / wisdom.

1016. Smith, Charlotte Ann. *A Study of the Relationship Between the Use of Proverbs and Ego Development Levels.* Diss. University of Arkansas, 1982. 83 pp.
Acquiescence / Bernard Bass / behavior / ego / emotion / maturity / proverbs test / psychology / student.

1017. Smith, Roger. "Use of the Proverbs Test for the Identification of Psychotic Disorder." *Journal of Clinical Psychology*, 27 (1971), 227.
Abstraction / brain / disorder / Donald R. Gorham / psychiatry / psychology.

1018. Soboleva, O.V. "O ponimanii mini–teksta, ili poslovitsa vek ne slomitsia." *Voprosy psikhologii*, no volume given, no. 1 (1995), 46–52.
Cognition / comprehension / figurativeness / literalness / psycholinguistics.

1019. Soler i Marcet, Maria–Lourdes. "Die Volksmedizin in der katalanischen Folklore unter besonderer Berücksichtigung der Parömiologie." *Iberoromania*, 39 (1994), 119–131.

Belief / Catalan / culture / disease / experience / folklore / health / medicine.

1020. Soliva, Claudio. "Ein Bibelwort in Geschichte und Recht." *"Unser Weg". Werkblatt der Schweizerischen Weggefährtinnen*, no volume given, nos. 6–7 (1964), 51–57.
Bible / categorical imperative / "Golden Rule" / history / Immanuel Kant / law / "Was du nicht willst, daß man dir tu, das füg auch keinem andern zu."

1021. Soriano, Marc. "L'enfant du XVIIe siècle à travers les proverbes." *Enfance et littérature au XVIIe siècle*. Ed. Andrée Mansau. Paris: Klincksieck, 1991. 59–65 (= *Littératures classiques*, no volume given, no. 14 [1991], 59–65).
Adult / authority / children / collection / didacticism / education / French / history / life / pedagogy / psychology / society / worldview.

1022. Spiewok, Wolfgang, and Danielle Buschinger (eds.). *Der Hahnrei im Mittelalter / Le cou au moyen âge*. Greifswald: Reineke–Verlag, 1994. 116 pp. With 6 illustrations.
Adultery / cuckold / culture / folklore / French / gender / German / iconography / literature / marriage / men / sex / women / "Ein Hahnrei sein."

1023. Srivastava, Sahab Lal. "Caste in Indian Proverbs." *Proverbium*, 14 (1969), 408–409.
Anthropology / behavior / caste / culture / Indian / profession / society / stereotype.

1024. Stafford, A.O. "The Mind of the African Negro as Reflected in His Proverbs." *Journal of Negro History*, 1 (1916), 42–48.
African / attitude / content / life / mentality / psychology / worldview.

1025. Stahl, Sandra K.D. "Cursing and Its Euphemisms: Power, Irreverence, and the Unpardonable Sin." *Midwestern Journal of Language and Folklore*, 3, no. 2 (1977), 54–68.
Curse / euphemism / folklore / language / power / religion / sociolinguistics / superstition / taboo.

1026. Stanciu, Dumitru. "Paremic Universalia." *Cahiers roumains d'études littéraires*, 1 (1984), 79–84.

Epistemology / Matti Kuusi / logic / metaphorization / paremiology / Grigorii L'vovich Permiakov / semantics / structure / universality / variability.

1027. Stanciu, Dumitru. "A Possible Model for the Construction of Proverbs." *Proverbium*, 13 (1996), 321–330.
Folklore / logic / metaphor / semantics / semiotics / structure / variant.

1028. Stanzel, Franz K. *Europäer: Ein imagologischer Essay.* Heidelberg: Carl Winter, 1997. 113 pp. With 11 illustrations.
Blason populaire / culture / ethnicity / ethnography / European / history / iconography / national character / origin / politics / prejudice / slur / society / stereotype / "Völkertafel" / worldview.

1029. Stanzel, Franz K. (ed.). *Europäischer Völkerspiegel: Imagologisch–ethnographische Studien zu den Völkertafeln des frühen 18. Jahrhunderts.* Heidelberg: Carl Winter, 1999. 324 pp. With 11 illustrations.
Blason populaire / culture / ethnicity / ethnography / European / history / iconography / language / mentality / national character / origin / politics / prejudice / psycholinguistics / slur / society / stereotype / "Völkertafel" / worldview.

1030. Stedje, Astrid. "Sprecherstrategien im Spiegel der Phraseologie." *Beiträge zur allgemeinen und germanistischen Phraseologieforschung.* Ed. Jarmo Korhonen. Oulu: Oulun Yliopisto, 1987. 91–109.
Collectivity / competence / context / discourse / function / knowledge / linguistics / norm / phraseology / semantics / speech act / strategy.

1031. Stedje, Astrid. "Beherztes Eingreifen oder ungebetenes Sich–Einmischen. Kontrastive Studien zu einer ethnolinguistischen Phraseologieforschung." *Europhras 88. Phraséologie Contrastive. Actes du Colloque International Klingenthal–Strasbourg, 12–16 mai 1988.* Ed. Gertrud Gréciano. Strasbourg: Université des Sciences Humaines, 1989. 441–452.
Behavior / ethnolinguistics / German / norm / phraseology / society / Swedish.

1032. Stedje, Astrid. "Rosen, Lilien und Veilchen sprechen. Zur Semiotik der Blumen in deutscher Phraseologie." *Europhras 90. Akten der internationalen Tagung zur germanistischen Phra-*

seologieforschung, Aske/Schweden 12.–15. Juni 1990. Ed. Christine Palm. Uppsala: Acta Universitatis Upsaliensis, 1991. 253–264.
Emotion / flower / folklore / German / love / metaphor / phraseology / poetry / semiotics / symbolism / women.

1033. Steigüber, Barbara. *Soziale Sprache und synthetische Zeit: Temporal–Adverbien in Sprichwörtern.* Diss. University of Paderborn, 1988. 276 pp.
Ambivalence / context / culture / function / society / sociolinguistics / time / worldview.

1034. Stein, Stephan. *Formelhafte Sprache. Untersuchungen zu ihren pragmatischen und kognitiven Funktionen im gegenwärtigen Deutsch.* Frankfurt am Main: Peter Lang, 1995. 375 pp.
Cognition / communication / context / discourse / formula / function / German / linguistics / pragmatics / reproduction / routine formula / speech act.

1035. Stern, Josef Peter. "Manipulation durch das Klischee." *Sprache und Gesellschaft.* Ed. Annamaria Rucktäschel. München: Wilhelm Fink, 1972. 260–274.
Cliché / emotion / generalization / language / manipulation / phraseologism / politics / society.

1036. Sternkopf, Jochen. "Redensart und Leitbegriff." *Methodologische Aspekte der Semantikforschung.* Ed. Inge Pohl. Frankfurt am Main: Peter Lang, 1997. 283–295.
Comprehension / foreign language / idiomaticity / pedagogy / phraseologism / semantics / speech act / teaching.

1037. Stewart, Susan Alice. *Nonsense: Aspects of Intertextuality in Folklore and Literature.* Diss. University of Pennsylvania, 1978. 360 pp. Baltimore, Maryland: Johns Hopkins University Press, 1978. 228 pp.
Common sense / context / folklore / indirection / intertextuality / literature / metaphor / metonymy / nonsense.

1038. Stewart, Susan Alice. "Notes on Distressed Genres." *Journal of American Folklore,* 104 (1991), 5–31.
Culture / fable / folklore / genre / Georg Wilhelm Friedrich Hegel / literature / modernity / obsoleteness / tradition / validity.

1039. Stock, Oliviero, John Slack, and Andrew Ortony. "Building Castles in the Air: Some Computational and Theoretical Issues in Idiom Comprehension." *Idioms: Processing, Structure, and Interpretation.* Eds. Cristina Cacciari and Patrizia Tabossi. Hillsdale, New Jersey: Lawrence Erlbaum Associates, 1993. 229–247.
Cognition / comprehension / idiom / psycholinguistics / semantics / syntax.

1040. Stone, Judith. "The Proverbial Story." *Hippocrates: The Magazine of Health and Medicine,* 6, no. 1 (January 1992), 70–74.
Contradiction / health / meaning / medicine / metaphor / science / truth / validity.

1041. Storm, Hiroko. "Women in Japanese Proverbs." *Asian Folklore,* 51, no. 2 (1992), 167–182.
Anti–feminism / culture / empiricism / folklore / gender / Japanese / misogyny / prejudice / statistics / stereotype / women / worldview.

1042. Streltsyna, M.S. "K voprosu o tipakh narushenii ponimaniia rechi pri afazii." *Voprosy Psikhologii,* no. 2 (1982), 121–125.
Aphasia / brain / comprehension / neuropsychology / psychiatry / psychology.

1043. Strube, Werner. "Zur Geschichte des Sprichworts 'Über den Geschmack läßt sich nicht streiten'." *Zeitschrift für Ästhetik und Allgemeine Kunstwissenschaft,* 30 (1985), 158–185.
Aesthetics / German / history / Immanuel Kant / meaning / philosophy / validity / wisdom / "Über den Geschmack läßt sich nicht streiten."

1044. Sullivan, Constance. "Gender Markers in Traditional Spanish Proverbs." *Literature Among Discourses: The Spanish Golden Age.* Ed. Wlad Godzich and Nicholas Spadaccini. Minneapolis, Minnesota: University of Minnesota Press, 1986. 82–102 and 160–165 (notes).
Attitude / culture / folklore / gender / men / norm / prejudice / society / socio–linguistics / Spanish / stereotype / tradition / women.

1045. Sullivan, Helen S., Frank X. Acosta, and Lowell H. Storms. "Modification of Chronic Schizophrenics' Abstractions Through Enriched Stimuli and Social Censure." *Journal of Clinical Psychology,* 36 (1980), 852–858.

Abstraction / brain / Donald R. Gorham / meaning / proverbs test / psychiatry / psychology / schizophrenia / society.

1046. Swinney, David A., and Anne Cutler. "The Access and Processing of Idiomatic Expressions." *Journal of Verbal Learning and Verbal Behavior*, 18 (1979), 523–534.
Cognition / comprehension / idiom / meaning / proverbs test / psycholinguistics.

1047. Syrotinski, Michael Friedrich Joseph. *Reinventing Figures: Jean Paulhan and the Critical Mystery of Literature.* Diss. Yale University, 1989. 269 pp.
Acquisition / competence / comprehension / language / literature / Malagasy / orality / Jean Paulhan / semiotics.

1048. Szemerkényi, Agnes. "A Semiotic Approach to the Study of Proverbs." *Proverbium*, 24 (1974), 934–936.
Communication / definition / function / life / linguistics / paremiology / Grigorii L'vovich Permiakov / pragmatics / semantics / semiotics / society / speech act.

T

1049. Tabossi, Patrizia, and Francesco Zardon. "The Activation of Idiomatic Meaning in Spoken Language Comprehension." *Idioms: Processing, Structure, and Interpretation*. Eds. Cristina Cacciari and Patrizia Tabossi. Hillsdale, New Jersey: Lawrence Erlbaum Associates, 1993. 145– 162.
Activation / comprehension / discourse / empiricism / idiom / informant / language / meaning / psycholinguistics / speech act / student.

1050. Tabossi, Patrizia, and Francesco Zardon. "The Activation of Idiomatic Meaning." *Idioms: Structural and Psychological Perspectives*. Eds. Martin Everaert, Erik–Jan van der Linden, André Schenk, and Rob Schreuder. Hillsdale, New Jersey: Lawrence Erlbaum Associates, 1995. 273– 282.
Activation / comprehension / discourse / identification / idiom / meaning / psycholinguistics / recognition / speech act.

1051. Tafel, Karin. "Zum Zusammenhang zwischen Nationalitätenstereotypen und Geschlechterstereotypen (an russischen und deutschen Beispielen)." *Wörter in Bildern – Bilder in Wörtern: Beiträge zur Phraseologie und Sprichwortforschung aus dem Westfälischen Arbeitskreis*. Eds. Rupprecht S. Baur, Christoph Chlosta, and Elisabeth Piirainen. Baltmannsweiler: Schneider Verlag Hohengehren, 1999. 389–403.
Blason populaire / ethnicity / gender / German / national character / phraseologism / prejudice / Russian / slur / stereotype.

1052. Tavernier–Almada, Linda. "Prejudice, Power, and Poverty in Haiti: A Study of a Nation's Culture as Seen Through Its Proverbs." *Proverbium*, 16 (1999), 325–350.
Creole / culture / national character / poverty / power / prejudice / worldview.

1053. Taylor, Archer. *The Proverb*. Cambridge, Massachusetts: Harvard University Press, 1931. 223 pp. Rpt. as *The Proverb and an Index to The Proverb*. Hatboro, Pennsylvania: Folklore Associates, 1962. 328 pp. Rpt. again with an introduction and a bibliography by Wolfgang Mieder. Bern: Peter Lang, 1985. 381 pp.
Antiquity / Bible / bibliography / blason populaire / collection / content / custom / definition / ethics / ethnicity / folklore / form / genre / history / language / law / literature / loan translation / medicine / metaphor / narrative / national character /

obscenity / origin / paremiology / structure / style / superstition / variation / wellerism.

1054. Taylor, Archer. *Selected Writings on Proverbs.* Ed. Wolfgang Mieder. FFC 216. Helsinki: Suomalainen Tiedeakatemia, 1975. 204 pp.
Bibliography / collection / culture / definition / folklore / formula / history / language / meaning / name / narrative / origin / paremiology / structure / wellerism.

1055. Tê', Huynh Dinh. *Vietnamese Cultural Patterns and Values as Expressed in Proverbs.* Diss. Columbia University, 1963. 254 pp.
Attitude / Chinese / content / culture / form / origin / society / value / Vietnamese / worldview.

1056. Teigen, Karl Halvor. "Old Truths or Fresh Insights? A Study of Students' Evaluations of Proverbs." *British Journal of Social Psychology,* 25 (1986), 43–49.
Contradiction / proverbs test / psycholinguistics / student / tradition / truth / value.

1057. Telija, Veronika N. "Phraseological Entities as a Language of Culture (Methodological Aspects)." *Europhras 95: Europäische Phraseologie im Vergleich: Gemeinsames Erbe und kulturelle Vielfalt.* Ed. Wolfgang Eismann. Bochum: Norbert Brockmeyer, 1998. 783–794.
Culture / imagery / language / mentality / phraseologism / semantics / semiotics / worldview.

1058. Telija, Veronika N., Natalya Bragina, Elena Oparina, and Irina Sandormirskaya. "Phraseology as a Language of Culture: Its Role in the Representation of Collective Mentality." *Phraseology: Theory, Analysis, and Applications.* Ed. A.P. Cowie. Oxford: Oxford University Press, 1998. 55–75.
Collectivity / culture / discourse / language / mentality / metaphor / phraseology / society / stereotype.

1059. Temple, Jon G. *You Must Walk before You Can Run: The Multi–Stage Model and the Primacy of Literal Meaning.* Diss. University of Cincinnati, 1993. 105 pp.
Comprehension / context / figurativeness / literalness / meaning / metaphor / psycholinguistics / psychology.

1060. Temple, Jon G., and Richard P. Honeck. "Literal Versus Nonliteral Reminders for Proverbs." *Bulletin of the Psychonomic Society*, 30, no. 1 (1992), 67–70.
Comprehension / figurativeness / literalness / memory / psycholinguistics / psychology / recall.

1061. Temple, Jon G., and Richard P. Honeck. "Proverb Comprehension: The Primacy of Literal Meaning." *Journal of Psycholinguistic Research*, 28, no. 1 (1999), 41–70.
Comprehension / figurativeness / literalness / meaning / psycholinguistics / psychology.

1062. Tercedor Sánchez, Maribel. "Hacia una taxonomia de unidades fraseológicas en el discurso biomédico." *Trabajos de lexicografía y fraseología contrastivas*. Eds. Antonio Pamies Bertrán and Juan de Dios Luque Durán. Granada: Departamento de Lingüística General y Teoría de la Literatura de la Universidad de Granada, 2000. 145–156.
Collocation / content / discourse / lexicology / linguistics / medicine / metaphor / phraseologism / science.

1063. Thiele, Johannes. "'Buey viejo, surco derecho' – 'Alte Esel wissen viel' oder: Die Rollenverteilung in der Tiersymbolik in Redensarten und Sprichwörtern." *Über Texte: Festschrift für Karl–Ludwig Selig*. Eds. Peter–Eckhard Knabe and J. Thiele. Tübingen: Stauffenberg, 1997. 255–261.
Animal / anthropomorphism / behavior / equivalent / French / German / metaphor / phraseologism / semiotics / Spanish / symbolism.

1064. Thierfelder, Franz. "Sprich- und Schlagwörter zwischen den Völkern." *Welt und Wort*, 11 (1956), 369–370 and 373.
Blason populaire / ethnicity / national character / slur / stereotype / validity.

1065. Thoren, Krista Helene. *Learner and Native Speaker Intuitions for Universal Linguistic Structures in French Proverbs*. M.A. Thesis University of Texas at Austin, 1985. 36 pp.
Attitude / French / linguistics / proverbs test / psycholinguistics / structure.

1066. Thorndike, Edward L., and G.J. Ruger. "The Effects of Outside Air and Recirculated Air upon Intellectual Achievement and Improvement of School Pupils." *School and Society*, 4 (1916), 260–264.

African / education / learning / proverbs test / society / student / teaching.

1067. Tóthné Litovkina, Anna. "The Use of Proverbs in Contemporary Hungarian Society: A Study of National Identity Among Hungarians of Tolna County Through Proverbs." *European Journal for Semiotic Studies*, 4, nos. 1–2 (1992), 289–316.
Age / education / empiricism / familiarity / gender / Hungarian / identity / informant / knowledge / society / sociolinguistics / statistics / use.

1068. Tóthné Litovkina, Anna. "The Most Powerful Markers of Proverbiality: Perception of Proverbs and Familiarity with Them Among 40 Americans." *Semiotische Berichte*, nos. 1–4 (1994), 327–353.
American / empiricism / familiarity / informant / marker / metaphor / perception / poetics / proverbiality / repetition / statistics.

1069. Tóthné Litovkina, Anna. "How Do Sex, Age, Settlement Type, Education and Parental Background Influence the Knowledge of Proverbs in Hungary?" *Semiotics Around the World: Synthesis in Diversity*. Eds. Irmengard Rauch and Gerald F. Carr. Berlin: Walter de Gruyer, 1997. 1147–1150.
Age / education / empiricism / familiarity / gender / Hungarian / informant / knowledge / parents / statistics.

1070. Tóthné Litovkina, Anna. "Perception of Proverbs and Familiarity with Them: Figurativeness as One of the Most Powerful Markers of Proverbiality." *Semiotics Around the World: Synthesis in Diversity*. Eds. Irmengard Rauch and Gerald F. Carr. Berlin: Walter de Gruyer, 1997. 215–218.
American / empiricism / familiarity / figurativeness / marker / metaphor / perception / poetics / proverbiality / statistics / student.

1071. Tóthné Litovkina, Anna. "An Analysis of Popular American Proverbs and Their Use in Language Teaching." *Die heutige Bedeutung oraler Tradition: Ihre Archivierung, Publikation und Index–Erschließung*. Eds. Walther Heissig and Rüdiger Schott. Opladen: Westdeutscher Verlag, 1998. 131–158.
American / culture / familiarity / foreign language / frequency / grammar / Hungarian / marker / pedagogy / poetics / proverbiality / teaching / syntax.

1072. Tóthné Litovkina, Anna. "How Many and What Proverbs Are Still Commonly Familiar Among Hungarian Children and Adolescents?" *Europhras 95: Europäische Phraseologie im Vergleich: Gemeinsames Erbe und kulturelle Vielfalt.* Ed. Wolfgang Eismann. Bochum: Norbert Brockmeyer, 1998. 807–821.
Adolescent / children / currency / empiricism / familiarity / Hungarian / informant / statistics / youth.

1073. Tóthné Litvokina, Anna. "If You Are not Interested in Being Healthy, Wealthy and Wise – How About Early to Bed? Sexual Proverb Transformations." *Semiotische Berichte*, 23, nos. 1–4 (1999), 387–412.
Anti–proverb / collection / content / graffiti / Wolfgang Mieder / obscenity / parody / sex / transformation / variation.

1074. Tóthné Litovkina, Anna. "'Spare the Rod and Spoil the Child': Sexuality in Proverbs, Sayings and Idioms." *Proverbium*, 16 (1999), 141–165.
American / anti–proverb / English / equivalent / Hungarian / idiom / obscenity / parody / phraseologism / Russian / sex / structure.

1075. Tóthné Litvokina, Anna. *A Proverb a Day Keeps Boredom Away.* Szekszárd: IPF–Könyvek, 2000. 386 pp.
American / anti–proverb / content / context / culture / education / equivalent / foreign language / form / genre / Hungarian / iconography / literature / mass media / pedagogy / poetics / poetry / structure / student / teaching.

1076. Tow, Patrick K., and Steve Tonelson. "An Exercise on Enacting Proverbs in Health Education." *Journal of Health Education*, 25, no. 4 (1994), 247–248.
Charade / education / experience / health / life / pedagogy / student / teaching.

1077. Traugott, Elizabeth Closs. "'Conventional' and 'Dead' Metaphors Revisited." *The Ubiquity of Metaphor: Metaphor in Language and Thought.* Eds. Wolf Paprotté and René Dirven. Amsterdam: John Benjamins Publishing, 1985. 17–53.
Currency / experience / figurativeness / literalness / language / metaphor / phraseologism / time.

1078. Tupper, Martin Farquahar. *Proverbial Philosophy: A Book of Thoughts and Arguments, Originally Treated. With an Essay*

on *"The Philosophy of Proverbs"*. Philadelphia: E.H. Butler, 1852. 276 pp. (the essay is on pp. ix–xxxvi).
Communication / definition / diachronic / form / function / genre / history / narrative / orality / origin / paremiology / philosophy / worldview.

1079. Turner, Mark. "Figure." In Albert N. Katz, Cristina Cacciari, Raymond W. Gibbs, and Mark Turner. *Figurative Language and Thought.* New York: Oxford University Press, 1998. 44–87.
Cognition / figurativeness / figure / grammar / language / linguistics / literalness / psycholinguistics / rhetoric / symmetry.

1080. Turner, Nigel E. *The Role of Literal Meaning in Proverb Comprehension.* Diss. University of Western Ontario, 1995. 294 pp.
Cognition / comprehension / familiarity / figurativeness / imagery / literalness / meaning / memory / psycholinguistics.

1081. Turner, Nigel E., and Albert N. Katz. "The Availability of Conventional and of Literal Meaning During the Comprehension of Proverbs." *Pragmatics & Cognition,* 5, no. 2 (1997), 199–233.
Cognition / comprehension / figurativeness / interpretation / literalness / meaning / psycholinguistics.

U

1082. Ugarte Ballester, Xus. "'A la galga y a la mujer no la des la carne a ver': traducción, misoginia y equivalencia." *Paremia*, 8 (1999), 511–516.
Anti–feminism / English / equivalent / French / gender / men / mentality / misogyny / prejudice / Spanish / stereotype / women.

1083. Ugochukwu, Françoise. "Les proverbes igbos d'hier à aujourd'hui: un tour d'horizon." *Cahiers de littérature orale*, no volume given, no. 13 (1983), 51–65.
Chinua Achebe / African / authority / content / context / culture / figurativeness / Igbo / literalness / orality / society / wisdom / worldview.

1084. Ugochukwu, Françoise. "Le proverbe igbo, perle du culture." *Cahiers d'études africaines*, 34, no. 4 (1994), 585–596.
African / culture / form / Igbo / metaphor / orality / society / structure.

1085. Ulatowska, Hanna K., and Gloria S. Olness. "Reflections on the Nature of Proverbs: Evidence from Aphasia." *Proverbium*, 15 (1998), 329–346.
Abstraction / aphasia / brain / cognition / competence / comprehension / context / culture / empiricism / meaning / metaphor / psycholinguistics / psychiatry / psychology.

1086. Upadhyaya, Hari S. "Attitude of Indian Proverbs Toward High Caste Hindus." *Proverbium*, 3 (1965), 46–56.
Attitude / caste / culture / folklore / Hindu / Indian / society / sociology.

1087. Upadhyaya, Hari S. "Craftsmen's and Tradesmen's Castes in Indian Proverbs." *Proverbium*, 4 (1966), 71–83.
Blason populaire / caste / culture / economics / folklore / Indian / profession / society / stereotype / worldview.

V

1088. Vajičková, Mária. "How Many Idioms Does One Need? Or How Many Idioms Does the Learner Need in Foreign Language Learning?" *Europhras 97: Phraseology and Paremiology*. Ed. Peter Ďurčo. Bratislava: Akadémia PZ, 1998. 346–351.
Competence / foreign language / German / idiom / learning / mass media / modification / pedagogy / style / teaching.

1089. Valle Domenech, Carlos del. "La idea de previsión en el refranero popular español." *Actas de Congresso Internacional de Etnografia, Santo Tirso de 10 a 18 de julho de 1963*. No editor given. Lisboa: Imprensa Portuguesa, 1965. III, 637–642.
Didacticism / experience / foresight / life / prudence / Spanish / worldview.

1090. Vallini, Cristina. "Proverbi: Ossessioni ed esorcismi." *La pratica e la grammatica: Viaggio nella linguistica del proverbio*. Ed. C. Vallini. Napoli: Istituto Universitario Orientale, 1989. 5–9.
Definition / form / linguistics / poetics / proverbiality / semantics / structure.

1091. Van de Voort, Marlies E.C., and Wietske Vonk. "You Don't Die Immediately When You Kick an Empty Bucket: A Processing View on Semantic and Syntactic Characteristics of Idioms." *Idioms: Structural and Psychological Perspectives*. Eds. Martin Everaert, Erik–Jan van der Linden, André Schenk, and Rob Schreuder. Hillsdale, New Jersey: Lawrence Erlbaum Associates, 1995. 283–299.
Comprehension / figurativeness / idiom / literalness / psycholinguistics / semantics / syntax.

1092. Van Lancker, Diana. "The Neurology of Proverbs." *Behavioural Neurology*, 3 (1990), 169–187. With 2 illustrations.
Aphasia / brain / cognition / comprehension / familiarity / figurativeness / idiom / literalness / meaning / neurology / proverbs test / psycholinguistics / psychology.

1093. Van Lancker, Diana. "A Neurolinguistic Perspective on Proverbs and the Laws of Life." *Understanding Wisdom: Sources, Science & Society*. Ed. Warren S. Brown. Philadelphia: Templeton Foundation Press, 2000. 215–243.

Abstraction / brain / classification / competence / comprehension / familiarity / figurativeness / frequency / law / life / neurolinguistics / psycholinguistics / use.

1094. Van Lancker, Diana, and Daniel Kempler. "Comprehension of Familiar Phrases by Left- but Not by Right–Hemisphere Damaged Patients." *Brain and Language*, 32 (1987), 265–277. With 1 illustration.
Brain / cognition / comprehension / familiarity / figurativeness / idiom / literalness / meaning / neurolinguistics / psycholinguistics / psychology.

1095. Venedey, Jacob. *Die Deutschen und Franzosen nach dem Geiste ihrer Sprachen und Sprüchwörter.* Heidelberg: Carl Winter, 1842. 176 pp.
Content / culture / equivalent / French / German / history / national character / society / stereotype / worldview.

1096. Vila Rubio, Nieves. "El refrán: un artefacto cultural." *Revista de dialectologia y tradiciones populares*, 45 (1990), 211–224.
Allegory / classification / culture / ethnolinguistics / function / language / marriage / Spanish / value / worldview.

1097. Vinken, P.J. "Some Observations on the Symbolism of 'The Broken Pot' in Art and Literature." *American Imago*, 15 (1958), 149–174.
Defloration / Jean–Baptiste Greuze / iconography / Heinrich von Kleist / literature / psychoanalysis / sex / symbolism / virginity / women / "The pitcher (pot) goes to the well until it is broken at last."

1098. Voegtle, Katherine H. *Categorization of Figurative Concepts.* Diss. University of Cincinnati, 1983. 146 pp.
Abstraction / acquisition / context / figurativeness / interpretation / meaning / proverbs test / psycholinguistics.

1099. Voigt, Vilmos. "Les niveaux des variantes de proverbes." *Acta Linguistica Academiae Scientiarum Hungaricae*, 20 (1970), 357–364. Published in shortened form in German as "Variantenschichten eines ungarischen Proverbiums." *Proverbium*, 15 (1970), 541–544; in Hungarian as "A szólások változatainak szintjei." *Magyar Nyelvör*, 95 (1971), 29–34; in Finnish as "Sananlaskujen variantit kielen eri tasorakenteissa." *Lalevalasseuran Vuosikirja*, 54 (1974), 529–538; and once again in French as "Sur les niveaux des variantes de proverbs." *Atti del*

simposio internazionale "Strutture e generi delle letterature etniche". Ed. Janne Vibaek. Palermo: Flaccovio, 1978. 209–218.
Folklore / form / function / linguistics / paremiology / semantics / structure / variant / variation.

1100. Vorlat, Emma. "'Your Marriage is Going Through a Rocky Patch'. On Idioms in the Lonely Hearts Columns." *Communiquer et traduire. Hommages à Jean Dierickx.* Eds. G. Debusscher and J.P. van Noppen. Bruxelles: Éditions de l'Université de Bruxelles, 1985. 103–108.
Communication / emotion / frequency / function / idiom / letter / love / marriage / mass media / metaphor / psychology / use / women.

W

1101. Wagener, A. Pelzer. "On 'Putting the Best Foot Forward'." *Transactions and Proceedings of the American Philological Society*, 66 (1935), 73–91.
Antiquity / belief / literature / loan translation / meaning / origin / phraseologism / "To put the best foot forward."

1102. Wakisaka, Yutaka. "Metapher, Idiom und Stereotypen – Pragmalinguistische Untersuchung der Interkulturalität." *Alte Welten – neue Welten. Akten des IX. Kongresses der Internationalen Vereinigung für germanische Sprach- und Literaturwissenschaft.* Ed. Michael S. Batts. Tübingen: Max Niemeyer, 1996. III, 138 (abstract).
Culture / idiom / linguistics / metaphor / pragmatics / semiotics / stereotype / worldview.

1103. Walsh, Mary–Elizabeth. *The Role of Imagery and Abstraction in Proverb Comprehension: A Dual–Coding Analysis of Figurative Language.* Diss. University of Western Ontario, 1988. 232 pp.
Abstraction / comprehension / figurativeness / imagery / interpretation / literalness / meaning / memory / proverbs test / psycholinguistics / psychology / recall.

1104. Walther, Andreas. "Volkhafte Sozialweisheit und Spitzenkultur." *Vom Geist der Dichtung. Gedächtnisschrift für Robert Petsch.* Ed. Fritz Martini. Hamburg: Hoffmann und Campe, 1949. 358–380.
Class / culture / history / intellectualism / profession / rule / society / sociology / truth / wisdom.

1105. Wamitila, Kyallo Wadi. "Towards Understanding Kiswahili Proverbs: An Examination of Schemes, Figurative Tropes and Contextual Issues." *Proverbium*, 17 (2000), 409–434.
African / classification / comprehension / context / figurativeness / folklore / function / Kiswahili / linguistics / metaphor / paradox / pragmatics / semantics / structure / universality.

1106. Wang, Juan. "Fatalism Seen Through Chinese Proverbial Expressions and Folk Beliefs." *Folk Narrative and World View. Vorträge des 10. Kongresses der Internationalen Gesellschaft für Volkserzählungsforschung. Innsbruck 1992.* Ed. Leander Petzoldt. Frankfurt am Main: Peter Lang, 1996. 823–834.

Belief / Chinese / culture / fatalism / mentality / phraseologism / worldview.

1107. Wanjohi, Gerald J. "The Philosophy of Gikuyu Proverbs: An Epistemological Contribution." *Denken unterwegs. Philosophie im Kräftefeld sozialen und politischen Engagements.* Eds. Henk Oosterling and Frans de Jong. Amsterdam: B.R. Grüner, 1990. 383–394.
African / empiricism / epistemology / Gikuyu / knowledge / meaning / philosophy / rationalism.

1108. Wanjohi, Gerald J. "The Philosophy of Gikuyu Proverbs and Other Sayings With Particular Reference to Ethics." *Relations Between Cultures.* Eds. George F. McLean and John Kromkowski. Washington, D.C.: The Council for Research in Values and Philosophy, 1991. 53–59.
African / content / contradiction / ethics / form / Gikuyu / morality / philosophy.

1109. Wanjohi, Gerald J. "The Ontology, Epistemology, and Ethics Inherent in Proverbs: The Case of the Gikuyu." *Embracing the Baobab Tree: The African Proverb in the 21st Century.* Ed. Willem Saayman. Pretoria: University of South Africa, 1997. 72–83.
African / empiricism / epistemology / ethics / Gikuyu / knowledge / metaphysics / ontology / philosophy / rationalism.

1110. Wanjohi, Gerald J. *The Wisdom and the Philosophy of the Gikuyu Proverbs.* Nairobi, Kenya: Paulines Publications Africa, 1997. 271 pp.
African / classification / contradiction / education / epistemology / ethics / generalization / Gikuyu / metaphor / metaphysics / peace / philosophy / politics / religion / society / structure / wisdom / worldview.

1111. Ward, Donald. "The Wolf: Proverbial Ambivalence." *Proverbium,* 4 (1987), 211–224.
Ambivalence / animal / culture / etymology / folklore / Wilhelm Grimm / metaphor / mythology / wolf.

1112. Wasserstein, David J. "A West–East Puzzle: On the History of the Proverb 'Speech is Silver, Silence is Golden'." *Israel Oriental Studies,* 19 (1999), 239–259.

Antiquity / Arabic / culture / distribution / Hebrew / history / loan translation / silence / society / speech / worldview / "Speech is silver, silence is golden."

1113. Watson, Charles G. "Abstract Thinking Deficit and Autism in Process and Reactive Schizophrenics." *Journal of Abnormal Psychology*, 82 (1973), 399–403.
Abstraction / autism / brain / disorder / proverbs test / psychiatry / psychology / schizophrenia.

1114. Watson, Charles G., Duane Plemel, and Marcia Burke. "Proverb [sic] Test Deficit in Schizophrenic and Brain–Damaged Patients." *Journal of Nervous and Mental Diseases*, 167, no. 9 (1979), 561–565.
Abstraction / autism / brain / concreteness / disorder / proverbs test / psychiatry / psychology / schizophrenia.

1115. Weber–Kellermann, Ingeborg. "Die Bedeutung des Formelhaften im volkstümlichen Denken." *Völkerforschung, Vorträge der Tagung für Völkerkunde an der Humboldt–Universität Berlin vom 25.–27. April 1952*. Ed. Wolfgang Steinitz. Berlin: Akademie–Verlag, 1954. 187–199.
Folklore / formula / meaning / mentality / narrative / structure / style / wisdom.

1116. Webster, Sheila K. "Women, Sex, and Marriage in Moroccan Proverbs." *International Journal of Middle East Studies*, 14 (1982), 173–184.
Anti–feminism / Arabic / culture / family / marriage / misogyny / morality / Moroccan / sex / sexuality / society / stereotype / Edward Westermarck / women.

1117. Webster, Sheila K. *The Shadow of a Noble Man: Honor and Shame in Arabic Proverbs*. Diss. Indiana University, 1984. 222 pp.
Anthropology / Arabic / behavior / context / culture / emotion / family / folklore / gender / honor / ethnography / men / origin / shame / stereotype / structure / style / women.

1118. Wegrocki, Henry J. "Generalizing Ability in Schizophrenia: An Inquiry into the Disorders of Problem Thinking in Schizophrenia." *Archives of Psychology*, 36 (1940), 1–76 (esp. pp. 17–24).
Abstraction / brain / disorder / proverbs test / psychiatry / psychology / schizophrenia.

1119. Weinreich, Uriel. "Problems in the Analysis of Idioms." *Substance and Structure of Language*. Ed. Jaan Puhvel. Berkeley, California: University of California Press, 1969. 23–81. Also published in German translation as "Probleme bei der Analyse von Idiomen." *Semantik und generative Grammatik*. Ed. Ferenc Kiefer. Frankfurt am Main: Athenäum, 1972. II, 415–474.
Ambiguity / dictionary / function / grammar / idiom / lexicography / linguistics / metaphor / phraseologism / semantics / structure.

1120. Weissman, Herbert, and Albert Kostlan. "Use of the Proverbs Test in Differential Diagnosis in the Intensive Treatment Setting." *Newsletter for Research in Psychology*, 7 (1965), 33–34.
Abstraction / brain / disorder / Donald R. Gorham / proverbs test / psychiatry / psychology / schizophrenia.

1121. Wenzel, Angelika. *Stereotype in gesprochener Sprache. Form, Vorkommen und Funktion in Dialogen*. München: Max Huber, 1978. 179 pp.
Communication / definition / field research / form / function / national character / orality / psychology / society / sociology / speech act / stereotype.

1122. Werlen, Iwar. "Vermeidungsritual und Höflichkeit. Zu einigen Formen konventionalisierter indirekter Sprechakte im Deutschen." *Deutsche Sprache*, 11 (1983), 193–218.
Aggression / emotion / formula / indirection / linguistics / phraseologism / politeness / ritual / society / sociolinguistics / speech act.

1123. Westermarck, Edward. "On the Study of Popular Sayings." *Nature*, 122 (November 3, 1928), 701–703.
Anthropology / folklore / history / paremiology / psychology / sociology.

1124. Westermarck, Edward. "The Study of Popular Sayings." *The Frazer Lectures 1922–1932 by Divers Hands*. Ed. Warren R. Dawson. London: Macmillan, 1932. 190–211.
Anthropology / context / culture / definition / figurativeness / form / meaning / Moroccan / sociology.

1125. Whaley, Bryan B. "When 'Try, Try Again' Turns to 'You're Beating a Dead Horse': The Rhetorical Characteristics of Proverbs and Their Potential for Influencing Therapeutic

Change." *Metaphor and Symbolic Activity*, 8, no. 2 (1993), 127–139.
Analogy / behavior / contradiction / function / metaphor / poetics / psychology / rhetoric / society / speech act / therapy.

1126. White, Geoffrey M. "Proverbs and Cultural Models: An American Psychology of Problem Solving." *Cultural Models in Language and Thought*. Eds. Dorothy Holland and Naomi Quinn. Cambridge: Cambridge University Press, 1987. 151–172.
American / behavior / common sense / comprehension / culture / ethnopsychology / experience / instantiation / psychology / wisdom.

1127. Whiting, Bartlett Jere. "The Origin of the Proverb." *Harvard Studies and Notes in Philology and Literature*, 13 (1931), 47–80; "The Nature of the Proverb." *Harvard Studies and Notes in Philology and Literature*, 14 (1932), 273–307; and with Francis W. Bradley, Richard Jente, Archer Taylor, and Morris Palmer Tilley, "The Study of Proverbs." *Modern Language Forum*, 24 (1939), 57–83. All three major essays are now available as Bartlett Jere Whiting, *"When Evensong and Morrowsong Accord": Three Essays on the Proverb*. Eds. Joseph Harris and Wolfgang Mieder. Cambridge, Massachusetts: Department of English and American Literature and Language, Harvard University, 1994. 130 pp. With 2 illustrations.
American / anthropology / bibliography / collection / content / context / definition / Susan E. Deskis / didacticism / folklore / form / function / genre / history / language / law / life / literature / mass media / national character / origin / paremiology / pedagogy / phraseologism / rhetoric / semantics / structure / style / variant / wellerism / wisdom.

1128. Widdowson, John D.A. "Language, Tradition and Regional Identity: Blason Populaire and Social Control." *Language, Culture and Tradition*. Eds. A.E. Green and J. Widdowson. Sheffield: University of Sheffield, 1981. 33–46.
Blason populaire / culture / English / identity / language / national character / prejudice / society / stereotype / tradition.

1129. Wienker–Piepho, Sabine. "Sozialisation durch Sprichwörter: Am Beispiel eines anglo–amerikanischen Bestsellers." *Proverbium*, 8 (1991), 179–189.

American / anti–proverb / behavior / collection / currency / English / innovation / pseudo–proverb / Michele Slung / socialization / wisdom.

1130. Wilkins, Eliza Gregory. *"Know Thyself" in Greek and Latin Literature.* Diss. University of Chicago, 1917. Chicago: University of Chicago Libraries, 1917. 104 pp.
Antiquity / context / ethics / history / literature / meaning / philosophy / use / wisdom / "Know thyself."

1131. Williams, Fionnuala. "'Bachelors' Wives and Old Maids' Children': A Look at the Men and Women in Irish Proverbs." *Ulster Folklore*, 30 (1984), 78–88.
Anti–feminism / attitude / behavior / culture / experience / folklore / gender / Irish / marriage / men / misogyny / society / stereotype / women.

1132. Williams. Fionnuala. "'To Kill Two Birds with One Stone': Variants in a War of Words." *Proverbium*, 8 (1991), 199–201. With 2 illustrations.
Graffiti / iconography / Irish / modification / phraseologism / politics / variant / war / "To kill two birds with one stone."

1133. Winick, Stephen D. *The Proverb Process: Intertextuality and Proverbial Innovation in Popular Culture.* Diss. University of Pennsylvania, 1998. 360 pp. With 92 illustrations.
Advertisement / ambiguity / American / anti–proverb / common sense / culture / definition / discourse / iconography / innovation / intertextuality / Gary Larson / mass media / metaphor / modernity / modification / nonsense / origin / poetics.

1134. Winick, Stephen D. "'Garbage In, Garbage Out,' and Other Dangers: Using Computer Databases to Study Proverbs." *Proverbium*, 18 (2001), 353–364.
Computer / context / database / frequency / function / Kimberly J. Lau / mass media / popularity / semantics / variant.

1135. Winton, Alan P. *The Proverbs of Jesus. Issues of History and Rhetoric.* Sheffield: Sheffield Academic Press, 1990. 236 pp.
Bible / bibliography / context / function / history / Jesus / literature / meaning / New Testament / religion / rhetoric / structure / use / wisdom.

1136. Wirrer, Jan. "Phraseologismen in der Argumentation." *Phraseologismen in Text und Kontext. Phrasemata I.* Ed. Jan Wirrer. Bielefeld: Aisthesis Verlag, 1998. 121–148.
Argumentation / enthymeme / phraseologism / politics / rhetoric / semantics / sententious remark / topos.

1137. Wirrer, Jan. "Phraseologie und Rhetorik." *Wörter in Bildern – Bilder in Wörtern: Beiträge zur Phraseologie und Sprichwortforschung aus dem Westfälischen Arbeitskreis.* Eds. Rupprecht S. Baur, Christoph Chlosta, and Elisabeth Piirainen. Baltmannsweiler: Schneider Verlag Hohengehren, 1999. 421–455.
Argumentation / communication / context / function / linguistics / phraseology / politics / rhetoric / semantics / structure.

1138. Wirrer, Jan. "Phraseologie und Pragmatik." *"Wer A sägt, muss auch B sägen": Beiträge zur Phraseologie und Sprichwortforschung aus dem Westfälischen Arbeitskreis.* Eds. Dietrich Hartmann and Jan Wirrer. Baltmannsweiler: Schneider Verlag Hohengehren, 2002. 445–448.
Context / equivalent / foreign language / function / linguistics / phraseology / pragmatics / syntax / use.

1139. Wittstock, Albert. *Die Erziehung im Sprichwort oder Die deutsche Volks–Pädagogik.* Leipzig: C.G. Naumann, 1889. 281 pp.
Children / education / ethics / German / pedagogy / society / student / teaching.

1140. Wolfrum, Erich. "Das sprachliche Bild als Phantasie- und Denkimpuls. Stufen und Formen des reifenden Sinnverständnisses (Sprichwort)." *Taschenbuch des Deutschunterrichts. Grundfragen und Praxis der Sprach- und Literaturpädagogik.* Ed. E. Wolfrum. Baltmannsweiler: Wilhelm Schneider, 1976. 547–564.
Children / cognition / competence / comprehension / education / meaning / metaphor / pedagogy / proverbs test / psycholinguistics / teaching.

1141. Woodburn, Roland Rickey. *Proverbs in Health Books of the English Renaissance.* Diss. Texas Tech University, 1975. 99 pp.
Disease / English / health / literature / medicine / rhetoric / science / wisdom.

1142. Workman, Mark E. "Proverbs for the Pious and the Paranoid: The Social Use of Metaphor." *Proverbium*, 4 (1987), 225–241.
Chinua Achebe / culture / Feodor Mikhailovich Dostoevsky / function / literature / metaphor / psychology / Thomas Pynchon / religion / rhetoric / Peter Seitel / society / use.

1143. Wotjak, Barbara. *Verbale Phraseolexeme in System und Text*. Tübingen: Max Niemeyer, 1992. 202 pp.
Anti–proverb / communication / context / function / mass media / modification / phraseologism / politics / semantics / slogan / structure / syntax / wordplay.

1144. Wulff, Michal [sic]. *Das Sprichwort im Kontext der Erziehungstradition. Dargestellt am Beispiel deutsch–jüdischer Sprichwörter*. Frankfurt am Main: Peter Lang, 1990. 317 pp.
Content / context / culture / education / ethics / function / German / Jewish / national character / pedagogy / religion / worldview / Yiddish.

Y

1145. Yan, Hairong. "The Concept of 'Face' in Chinese Proverbs and Phrases." *Proverbium*, 12 (1995), 357–373.
Chinese / culture / face / metaphor / phraseologism / society / somatism / worldview.

1146. Yanga, Tshimpaka. "Inside the Proverbs: A Sociolinguistic Approach." *African Languages/Langues Africaines*, 3 (1977), 130–157.
African / communication / ethnography / Luba / society / sociolinguistics / speech act / structure / truth.

1147. Yankah, Kwesi. "The Proverb and the Western–Educated African: Use or Neglect?" *Folklore Forum*, 15 (1982), 143–158.
African / context / field research / folklore / frequency / informant / student / tradition / value / wisdom.

1148. Yankah, Kwesi. "Toward a Performance–Centered Theory of the Proverb." *Critical Arts*, 3, no. 1 (1983), 29–43.
Aesthetics / African / Akan / cognition / context / discourse / foregrounding / linguistics / performance / speech act / structure / use.

1149. Yankah, Kwesi. "Do Proverbs Contradict?" *Folklore Forum*, 17 (1984), 2–19. Also in *Wise Words: Essays on the Proverb*. Ed. Wolfgang Mieder. New York: Garland Publishing, 1994. 127–142.
African / Akan / context / contradiction / culture / discourse / meaning / truth.

1150. Yankah, Kwesi. *The Proverb in Context of Akan Rhetoric*. Diss. Indiana University, 1985. 455 pp. Also published as *The Proverb in the Context of Akan Rhetoric. A Theory of Proverb Praxis*. Bern: Peter Lang, 1989. 313 pp. With 4 illustrations.
African / Akan / anthropology / cognition / context / culture / discourse / ethnography / field research / folklore / iconography / indirection / law / narrative / performance / pragmatics / rhetoric / society / speech act / tradition.

1151. Yankah, Kwesi. "Proverb Speaking as a Creative Process: The Akan of Ghana." *Proverbium*, 3 (1986), 195–230.
African / Akan / ambiguity / context / creativity / discourse / fixity / performance / pragmatics / speech act / variability.

1152. Yankah, Kwesi. "Proverbs: The Aesthetics of Traditional Communication." *Research in African Literature*, 20, no. 3 (1989), 325–346.
Aesthetics / African / Akan / communication / context / law / orality / politics / rhetoric / society / tradition.

1153. Yao–Weyrauch, Wan–Hsuan. *Die Rolle der Frau im deutschen und chinesischen Sprichwort*. Bochum: Norbert Brockmeyer, 1990. 177 pp.
Anti–feminism / Chinese / culture / equivalent / German / misogyny / prejudice / stereotype / women / worldview.

1154. Yéo, Lacina. "'Mohr', 'Neger', 'Schwarzer', 'Afrikaner', 'Schwarzafrikaner', 'Farbiger' – abfällige oder neutrale Zuschreibungen? Eine Analyse der Ethnika und Ethnophaulismen zur Bezeichnung von Afrikanern und dunkelhäutigen Menschen afrikanischer Abstammung." *Muttersprache*, 111, no. 2 (2001), 110–146.
African / African American / ethnicity / ethnophaulism / etymology / negro / prejudice / semantics / slur / society / sociolinguistics / stereotype.

1155. Yoshikatsu, Kitamura. "Unouto kotowazana gengo. [Right Brain and the Language of Proverbs]." *Gengo*, 25, no. 7 (1996), 41–47 (in Japanese).
Brain / cognition / comprehension / figurativeness / language / psycholinguistics.

1156. Yusuf, Yisa Kehinde. "Proverbs and Misogyny." *Working Papers on Language, Gender and Sexism*, 4, no. 2 (1994), 25–45.
African / anti–feminism / gender / misogyny / prejudice / stereotype / women.

1157. Yusuf, Yisa Kehinde. "The Ethical Value of Women's Speech in Yoruba Proverbs." *Proverbium*, 11 (1994), 283–291.
African / communication / culture / ethics / speech / value / women / Yoruba.

1158. Yusuf, Yisa Kehinde. "Contradictory Yoruba Proverbs about Women: Their Significance for Social Change." *Nigerian Women in Social Change*. Eds. Simi Afonja and Bisi Aina. Ile–Ife: Programme in Women's Studies, Obafemi Awolowo University Press, 1995. 206–215.

African / ambivalence / anti–feminism / contradiction / gender / misogyny / prejudice / society / stereotype / value / women / Yoruba.

1159. Yusuf, Yisa Kehinde. "English and Yoruba Proverbs and the Spiritual Denigration of Women." *Research in Yoruba Language and Literature*, 8 (1996), 1–8.
African / anti–feminism / English / misogyny / prejudice / religion / stereotype / women / Yoruba.

1160. Yusuf, Yisa Kehinde. "Rape–Related English and Yoruba Proverbs." *Women and Language*, 21, no. 2 (1998), 39–42.
African / English / misogyny / rape / sex / society / sociolinguistics / women / Yoruba.

1161. Yusuf, Yisa Kehinde. "A Semantics Classroom Connection of Connotations, Stereotypes and Misogynous Proverbs." *Proverbium*, 18 (2001), 365–374.
African / connotation / misogyny / semantics / society / stereotype / student / teaching / women / Yoruba.

Z

1162. Zahler, Diane and Kathy A. "A Well–Turned Phrase: Quotes, Phrases, and Aphorisms." In D. and K.A. Zahler. *Test Your Cultural Literacy*. New York: Prentice Hall, 1993. 141–156 and 311–312.
Aphorism / culture / familiarity / history / knowledge / phraseologism / proverbs test / quotation.

1163. Zapf, Hubert. "Gaps in the Wall: Determinacy and Indeterminacy in Robert Frost's 'Mending Wall'." *Zeitschrift für Anglistik und Amerikanistik*, 39, no. 3 (1991), 250–253.
American / behavior / convention / deautomatization / Robert Frost / literature / poetry / tradition / "Good fences make good neighbors."

1164. Zeevat, Henk. "Idiomatic Blocking and the Elsewhere Principle." *Idioms: Structural and Psychological Perspectives*. Eds. Martin Everaert, Erik–Jan van der Linden, André Schenk, and Rob Schreuder. Hillsdale, New Jersey: Lawrence Erlbaum Associates, 1995. 301–316.
Blocking / competence / grammar / idiom / linguistics / meaning / performance.

1165. Zenner, Walter P. "Ethnic Stereotyping in Arabic Proverbs." *Journal of American Folklore*, 83 (1970), 417–429.
Arabic / ethnicity / folklore / Lebanese / prejudice / slur / stereotype.

1166. Zhang, Hong. "'Spare Women a Beating for Three Days, They Will Stand on the Roof and Tear the House Apart': Images of Women in Chinese Proverbs." *Locating Power: Proceedings of the Second Berkeley Women and Language Conference, April 4 and 5, 1992*. Eds. Kira Hall, Mary Bucholtz, and Birch Moonwomon. Berkeley, California: Berkeley Women and Language Group, University of California, 1992. II, 601– 609.
Anti–feminism / Chinese / culture / gender / men / misogyny / prejudice / stereotype / women.

1167. Zholkovskii, Aleksandr K. "At the Intersection of Linguistics, Paremiology and Poetics: On the Literary Structure of Proverbs." *Poetics*, 7 (1978), 309–332.
Linguistics / paremiology / Grigorii L'vovich Permiakov / phraseology / poetics / semantics / semiotics / structure.

1168. Zick, Gisela. "Der zerbrochene Krug als Bildmotiv des 18. Jahrhunderts." *Wallraf–Richartz Jahrbuch*, 31 (1969), 149–204. With 40 illustrations.
Jean–Baptiste Greuze / iconography / Heinrich von Kleist / literature / psychoanalysis / sex / symbolism / virginity / women / "The pitcher (pot) goes to the well until it is broken at last."

1169. Zittlau, Jörg. "'Ein Unglück kommt selten allein': In seinen Sprichwörtern ist der Deutsche ein echter Pessimist." *Psychologie heute*, no volume given, no. 5 (1996), 8–9. With 1 illustration.
Culture / frequency / German / iconography / national character / pessimism / psychology / worldview.

NAME INDEX

Those scholars whose publications are annotated in alphabetical order in this bibliography are not listed here. However, second or third authors of any particular entry are included. This index also registers all names mentioned in the titles of the bibliographical entries and in the key-word annotations. All numbers refer to the entries and not to page numbers.

Achebe, Chinua 1083, 1142
Acosta, Frank X. 1045
Albert, Marilyn S. 586
Allen, Melissa M. 757
Althof, Stanley E. 468
Ammons, C.H. 20
Anderson, Walter 484
Anscombre, Jean-Claude 672
Antos, Gerd 603
Antos, Stephen J. 799
Aristophanes 713
Aristotle 48, 405
Arter, Judith A. 798

Babcock-Abrahams, Barbara 4
Bacon, Francis 1
Bakhtin, Mikhail M. 619
Baltes, Paul B. 804
Bass, Bernard 1016
Baudrillard, Jean 193
Beauvoir, Simone de 193
Beitel, Dinara 359
Bell, Susan M. 80
Benjamin, John D. 67, 68, 148, 149, 155, 417, 675, 828–831, 977
Bernstein, Ignaz (Ignace) 572
Blake, William 781
Böll, Heinrich 265
Bookin, Howard B. 374
Bosch, Hieronymus 718
Bragina, Natalya 1058
Brandt, Willy 703, 707, 708
Brecht, Bertolt 708
Brewer, William F. 81

Broida, Daniel 878
Brown, Malrie 839, 840
Brown, Mary 373
Brueghel, Pieter 682, 683, 695, 718, 832
Bryan, George B. 714, 715
Budnek, Jane E. 485
Buhofer, Annelies 130
Burger, Harald 445
Burgess, Curt 847
Burke, Kenneth 258
Burridge, Kate 12
Buschinger, Danielle 1022

Cacciari, Cristina 539, 541, 599
Caird, W.K. 828
Cameron, Richard 167
Campbell, Alfonso 212
Canellas de Castro Duarte, Denis 879
Carey, Gloria 922
Carlin, Kathleen 747
Carroll, L.T. 952
Carson, Eleanor 71
Čelakovský, František Ladislav 966
Cervantes Saavedra, Miguel de 159, 881
Champion, Selwyn 56
Chapman, Jean P. 475
Chapman, Loren J. 153, 475
Chaucer, Geoffrey 781
Chesterfield, Lord Philip 708
Chlosta, Christoph 426, 427, 966

Chomsky, Noam 164, 536, 635, 938
Church, Joseph 899
Churchill, Winston S. 696, 702, 714
Cicogna, Caterina 772
Cocke, Joseph G. 167
Cohen, Bertram D. 329
Cohen, Ronald Jay 552
Colin, Roland 86
Colston, Herbert L. 360, 361
Coste, Ellen L. 901
Cram, David 805
Cromwell, Rue L. 628
Cutler, Anne 89, 1046
Cutting, Cooper 363

Darwin, Charles 26
Daudet, Alphonse 26
Derrida, Jacques 553, 619
Deskis, Susan E. 1127
Detje, Frank 249
Diaz, Juan Carlos 990
Dickens, Charles 708
Dickinson, Emily 695
Dobrovol'skij, Dmitrij 51
Dodd, Beverly A. 186
Dorfmueller, Mark A. 505
Dostoevsky, Feodor Mikhailovich 1142
Dougherty, Kathleen C. 468
Douglass, Frederick 708, 710–712
Droppová, Zdena 1007
Dundes, Alan 30, 268, 416, 418, 536, 716

Edmonds, Ed M. 145
Edwards, Darrel 46
Emerson, Ralph Waldo 684
Epelbaum, Catherine 87
Erasmus of Rotterdam 394, 713
Erskin, Barbara J. 759

Fabrizi, Michael 863
Fanany, Rebecca 307
Farkaš, Gabriel 1008
Farrell, Calista 922

Féline, André 87
Ferretti, Todd R. 540
Fisher, James H. 317
Folly, Dennis 868, 869
Foucault, Michel 619
Foules, Edward F. 747
Frank, George H. 406
Franklin, Benjamin 665, 684, 691, 708
Franklin, L.R. 168
Fredenthal, Burton J. 329
Freire, Paulo 301
Freud, Sigmund 82, 258, 265, 284, 473, 886, 907, 973
Freund, A.M. 804
Friedlander, D. 829
Frommhold, Kris 72
Frost, Robert 493, 526, 639, 725, 1163
Fujiki, Martin 110

Gardner, Howard 224
George, E.I. 831
Gibbs, Raymond W. 539, 541, 732, 743
Gildea, Patricia 374
Glick, Ira D. 94
Glucksberg, Sam 141, 142
Goethe, Johann Wolfgang von 433–435
Gorham, Donald R. 20, 94, 99, 153, 167, 208, 211, 288, 319, 366, 379, 380, 417, 432, 455, 459, 460, 474, 475, 482, 495, 530, 589, 609, 675, 797, 839, 840, 867, 885, 952, 964, 1006, 1017, 1045, 1120
Goya, Francisco de 718
Grass, Günter 265
Greenberg, Harvey R. 948
Greenblatt, Milton 663
Greuze, Jean-Baptiste 1097, 1168
Griffin, Peggy 94
Griffith, Clay 606
Grimm, Wilhelm 1111
Grisell, James L. 329
Grober-Glück, Gerda 680

Grossman, Linda S. 459
Grzybek, Peter 179, 180, 412, 413
Guardiola, Elena 49
Guicciardini, Francesco 749
Gurudas, S. 532
Gynther, Malcolm D. 996, 997

Hama, Haruyo 721
Hammond, N.V. 53
Haq, Faridah Serajul 758
Harkins, Stephen 590
Harris, Joseph 1127
Harrison, K. 797
Harrow, Martin 562
Hasan-Rokem, Galit 10, 11
Hatakenaka, Y. 741
Hattemer, K. 680
Haug, F. 494
Hayes, Jeffrey C. 908
Hayley, Coralie B. 186
Healy, Alice F. 347
Hegel, Georg Wilhelm Friedrich 1038
Henke, Käthe 428
Herbert, George 1
Hewlett, J.H.G. 830
Hippocrates 50, 898
Hirsch, E.D. 690
Hitler, Adolf 677, 697, 698, 702, 708
Hobbes, Thomas 477
Hoff, Hebbel E. 50
Hoffman, Robert R. 500, 505
Höller, Herwig 228
Holmes, Deborah 673, 717
Holt, Eilsabeth 253, 254
Honeck, Richard P. 192, 247, 417, 488, 489, 1060, 1061
Horkovič, Gabriel 1007
Howell, Robert J. 455
Humboldt, Wilhelm von 234
Ikeda, H. 741
Iekda, M. 741
Inoue, N. 741
Ito, K. 741

Jacob, Teresa C. 839, 840
Jaime Gómez, José de 618
Jesus 583, 656, 658, 1135
Jimenez, Beatrice C. 97
Johnson, Lyndon Baines 85
Johnson, Mark 575, 587
Johnson, Michael D. 360, 361
Jolles, André 416, 418, 420
Judas Iscariot 453
Jurado Merelo, Javier 648

Kafka, Franz 411
Kant, Immanuel 477, 1020, 1043
Kanyó, Zoltán 902
Kaplan, Joni 482
Katz, Albert N. 1081
Kazui, H. 741
Keenan, Tom 72
Kemper, Susan 299
Kempler, Daniel 1094
Kibler, Clare T. 499, 502
Kirsch, Dixon I. 757
Kleiber, Georges 672
Kleist, Heinrich von 1097, 1168
Klemperer, Victor 708
Krikmann, Arvo 484
Kuusi, Matti 1026

La Rochefoucauld, François 749
Lakemper, Udo 205
Lakoff, George 575, 652, 672
Lanin-Kettering, Ilene 460
Larson, Gary 1133
Larson-Shapiro, Nancy 800
Laskaris, Jane B. 647
Lau, Kimberly J. 1134
Laverty, S.G. 828
Leach, Edwin A. 612
Lima, Susan D. 207
Lincoln, Abraham 528, 703, 707–709
Lowe, Sandra A. 186
Luther, Martin 265, 683

Macaulay, Peter S. 93
Mackey, Teresa A. 110

MacLean, A. 53
Maimonides, Moses 50
Maingueneau, Dominique 407
Mal Lara, Juan de 158
Manaster, Guy J. 331
Manelis, Leon 509
Martin, Stephanie A. 759
Mattussek, P. 831
Maw, Ethel W. 646, 647
McCabe, Neil 63
McGlone, Matthew S. 373
McIntire, D.D. 168
McRae, Ken 864
Mellsop, Graham W. 458
Meltzer, Herbert 459
Merwin, William Stanley 588
Mieder, Wolfgang 528, 657, 673, 811, 923, 1053, 1054, 1073, 1127
Millard, Richard J. 483
Miller, Joan G. 460, 461
Mine, Hiroshi 721
Minkes, A.L. 13
Moates, Danny R. 979
Mokienko, Valerij 284
Moran, Louis J. 495
Morton, J. 53
Mozart, Wolfgang Amadeus 265
Muckenheim, Ron 72
Mueller, Dierk 72
Mukařovský, Jan 835
Murphy, Shannon J. 870
Myers, Jerome L. 998

Nayak, Nandini P. 362, 363

O'Brien, Jennifer E. 364
Olness, Gloria S. 1085
Oparina, Elena 1058
Ortony, Andrew 1039
Ostermann, Torsten 65, 181

Page, Mary 62
Palúchová, Luba 1008
Pamies Bertrán, Antonio 638
Partridge, Eric 1005
Paulhan, Jean 1047
Pazos, Juan 89

Peel, Bettina 250
Pepicello, William 405
Pérez, Alicia M. 89
Permiakov, Grigorii L'vovich 133, 134, 415, 416, 418, 420, 421, 424, 426, 427, 536, 616, 617, 680, 690, 1026, 1048, 1167
Perris, C. 107
Piaget, Jean 194
Piirainen, Elisabeth 241–243
Pope, Alexander 975
Powell, Colin 749
Prahlad, Sw. Anand 320, 321
Pritchett, Thomas 167
Prosen, Mel 460
Pynchon, Thomas 1142

Ragin, Ann B. 562
Resnick, Phillip J. 468
Reynolds, Ralph E. 798, 799
Richard, Philippe 623, 624
Richter, Gregory C. 392
Ridley, Stanley E. 212
Riechmann, Paul 500
Riedel, Albert F. 606
Riggs, Ann 604
Ríos, Juan 89
Robbins, Anthony 295, 296
Rodange, Michel 490
Rogers, Tim 687
Rosenbaum, Gerald 628
Ross, Undine 180
Rudzinski, Michelle 760
Ruger, G.J. 1066
Rukuni, Margaret 651

Sainte-Beuve, Charles Augusta 322
Salzman, Leonard F. 379, 380
Sandormirskaya, Irina 1058
Sanjuan, Pedro 995
Sartre, Jean Paul 193
Sawada, T. 741
Schallert, Diane L. 799
Schenk, André 300
Scheuch, E.K. 466, 680
Schloss, Patrick 517

Schreuder, Rob 300
Schwarz, Ilsa E. 762
Schweigert, Wendy A. 207
Seitel, Peter 1142
Shakespeare, William 1, 117, 716, 765, 781
Shiraishi, J. 741
Shobe, A.E. 168
Sialm, Ambros 130
Silberstein, Lisa 224
Silverstein, Marshall 459
Sills, Abigail 863
Simmons, Belvin A. 606
Simopoulos, Gregory 552
Simrock, Karl 180, 966
Škarbová, Otilia 1009
Slack, John 1039
Slung, Michele 1129
Smith, Maureen 517
Smith, Michael 863
Smith, Kathleen 996, 997
Sobieski, Janet 718
Solomon, Harry C. 663
Sowry, Brenda M. 501, 506
Spelman, Michael S. 458
Spencer, Herbert 26
Steen, Francis 472
Storms, Lowell H. 1045
Streiff, Michael B. 268
Stupavská, L'ubica 1010
Sugar, Judith 502
Sybertz, Donald 469
Szirtes, József 642

Tabossi, Patrizia 143
Tanabe, H. 741
Taylor, Archer 416, 418, 699, 811
Taylor, Catherine L. 761
Taylor, Henry 749
Temple, Jon G. 503, 504, 508

Thompson, J.L. 168
Tofighbakhsh, Jessica 653
Tonelson, Steve 1076
Tóthné Litovkina, Anna 413
Truman, Harry S. 702, 715
Turner, Mark 539, 541, 575, 588, 672
Turner, Terence J. 800

Uhden, Linda D. 762
Ulatowska, Hanna K. 168

Van Brussel, P. 916
Van den Haag, Ernest 887
van der Linden, Erik-Jan 300
Van Lancker, Diana 546
Voegtle, Katherine 501, 505, 506
Vonk, Wietske 1091

Waehler, Charles A. 432
Warshaw, Mimi 492
Washington, Nancy D. 812
Watson, Wilfred 660
Webster, Daniel 703
Welge, Jeffrey 507, 508
Westermarck, Edward 1116
Wenzel, Joseph W. 385
White, June Miller 317
Whiting, Bartlett Jere 690, 811
Williams, Kipling 590
Winner, Ellen 224
Wise, Linda K. 485
Wundt, Wilhelm 119

Yoshida, Teigo 316

Zahler, Kathy A. 1162
Zardon, Francesco 1049, 1050
Zumwalt, Rosemary Levy 600, 601
Zur Oeveste, Hans 609

SUBJECT INDEX

This index is based on the key-words in the titles of the bibliographical entries and also refers to all of the key-words in the annotations. The term "proverb" has not been used in the annotations and the index since it would be referring to almost every entry. All numbers refer to the entries and not to pages.

abstraction 46, 67, 68, 73, 94, 98–100, 103–107, 115, 137, 140, 148, 149, 153, 154, 168, 176, 177, 191, 208, 211, 269, 279, 288, 292, 303, 329, 340, 359, 366, 380, 386–390, 432, 447, 454, 455, 468, 474, 475, 482, 489, 494, 500, 502, 505, 506, 550, 552, 577, 594, 604, 606, 607, 613, 628, 663, 717, 734, 758, 762, 797, 806, 810, 822–824, 828–831, 839, 840, 884, 890, 891, 927, 948, 951, 964, 977, 996, 997, 1014, 1017, 1045, 1085, 1093, 1098, 1103, 1113, 1114, 1118, 1120
absurdity 576
abuse 19
academe 36
accuracy 653
achievement 60
acknowledgement 2
acoustics 70
acquiescence 58, 1016
acquisition 65, 108, 120, 123, 125, 143, 271, 440, 497, 499, 500, 514–516, 546, 579, 598, 599, 612, 783, 826, 844, 900, 954, 967–969, 1047, 1098
action 225–227, 249
activation 1049, 1050
adage 641, 989
addiction 61, 198, 919, 920
administration 13, 187, 218, 1004
adolescence 318, 329, 755–762
adolescent 1072
adult 762, 770, 899, 1021

adultery 306, 392, 1022
advertisement 126, 466, 564, 603, 657, 679, 682, 713, 716, 1133
advertising 328, 435, 691
advice 338, 339, 446, 472, 834, 835, 896
aesthetics 321, 869, 1043, 1148, 1152
affection 721
affirmation 845
Afghanistan 55
African 2, 7, 17, 18, 24, 25, 29, 30, 40, 54, 74, 86, 114, 144, 160, 161, 178, 189, 214–216, 245, 274, 277, 278, 297, 301, 302, 320, 321, 333, 340, 343, 409, 410, 449, 468, 469, 476, 511, 513, 519, 533–535, 553, 565, 578, 585, 592, 613, 647, 650, 651, 657, 662, 684, 708, 710–713, 716, 723, 726–729, 731, 738, 744, 769, 774–780, 782, 784, 786, 788–790, 795, 796, 807, 808, 812, 819–821, 833–837, 839, 840, 869, 880, 909, 917, 931, 941, 943, 953, 985–987, 992–994, 1011, 1024, 1066, 1083, 1084, 1105, 1107–1110, 1146–1152, 1154, 1156–1161
African American 54, 215, 216, 320, 321, 449, 468, 519, 647, 657, 662, 684, 708, 710–713, 812, 839, 840, 869, 909, 1154
age 76, 100–102, 106–108, 110, 138, 165, 194, 210, 224, 231,

250, 269, 412, 421, 466, 470, 523, 529, 551, 620, 624, 680, 704, 755–762, 849, 867, 877, 890, 899, 931, 957, 962, 968, 969, 1067, 1069
aggression 19, 60, 66, 937, 1122
aging 704, 770, 877, 957
Akamba 738
Akan 29, 114, 274, 343, 782, 1148–1152
Akkadian 15
alcohol 1
alcoholism 61, 198, 920
alienation 448
allegory 1096
allusion 275, 371, 982
Alzheimer's 92, 168, 586
amassment 395
ambiguity 80, 96, 143, 190, 405, 540, 573, 578, 608, 634, 646, 695, 765, 809, 827, 1119, 1133, 1151
ambivalence 617, 1033, 1111, 1158
American 8, 36, 38, 39, 54, 63, 85, 88, 111, 112, 116, 215, 216, 223, 259–262, 264, 267, 268, 275, 295, 296, 320, 321, 391, 449, 468, 493, 519, 526, 547, 591, 639, 647, 657, 660, 662, 665, 673, 684, 689–694, 700, 701, 703, 707–713, 715, 720, 725, 753, 773, 812, 838–840, 866, 868, 869, 904, 909, 913, 922, 924, 937, 945, 1068, 1070, 1071, 1074, 1075, 1126, 1127, 1129, 1133, 1154, 1163
amplification 730
amusement 54
anality 259, 265, 674
analogy 9, 113, 118, 119, 269, 314, 373, 395, 405, 410, 499, 506, 581, 608, 640, 695, 725, 759, 798, 805, 822, 849, 890, 914–916, 950, 976, 1125
analyticity 383
anatomy 446

animal 25, 48, 93, 117, 135, 221, 241, 243, 304, 333, 404, 410, 511, 524, 576, 648, 649, 664, 767, 785, 846, 850–852, 855, 859, 860, 865, 925, 945, 1063, 1111
Annang 297
anomaly 791, 792
anomia 1003
anonymity 71
anthroplogy 942
anthropocentrism 11
anthropology 30, 74, 95, 109, 114, 260, 261, 265, 304, 315, 325, 367, 391, 522, 532, 579, 592, 613, 659, 695, 699, 705, 706, 774, 782, 784, 789, 834, 835, 908, 917, 943, 960, 985–987, 995, 1011, 1023, 1117, 1123, 1124, 1127, 1150
anthropomorphism 162, 722, 1063
antiquity 92, 294, 394, 583, 682, 713, 894, 975, 1053, 1101, 1112, 1130
antithesis 1014
anti-feminism 6, 17, 40, 146, 156, 206, 245, 305, 310, 369, 547, 585, 629–632, 638, 679, 683, 790, 832, 841, 858, 879, 904, 945, 988, 1000, 1041, 1082, 1116, 1131, 1153, 1156, 1158, 1159, 1166
anti-proverb 217, 407, 470, 551, 603, 684, 735, 753, 857, 858, 889, 982, 1073–1075, 1129, 1133, 1143
anti-Semitism 244, 265, 677, 691, 697, 698, 708, 929
antonym 336, 567
antonymy 395, 396
anxiety 455, 644
aphasia 115, 168, 741, 1042, 1085, 1092
aphorism 50, 344, 595, 653, 898, 922, 973, 989, 1162
appearance 471, 752
appreciation 347

approbation 74
Arabic 6, 287, 304, 375, 464, 548, 549, 719, 865, 908, 924, 999, 1000, 1112, 1116, 1117, 1165
arbitrariness 636
archaism 580
archetype 660, 894
archive 65
argument 16, 385, 876, 930, 970
argumentation 28, 69, 554, 603, 626, 665, 728, 805, 838, 938, 1136, 1137
art 343
Asante 784
Ashanti 784
assessment 75
association 438, 1013
atlas 205
attitude 58–60, 64, 132, 166, 182, 223, 267, 274, 331, 336, 345, 436, 437, 476, 527, 590, 643, 646, 647, 649, 661, 680, 721, 734, 735, 748, 796, 808, 878, 881, 882, 892, 918, 919, 924, 928, 939, 971, 992, 995, 1000, 1024, 1044, 1055, 1065, 1086, 1131
Austrian 570
authenticity 433, 434
authority 39, 85, 88, 307, 320, 619, 730, 834, 835, 882, 981, 1021, 1083
autism 99, 153, 495, 997, 1113, 1114
Baluba 144
Bamana 565
Bambara 189
bear 243
behavior 3, 4, 29, 46, 48, 58, 61, 72, 74, 93, 106, 147, 169, 218, 223, 225–227, 230, 248, 249, 256, 286, 287, 290, 291, 295, 296, 302, 304, 323, 325, 346, 428, 437, 461, 472, 505, 511, 524, 531, 561, 576, 605, 646–648, 653, 664, 666, 682, 708, 717, 721, 722, 734, 742, 747, 748, 763, 770, 771, 784–786, 795, 796, 803, 811, 812, 819–821, 834, 836, 846, 892, 894, 909, 918, 919, 925, 928, 941, 949, 950, 952, 981, 994, 1014, 1016, 1023, 1031, 1063, 1117, 1125, 1126, 1129, 1131, 1163
belief 114, 264, 266, 291, 295, 296, 316, 323, 327, 349, 393, 408, 437, 600, 651, 654, 661, 662, 752, 836, 907, 929, 999, 1019, 1101, 1106
Bemba 114
benediction 266
Beta-Israel 942
Bible 121, 150, 188, 330, 394, 453, 469, 477, 521, 528, 567, 583, 656–658, 695, 703, 707, 709, 716, 729, 737, 738, 745, 888, 894, 937, 981, 982, 1020, 1053, 1135
bibliography 20, 105, 106, 131, 324, 345, 359, 389, 396, 416–418, 433, 467, 487, 505, 537, 538, 624, 637, 675, 676, 684, 695, 705, 706, 718, 755, 765, 798, 921, 923, 927, 1001, 1053, 1054, 1127, 1135
bilingualism 794
biography 433, 434
blason populaire 77, 152, 263, 280, 282, 298, 404, 422, 496, 787, 872, 924, 958, 972, 1028, 1029, 1051, 1053, 1064, 1087, 1128
blasphemy 19
blessing 644
blocking 1164
body 624
brain 20, 23, 67, 68, 73, 87, 92, 106, 115, 131, 137, 153, 154, 168, 184, 186, 192, 208, 288, 292, 313, 319, 340, 364, 378–380, 386–390, 406, 432, 447, 454, 458–461, 468, 482, 494, 498, 546, 562, 586, 594, 604, 606, 607, 627, 628, 642, 663,

732, 741, 797, 828–831, 870, 884, 919, 927, 948, 951, 952, 964, 977, 996, 997, 1017, 1042, 1045, 1085, 1092–1094, 1113, 1114, 1118, 1120, 1155
Brazilian 27
Builsa 729
Bulgarian 621

canonization 251
cardiology 401
caregiver 302
caregiving 62
Caribbean 38
cartoon 435
caste 724, 903, 924, 1023, 1086, 1087
castration 392
cat 93, 649, 785
Catalan 195, 1019
catch phrase 1005
categorical formulation 41–45
categorical imperative 1020
Central American 38
centrality 247
Chad 86
Chamula 391
change 8, 57, 102, 946
character 134, 152, 263, 265, 280, 282, 285, 286, 298, 325, 345, 365, 404, 419, 422, 436, 437, 471, 496, 524, 584, 695, 716, 717, 750, 752, 771, 773, 787, 801, 872, 881–883, 896, 905, 912, 924, 972, 1028, 1029, 1051–1053, 1064, 1095, 1121, 1127, 1128, 1144, 1169
charade 1076
chauvinism 172, 264, 679
chemistry 92
childrearing 813, 861, 880
children 5, 76, 86, 108, 110, 120, 121, 123, 125, 130, 138, 139, 150, 165, 175, 194, 197, 210, 219, 224, 231, 250, 269, 276, 294, 308, 318, 324, 325, 329, 354, 389, 440, 449, 501,

505, 512, 520, 599, 612, 620, 627, 637, 651, 662, 670, 671, 673, 708, 717, 755, 756, 758–761, 775, 784, 798, 800, 812, 813, 822–824, 837, 849, 861, 867, 869, 871, 880, 886, 890, 891, 899, 919, 962, 968, 969, 1021, 1072, 1139, 1140
Chinese 31, 32, 162, 166, 171, 174, 429–431, 566, 593, 636, 700, 716, 818, 838, 1055, 1106, 1145, 1153, 1166
Chinese American 700
Christian 548, 549
civil rights 710–712
Civil War 708, 709
class 185, 520, 777, 781, 883, 889, 980, 1104
classification 113, 127, 130, 213, 236, 280, 283, 423, 426, 480, 564, 567, 597, 616, 744, 802, 816, 843, 926, 936, 955, 969, 989, 1001, 1093, 1096, 1105, 1110
cliché 280, 396, 484, 522, 660, 842, 876, 1035
cloth 718
codification 70, 301, 440
cognition 5, 51, 76, 80, 87, 96, 100, 119, 120, 125, 131, 136, 138, 140, 143, 168, 176, 177, 184, 186, 192, 209, 211, 224, 231, 233, 236, 237, 240, 242, 247, 262, 279, 292, 311–313, 324, 329, 347, 350–364, 366, 368, 372–374, 378–380, 386–388, 390, 406, 417, 438, 439, 443, 456, 462, 468, 479, 498, 504, 507, 538, 539, 541, 559, 562, 575, 586, 603, 627, 637, 722, 734, 741, 755, 756, 794, 800, 806, 816, 822, 838, 849, 867, 870, 871, 890, 891, 899, 910, 918, 919, 927, 933, 964, 991, 1018, 1034, 1039, 1046, 1079–1081, 1085, 1092, 1094, 1140, 1148, 1150, 1155

Subject Index

Cold War 685, 701
collection 32, 56, 72, 92, 161, 180, 220, 251, 335, 375, 421–423, 433, 441, 521, 548, 549, 576, 616, 677, 692, 709, 711, 714, 715, 735, 744, 773, 781, 785, 816, 825, 866, 881, 903, 904, 911, 923, 934, 940, 966, 1014, 1021, 1053, 1054, 1073, 1127, 1129
collectivity 556, 557, 590, 592, 812, 876, 1002, 1030, 1058
collocation 791, 961, 1062
colloquialism 920
color 241, 252, 393, 404, 850–852
comics 435
committee 36
common sense 91, 749, 843, 880, 1037, 1126, 1133
commonality 621
communication 4, 29, 36, 39, 44, 45, 54, 71, 78, 114, 133, 169, 189, 195, 196, 216, 228, 256, 317, 324, 349, 409, 428–431, 456, 460, 487, 491, 495, 498, 510, 513, 525, 529, 553, 554, 561, 582, 610, 619, 645, 702, 728, 733, 739, 740, 747, 754, 776, 782, 788, 793, 808, 826, 827, 835, 862, 883, 919, 921, 947, 967, 970, 971, 1011, 1034, 1048, 1078, 1100, 1121, 1137, 1143, 1146, 1152, 1157
community 61, 325, 532, 535, 780, 786, 793
comparison 783
compensation 803, 804
competence 10, 70, 97, 123, 125, 196, 200, 202, 229, 237, 239, 272, 335, 356, 402, 450, 480, 514, 515, 546, 598, 599, 717, 816, 822, 844, 954, 990, 1030, 1047, 1085, 1088, 1093, 1140, 1164
complaint 253
composition 75

comprehension 5, 76, 80, 81, 84, 96, 98–100, 108, 110, 120, 121, 123, 130, 136, 138, 141–143, 157, 160, 161, 165, 184, 190–192, 194, 197, 210, 224, 226, 231, 239, 250, 257, 269, 276, 279, 299, 308, 314, 318, 347, 350–364, 368, 371–374, 378–380, 386–388, 390, 395, 396, 406, 417, 438, 439, 443, 445, 450, 451, 457, 482, 489, 492, 498, 499, 501–506, 508, 512, 514–517, 533, 540, 544–546, 550, 575, 579, 587, 598, 599, 607, 612, 627, 636, 637, 642, 652, 717, 720, 732, 741, 755–762, 794, 798–800, 803, 804, 816, 822–824, 847, 849, 863, 867, 870, 871, 875, 890, 891, 899–901, 919, 927, 933, 962, 978, 979, 991, 998, 1006, 1018, 1036, 1039, 1042, 1046, 1047, 1049, 1050, 1059–1061, 1080, 1081, 1085, 1091–1094, 1103, 1105, 1126, 1140, 1155
computer 53, 89, 181, 228, 582, 591, 692, 1134
concentration camp 244
conceptualization 587
concreteness 72, 105, 106, 137, 208, 269, 303, 432, 454, 468, 475, 577, 757, 758, 760–762, 977, 996, 997, 1114
conflict 464, 543, 578
conformity 54
Congo 144
connotation 814, 815, 1161
conservativeness 980
consolation 748
consumer 328
content 15, 21, 32, 49, 56, 57, 79, 91, 134, 147, 158, 161, 185, 213, 217, 218, 259–261, 287, 289, 305, 341, 342, 365, 371, 426, 486, 524, 604, 606, 614, 618, 621–624, 645, 650, 667, 670, 671, 678, 689, 704,

724, 735, 750, 768, 770, 771, 773, 802, 818, 825, 857, 877, 881, 882, 889, 895, 896, 903–905, 923, 931, 932, 963, 974, 992, 994, 995, 999, 1002, 1005, 1024, 1053, 1055, 1062, 1073, 1075, 1083, 1095, 1108, 1127, 1144

context 2, 3, 10, 30, 52, 55, 84, 85, 88, 108, 109, 123, 125–127, 130, 133, 157, 184, 190, 195, 199, 200, 204, 207, 210, 235, 247, 268, 301, 320, 321, 323, 334–336, 338, 347, 350, 354, 356, 361, 367, 370, 374, 377, 391, 396, 400, 402, 403, 405, 409, 411, 416, 418, 420, 424, 430, 440, 450, 451, 463–465, 469, 473, 480, 491, 500, 501, 503–505, 508, 525, 532, 540, 542, 544, 545, 555, 558, 563, 571, 573, 582, 592, 598–600, 602, 603, 608, 610, 611, 625, 642, 645, 650, 675, 682, 684, 686, 687, 692, 695, 699, 717, 723, 724, 726–728, 738–740, 743, 744, 759, 765, 774, 781, 786, 798, 799, 805–807, 819, 821, 822, 834, 835, 837, 845, 863, 869, 897, 908, 919–921, 930, 933–936, 940, 943, 948, 956, 959, 962, 967, 970, 971, 975, 982, 985–987, 998, 1015, 1030, 1033, 1034, 1037, 1059, 1075, 1083, 1085, 1098, 1105, 1117, 1124, 1127, 1130, 1134, 1135, 1137, 1138, 1143, 1144, 1147–1152

contradiction 9, 87, 132, 203, 204, 290, 291, 334, 336, 338, 367, 542, 543, 571, 583, 605, 646, 647, 695, 699, 766, 779, 780, 805, 809, 838, 881, 921, 934, 1004, 1014, 1040, 1056, 1108, 1110, 1125, 1149, 1158

control 8, 47, 74
convention 385, 433, 1163
conventionalization 311
convergence 569
conversation 3, 253, 254, 350, 353, 403, 600
correlation 283
creation 507
creativity 503, 523, 793, 1151
Creole 1052
criminality 366, 614, 1006
criminology 471
Croatian 720, 1012, 1013
crying 630
cuckold 1022
cuckoldry 117, 306, 392
cult 63
cultural literacy 690, 691, 695
culture 7–9, 14, 21, 29, 48, 54, 57, 83, 92, 108, 111–113, 124, 128, 152, 158, 166, 169–172, 178, 185, 189, 193, 198, 206, 211, 214–216, 220, 223, 238, 240–243, 245, 248, 256, 259–262, 264, 265, 274, 275, 285, 287, 290, 293, 297, 301, 305, 306, 310, 311, 315, 316, 326, 332, 333, 335, 336, 342, 346, 349, 361, 365, 367, 375–377, 392, 413, 419–421, 425, 429–431, 433, 435, 449, 453, 465, 469, 470, 473, 476, 486, 504, 507, 510, 511, 513, 523–525, 527, 531, 534, 535, 543, 547–549, 551–554, 559, 572, 579, 584, 587, 588, 593, 600, 601, 603, 614, 617, 644, 661, 666, 680, 682, 684, 689–691, 699, 704, 708, 719, 722, 724, 729, 730, 738, 747, 754, 763, 769, 771, 773, 777, 778, 781, 785, 786, 796, 800, 802–804, 817, 826, 827, 833, 838, 842, 843, 848, 850, 852–856, 858–1029, 861, 865, 869, 874, 877, 879, 881, 882, 885, 894, 903–906, 908, 911, 912, 917, 918, 922, 925, 931, 932, 937, 941, 943, 946, 947, 953, 957, 960,

Subject Index

974, 980, 982–984, 987, 992–995, 999, 1000, 1002, 1012, 1019, 1022, 1023, 1028, 1029, 1033, 1038, 1041, 1044, 1052, 1054, 1055, 1057, 1058, 1071, 1075, 1083–1087, 1095, 1096, 1102, 1104, 1106, 1111, 1112, 1116, 1117, 1124, 1126, 1128, 1131, 1133, 1142, 1144, 1145, 1149, 1150, 1153, 1157, 1162, 1166, 1169
currency 35, 408, 415, 478, 507, 564, 686, 735, 915, 1072, 1077, 1129
curriculum 308
curse 452, 644, 1025
cursing 452
custom 266, 316, 392, 408, 929, 999, 1053
Czech 162, 965, 966

Dangme 114, 578
Danish 496
database 582, 591, 692, 1134
deafness 197
death 22, 856, 866, 907
deautomatization 935, 1163
debate 36
defeatism 527
definition 27, 28, 35, 52, 56, 114, 134, 151, 192, 199, 204, 227, 236, 275, 279, 283, 291, 309, 315, 323, 337, 395, 396, 419, 422, 423, 425, 472, 478, 489, 498, 510, 536, 556, 564, 587, 593, 597, 602, 625, 634, 640, 645, 669, 672, 681, 686, 691, 699, 706, 717, 734, 736, 744, 765, 802, 811, 816, 914, 916, 923, 926, 930, 955, 961, 985, 989, 1001, 1005, 1011, 1048, 1053, 1054, 1078, 1090, 1121, 1124, 1127, 1133
defloration 1097
dementia 115
denomination 556–558, 845
denotation 396, 573
dentistry 414
depression 94, 98-101, 106, 155, 562
deproverbialization 956
destiny 33, 34
development 76, 86, 123, 150, 165, 178, 194, 210, 215, 216, 219, 231, 250, 269
devil 787
diachronic 124, 127, 128, 130, 171, 252, 267, 281, 442, 510, 569, 688, 692, 781, 816, 846, 984, 1078
diagnostics 268
dialect 120, 129, 130, 205, 305, 441, 445, 569, 570, 855, 934, 961, 962, 968, 969
dialectics 838, 1011
dialogue 24, 464, 465
dictionary 127, 128, 163, 233, 236, 251, 255, 281, 480, 481, 567, 569, 692, 815, 844, 1119
didacticism 24, 39, 42, 43, 88, 175, 219, 225, 226, 320, 332, 425, 478, 510, 519, 521, 560, 578, 656, 658, 664, 665, 728, 765, 812, 813, 869, 880, 1021, 1089, 1127
diet 446, 595
differentiation 992
disability 627
disambiguation 608
discourse 16, 56, 66, 69, 123, 140, 169, 173, 182, 196, 199, 235, 255, 294, 320, 351, 353, 370, 376, 377, 403, 429–431, 463–465, 539, 565, 600, 626, 661, 669, 672, 696, 701, 702, 709, 714, 715, 739, 740, 772, 782, 862, 869, 910, 935, 936, 938, 944, 947, 956, 1030, 1034, 1049, 1050, 1058, 1062, 1133, 1148–1151
disease 91, 135, 144, 154, 158, 159, 168, 289, 319, 339, 344, 400, 414, 586, 594, 622–624,

628, 688, 919, 928, 932, 983, 984, 1019, 1141
disorder 23, 46, 67, 68, 73, 94, 107, 115, 131, 137, 155, 176, 186, 447, 454, 458–461, 494, 830, 831, 951, 964, 1017, 1113, 1114, 1118, 1120
dissemination 326, 394, 423, 569, 682, 700
distribution 408, 689, 923, 1112
divergence 569
divination 260
dog 785
dominoes 89
dream 82, 258, 284, 473, 906
drug 61, 63, 167, 919, 920
duel 27, 175, 216, 658
Dutch 524
dying 22, 856, 866
dysphemism 12

ear 596
economics 174, 731, 818, 1087
education 54, 71, 75, 86, 93, 114, 138, 193, 195, 219, 229, 276, 297, 301, 318, 412, 478, 615, 670, 671, 673, 708, 800, 890, 953, 962, 967, 993, 1021, 1066, 1067, 1069, 1075, 1076, 1110, 1139, 1140, 1144
egalitarianism 777
ego 1016
elder 7, 175, 376, 377, 620, 704, 770
emancipation 217
emigrant 65
emotion 64, 140, 630, 644, 667, 668, 721, 767, 814, 949, 950, 974, 1016, 1032, 1035, 1100, 1117, 1122
empiricism 8, 35, 41–43, 65, 72, 108, 129, 179–181, 184, 200, 201, 205, 227, 229, 235, 241, 270–272, 281, 314, 334, 352, 408, 412, 413, 415, 421, 425, 427, 439–441, 444, 445, 466, 470, 485, 489, 551, 564, 580, 585, 591, 605, 680, 699, 713, 717, 720, 733, 740, 794, 798, 803, 804, 864, 921, 965, 966, 968, 969, 978, 990, 1041, 1049, 1067–1070, 1072, 1085, 1107, 1109
enculturation 723
endorsement 436
English 22, 52, 72, 145, 209, 267, 289, 309, 414, 428, 485, 514, 516, 555, 563, 590, 594, 612, 633, 649, 655, 660, 688, 690, 691, 696, 708, 713, 714, 733, 753, 765, 776, 781, 846, 848, 868, 904, 905, 940, 983, 984, 1012, 1013, 1074, 1082, 1128, 1129, 1141, 1159, 1160
enthymeme 405, 1136
entrepreneurship 31
environment 685
epic 664
epigram 344
epistemology 114, 274, 291, 396, 513, 1026, 1107, 1109, 1110
equivalent 238, 242, 281, 441, 450, 451, 514, 524, 567, 569, 570, 667, 720, 742, 816, 844, 859, 860, 865, 877, 879, 959, 983, 984, 989, 1012, 1013, 1063, 1074, 1075, 1082, 1095, 1138, 1153
eroticism 259, 293, 343, 572
error 222
escapism 322
Estonian 484
ethics 114, 278, 315, 429, 477, 560, 613, 658, 665, 670, 671, 685, 717, 738, 767, 768, 773–775, 780, 788, 789, 795, 887, 888, 909, 1053, 1108–1110, 1130, 1139, 1144, 1157
Ethiopian 942
ethnicity 12, 19, 38, 77, 152, 215, 263, 280, 282, 298, 318, 320, 321, 391, 419, 422, 464, 465, 468, 548, 549, 647, 655,

684, 694, 695, 700, 702, 708, 710–713, 750, 776, 787, 796, 801, 817, 839, 840, 869, 872, 889, 903, 924, 929, 958, 972, 995, 1028, 1029, 1051, 1053, 1064, 1154, 1165
ethnocentrism 263
ethnography 30, 55, 215, 256, 367, 377, 492, 532, 565, 835, 908, 1028, 1029, 1117, 1146, 1150
ethnolinguistics 189, 199, 391, 1031, 1096
ethnology 113, 615, 623
ethnonym 958
ethnophaulism 924, 1154
ethnopsychology 1126
etymology 124, 128, 130, 306, 392, 1111, 1154
euphemism 12, 19, 22, 172, 294, 481, 856, 866, 1025
European 298, 333, 1028, 1029
evaluation 187, 949, 950
evangelization 114
Ewe 274, 277
expectancy 145
experience 9, 64, 95, 111, 112, 132, 140, 188, 214, 304, 326, 332, 410, 472, 476, 531, 543, 553, 558, 561, 571, 587, 605, 611, 617, 621, 659, 728, 745, 748, 793, 811, 812, 820, 826, 827, 862, 891, 894, 912, 939, 942, 953, 963, 981, 999, 1019, 1076, 1077, 1089, 1126, 1131
explanation 121
extension 179
eye 870

fable 151, 447, 454, 492, 664, 695, 842, 873, 1038
face 1145
fairy tale 873
fallacy 49, 204, 220, 277, 385, 650
falsehood 307, 563

familiarity 36, 41, 44, 45, 65, 72, 75, 97, 108, 129, 136, 142, 157, 168, 179, 180, 190, 200, 201, 205, 207, 210–212, 229, 271, 273, 279, 405, 408, 412, 413, 415, 421, 425, 427, 436, 437, 441, 443–445, 466, 468, 483, 489, 546, 564, 580, 599, 643, 680, 690, 717, 757, 758, 760–762, 840, 844, 864, 962, 965, 966, 978, 979, 1067–1072, 1080, 1092–1094, 1162
family 25, 62, 88, 147, 175, 219, 320, 324, 529, 651, 662, 738, 812, 813, 878, 913, 988, 1116, 1117
family proverb 88
fatalism 31, 584, 716, 1106
femininity 790
feminism 6, 17, 40, 114, 146, 156, 206, 245, 305, 310, 369, 547, 585, 629–632, 638, 679, 683, 790, 832, 841, 858, 879, 904, 945, 988, 1000, 1041, 1082, 1116, 1131, 1153, 1156, 1158, 1159, 1166
field research 10, 36, 54, 95, 109, 161, 189, 320, 367, 377, 391, 408, 413, 465, 511, 532, 549, 561, 600, 654, 655, 680, 724, 753, 782, 834, 835, 942, 962, 971, 1121, 1147, 1150
figurativeness 78, 80–81, 139, 140, 142, 143, 157, 169, 176, 191, 192, 194, 207, 210, 224, 242, 250, 276, 299, 300, 308, 317, 347, 350–355, 358–360, 362–364, 368, 372, 374, 378, 424, 438, 448, 457, 467, 487, 498, 502, 504–506, 508, 538–541, 544, 545, 550, 575, 577, 598, 612, 633, 640, 652, 732, 736, 743, 746, 755–758, 762, 765, 766, 769, 791, 792, 794, 799, 800, 849, 863, 864, 890, 901, 927, 978, 979, 986, 991, 1018, 1059–1061, 1070, 1077,

1079–1081, 1083, 1091–1094, 1098, 1103, 1105, 1124, 1155
figure 1079
film 435
Finnish 568–570, 580, 583–585, 629–632, 716, 785, 957, 958
fixididty 300
fixidity 28, 127, 348, 399, 456, 518, 746, 955, 956, 1001, 1151
flexibility 362, 371
flower 1032
folk belief 264
folk idea 261
folk medicine 158
folk speech 116, 267
folk value 261
folklore 30, 55, 57, 63, 77, 82, 83, 92, 95, 114, 116, 122, 130, 151, 152, 179, 204, 230, 251, 252, 256, 259–261, 263–268, 315, 316, 320, 321, 323, 325, 392, 393, 408, 464, 473, 484, 510, 512, 522, 525, 549, 576, 583, 600, 601, 608, 641, 649, 654, 655, 661, 677, 681–685, 687, 689, 691, 694, 695, 698, 699, 705–708, 710–713, 719, 724, 744, 747, 752, 764, 774, 776, 788, 796, 817, 833–835, 841, 842, 848, 861, 872–874, 880, 906, 907, 909, 913, 919, 923, 929, 932, 958, 971, 972, 983–987, 1003, 1019, 1022, 1025, 1027, 1032, 1037, 1038, 1041, 1044, 1053, 1054, 1086, 1087, 1099, 1105, 1111, 1115, 1117, 1123, 1127, 1131, 1147, 1150, 1165
Fon 245
food 446
foregrounding 1148
foreign language 65, 75, 130, 138, 169, 177, 183, 196, 271, 273, 415, 428, 429, 444, 450, 451, 514–516, 546, 625, 673, 720, 772, 826, 844, 881, 954, 1036, 1071, 1075, 1088, 1138

foreigner 787
foresight 1089
form 28, 41–45, 56, 130, 163, 259, 275, 283, 297, 330, 337, 339, 416, 418, 420, 422, 423, 478, 537, 602, 625, 653, 666, 669, 765, 783, 875, 893, 897, 916, 923, 936, 955, 963, 1053, 1055, 1075, 1078, 1084, 1090, 1099, 1108, 1121, 1124, 1127
formula 2, 33, 34, 109, 428, 429, 431, 556, 581, 625, 645, 740, 949, 950, 954–956, 1034, 1054, 1115, 1122
French 26, 28, 48, 78, 175, 183, 193, 220, 221, 333, 428, 452, 623, 624, 648, 877, 896, 905, 955, 989, 1002, 1021, 1022, 1063, 1065, 1082, 1095
frequency 129, 164, 207, 228, 229, 246, 273, 279, 415, 0427, 436, 466, 516, 551, 564, 568, 576, 580, 591, 599, 609, 620, 643, 680, 681, 690, 717, 785, 844, 864, 990, 1071, 1093, 1100, 1134, 1147, 1169
frustration 641
function 25, 36, 42, 43, 52, 54–56, 63, 69, 71, 85, 88, 95, 109, 114, 116, 120, 125, 132, 133, 140, 141, 151, 163, 171, 189, 193, 199, 216, 220, 235, 237, 253–255, 268, 284, 297, 315, 320, 321, 328, 335, 337, 371, 377, 396, 397, 403, 416, 418–420, 463, 464, 469, 470, 510, 521, 525, 528, 538, 539, 554, 566, 568, 574, 592, 602, 608, 645, 669, 683, 687, 699, 723, 726, 727, 730, 733, 744, 754, 763–765, 774, 781, 789, 819, 826, 827, 834, 835, 875, 876, 914–916, 936, 939, 959, 980, 982, 985, 986, 1030, 1033, 1034, 1048, 1078, 1096,

1099, 1100, 1105, 1119, 1121, 1125, 1127, 1134, 1135, 1137, 1138, 1142–1144
future 260

Ga 114, 578
game 89, 517
Gauchos 27
gender 17, 37, 106, 117, 156, 172, 200, 206, 217, 248, 264, 310, 466, 629–632, 638, 662, 679, 680, 770, 771, 784, 790, 832, 841, 850, 855, 858, 878, 879, 895, 904, 908, 943, 945, 988, 1000, 1022, 1041, 1044, 1051, 1067, 1069, 1082, 1117, 1131, 1156, 1158, 1166
generalization 58, 98, 99, 290, 291, 796, 981, 1035, 1110
generation 24, 62
generativity 247
genre 3, 6, 52, 261, 422, 423, 465, 484, 510, 645, 705, 706, 802, 816, 842, 872, 914–916, 923, 955, 985, 989, 990, 1038, 1053, 1075, 1078, 1127
geography 180, 205, 408
Georgian 465
German 6, 65, 118–121, 123, 125, 129, 130, 171, 180, 200, 205, 233–236, 244, 265, 271, 280, 293, 312, 327, 332, 335, 369, 395, 396, 408, 411, 421, 426, 429–431, 434, 435, 438, 441, 444, 450–452, 466, 470, 478, 496, 524, 527, 551, 564, 568–570, 602, 603, 629–632, 667, 668, 673, 677, 678, 680, 691, 692, 697, 698, 701, 703, 704, 707, 708, 735, 742, 752, 753, 801, 825, 855, 856, 859, 860, 865, 879, 923, 934, 957, 959, 962, 966, 968, 969, 983, 984, 1022, 1031, 1032, 1034, 1043, 1051, 1063, 1088, 1095, 1139, 1144, 1153, 1169
gerontology 62, 704, 770, 877, 957

gesture 162
Gikuyu 114, 1107–1110
globality 582
gnome 973
God 188
gold weight 343
Golden Rule 477, **888**, 1020
goodness 72
graffiti 217, 259, 470, 678, 685, 695, 718, 735, 753, 857, 889, 1073, 1132
grammar 96, 195, 403, 426, 492, 536–539, 751, 754, 843, 910, 938, 970, 1071, 1079, 1119, 1164
grandparents 662
Greek 206, 621, 622, 898
guitar 37
Gypsies 929
Haitian 333
hand 162
haptics 111, 112, 140, 262
Hausa 943
Haya 986, 987
headache 49
health 49, 62, 91, 135, 158, 159, 289, 302, 339, 344, 400, 401, 414, 446, 485, 595, 618, 622, 624, 688, 770, 877, 932, 983, 984, 1019, 1040, 1076, 1141
hearing-impaired 517
heart 257, 401
Hebrew 595, 906, 1112
hermeneutics 189, 610, 611, 790
heterodoxy 32
heuristics 89
Hindu 1086
history 1, 7, 15, 114, 121, 122, 124, 128, 130, 158, 193, 265, 294, 327, 333, 339, 344, 375, 423, 433, 528, 682, 694–696, 699, 702, 703, 707, 710–714, 777, 778, 781, 814, 874, **889**, 984, 1020, 1021, 1028, 1029, 1043, 1053, 1054, 1078, 1095, 1104, 1112, 1123, 1127, 1130, 1135, 1162
Holocaust 698

home 11
homonymy 668
homosexuality 267
honor 1117
horse 243
humor 36, 293, 678, 716, 753, 774, 895, 906, 974, 1005
Hungarian 345, 413, 1067, 1069, 1071, 1072, 1074, 1075
hyperbole 767

Ibibio 513
Ibo 778, 985
Icelandic 450, 451
iconography 244, 343, 673, 682–685, 688–693, 695, 699, 701–706, 713, 717, 718, 832, 1022, 1028, 1029, 1075, 1097, 1132, 1133, 1150, 1168, 1169
identification 1050
identity 10, 55, 464, 576, 872, 1067, 1128
ideology 16, 26, 29, 519, 619
idiom 5, 22, 80, 90, 96, 97, 110, 126, 138, 139, 141–143, 162, 163, 183, 190, 197, 207, 209, 222, 228, 233–240, 253, 254, 267, 271, 276, 299, 300, 309, 348, 350–355, 362–364, 368, 370–373, 394–398, 428, 431, 440, 442, 448, 450, 456, 481, 509, 514–516, 518, 546, 559, 567–570, 598, 599, 612, 625, 633–636, 652, 722, 732, 733, 743, 746, 751, 756, 760, 761, 796, 799, 845, 847, 863, 864, 871, 875, 910, 926, 938, 946, 954, 955, 959, 961, 968, 978, 979, 999, 1039, 1046, 1049, 1050, 1074, 1088, 1091, 1092, 1094, 1100, 1102, 1119, 1164
idiomaticity 70, 127, 143, 164, 183, 199, 209, 246, 300, 309, 355–357, 395, 396, 442, 634–636, 766, 791, 792, 814, 816, 944, 959, 960, 1001, 1036
idiomatization 128, 348, 871

idioms test 197
Idoma 17, 18
Igbo 278, 726–728, 774, 775, 777, 779, 780, 786, 795, 796, 834–837, 994, 1083, 1084
ill-formedness 90
image 57, 160, 161, 718, 767, 784, 813, 841, 868, 933, 960
imagery 71, 72, 142, 303, 307, 364, 424, 438, 467, 483, 487, 489, 499, 500, 505, 581, 728, 900, 901, 963, 1057, 1080, 1103
immigrant 77, 88
implication 411
improvisation 27
inadequacy 967
incantation 414
incongruence 370
inculturation 114
indefiniteness 573, 574
Indian 256, 532, 560, 615, 661, 724, 737, 903, 911, 924, 1023, 1086, 1087
indirection 42, 43, 55, 140, 398, 411, 456, 498, 539, 601, 611, 727, 739, 740, 747, 782, 808, 909, 1037, 1122, 1150
Indonesian 307
industry 654, 655
inference 385
informant 10, 24, 53, 60, 65, 95, 97, 115, 136, 157, 179, 180, 184, 200, 205, 270, 377, 412, 413, 421, 425, 427, 439–441, 444, 445, 466, 514, 516, 551, 782, 794, 803, 804, 833, 864, 868, 908, 942, 965, 978, 990, 998, 1049, 1067–1069, 1072, 1147
innovation 116, 813, 1129, 1133
insertion 348
inspiration 39
instantiation 499, 505, 506, 1126
instinct 93
instrument 37
insult 19, 833

intellectualism 322, 1104
intelligence 100–102, 105, 106, 118, 119, 313, 389, 417, 475, 498, 505, 530, 637, 675, 806, 885, 891, 919, 996, 1003, 1006
intelligentsia 36
interdependence 535
intermingling 460
internality 331
internet 181, 228
interpretation 5, 23, 50, 54, 68, 75, 98–104, 106, 107, 115, 131, 136, 143, 145, 153, 154, 167, 168, 183, 186, 194, 211, 212, 247, 257, 269, 284, 292, 299, 313, 319, 324, 329, 340, 351, 368, 384, 409, 458, 460, 473, 475, 482, 488, 494, 500, 540, 544, 545, 552, 562, 573, 577, 590, 594, 604, 607, 628, 637, 642, 743, 747, 769, 799, 822–824, 828–831, 840, 875, 899, 900, 948, 977, 996, 997, 1006, 1081, 1098, 1103
intertextuality 151, 1037, 1133
intervention 61
interview 10, 54, 65, 320, 782, 1003
introductory formula 2, 33, 34, 109, 429, 556, 645, 740
Iranian 895, 896
Irish 716, 912, 1131, 1132
Iron Curtain 701
Islam 55, 375
isolation 448
Israel 464, 465, 942
Italian 79, 113, 305, 748, 770–772, 1012, 1013

Japanese 21, 316, 721, 742, 802, 850, 1041
jargon 12
Jewish 10, 11, 77, 248, 463–465, 525, 548, 549, 572, 595, 600, 601, 677, 697, 698, 886, 906, 907, 929, 1144
joke 370, 886

Jordanian 6
Judeo-Spanish 600, 601
judgment 556, 557, 562
Jula 189
justice 887
justification 748
juxtaposition 745

Kaguru 114, 723
Kenyan 40
Kenyang 650
Kiswahili 1105
knowledge 108, 178, 274, 291, 371, 373, 400, 402, 405, 412, 413, 431, 513, 534, 743, 744, 803, 804, 806, 820, 993, 1030, 1067, 1069, 1107, 1109, 1162
Korean 182, 185
Kpelle 579
Krobo 511
Kuanyama Ambo 613

labor 341
language 12, 16, 48, 65, 66, 75, 77, 84, 108, 110, 120, 121, 124, 130, 138, 169, 177, 182, 183, 195, 196, 200, 224, 234, 241–243, 246, 258, 265, 267, 271, 273, 275, 308, 316, 317, 326, 328, 336, 349, 354, 358, 372, 375, 384, 402, 404, 415, 428, 429, 444, 450, 451, 470, 481, 487, 490, 498, 514–516, 523, 538–541, 546, 553, 593, 619, 625, 634, 635, 661, 673, 698, 708, 720, 722, 749, 755–757, 759, 765, 766, 768, 772, 776, 826, 827, 833, 844, 848, 853, 854, 858, 862, 881, 889, 894, 902, 910, 911, 916, 918, 923, 934, 935, 952, 954, 962, 967, 973, 1015, 1025, 1029, 1035, 1036, 1047, 1049, 1053, 1054, 1057, 1058, 1071, 1075, 1077, 1079, 1088, 1096, 1127, 1128, 1138, 1155

last word 433–435
Latin 156, 583, 945
Latin American 945
latrinalia 259
Latvian 529
laughter 630, 974
law 294, 327, 583, 613, 614, 723, 887, 982, 1006, 1014, 1020, 1053, 1093, 1127, 1150, 1152
learning 53, 1066, 1088
Lebanese 213, 287, 1165

legitimacy 253
letter 1100
lexicographgy 481
lexicography 163, 172, 181, 233, 236, 237, 251, 255, 273, 564, 567, 569, 815, 1119
lexicology 51, 202, 309, 371, 396, 399, 400, 442, 463, 518, 570, 736, 936, 946, 959, 1062
Liberian 579
life 3, 25, 31, 33, 34, 48, 132, 147, 185, 188, 213, 214, 223, 225–227, 249, 287, 302, 304, 315, 325, 332, 338, 365, 385, 410, 433, 476, 486, 528, 543, 553, 555, 558, 561, 571, 576, 578, 605, 611, 615, 621, 648, 744, 748, 762, 773, 802, 820, 886, 892, 894, 931, 941, 963, 999, 1021, 1024, 1048, 1076, 1089, 1093, 1127
linguistics 18, 28, 70, 122, 129, 130, 134, 143, 161, 163–165, 170, 183, 199, 202, 203, 205, 209, 221, 222, 232–237, 239, 240, 246, 247, 270, 272, 273, 281, 285, 300, 311, 330, 334, 348, 358, 371, 372, 381–383, 395–398, 409, 416, 418, 440, 441, 462, 470, 479, 481, 490, 518, 536–539, 554, 559, 564, 566–570, 573–575, 597, 602, 603, 616, 617, 619, 625, 626, 633–636, 645, 652, 666, 672, 674, 695, 699, 705, 706, 733, 735, 736, 746, 751, 754, 764–768, 772, 776, 779, 783, 791, 792, 805, 810, 842, 843, 853, 855, 857, 876, 902, 910, 926, 933, 938, 944, 946, 949, 950, 956, 959–961, 970, 971, 989, 1001, 1012, 1013, 1030, 1034, 1048, 1062, 1065, 1079, 1090, 1099, 1102, 1105, 1119, 1122, 1137, 1138, 1148, 1164, 1167
litany 63
literacy 55, 92, 228, 402, 690, 691, 695, 968, 969
literalization 871
literalness 73, 80, 81, 139, 141–143, 153, 154, 157, 191, 192, 207, 231, 257, 299, 300, 317, 350–354, 358–360, 362–364, 368, 372, 374, 432, 457, 475, 498, 505, 506, 508, 538–541, 544, 545, 550, 575, 577, 598, 612, 633, 640, 732, 746, 755–759, 765, 769, 799, 849, 863, 864, 890, 927, 978, 979, 1018, 1059–1061, 1077, 1079–1081, 1083, 1091, 1092, 1094, 1103
literature 22, 26, 39, 40, 93, 114, 117, 125, 130, 132, 159, 220, 258, 265, 278, 281, 322, 407, 411, 433–435, 473, 493, 496, 526, 533, 564, 569, 588, 639, 660, 665, 682–685, 693, 695, 699, 703, 704, 706–708, 710–713, 716, 725, 730, 763, 765, 781, 789, 910, 923, 973, 975, 1015, 1022, 1037, 1038, 1047, 1053, 1075, 1097, 1101, 1127, 1130, 1135, 1141, 1142, 1163, 1168
loafing 590
loan translation 330, 569, 691, 692, 713, 736, 975, 1053, 1101, 1112
lobotomy 101, 389
logic 9, 52, 79, 113, 133, 194, 202, 203, 337, 381–383, 385, 405, 426, 511, 537, 573, 610, 611, 640, 716, 745, 778, 779,

Subject Index 217

805, 827, 842, 843, 902, 1026, 1027
love 531, 572, 1032, 1100
LSD (drug) 63
Luba 1146
Luxemburgish 490
lying 825
Macedonian 326
Malagasy 592, 826, 827, 917, 1047
Malawi 114, 178
male 1000
malediction 19, 66
Mali 565
Maltese 719
management 13, 218
mania 458, 459, 964, 977
manipulation 244, 328, 619, 677, 1035
manners 999
Maori 315
marker 35, 41, 686, 855, 875, 1012, 1013, 1068, 1070, 1071
marriage 114, 531, 738, 790, 878, 943, 1000, 1022, 1096, 1100, 1116, 1131
mass media 116, 126, 127, 294, 335, 427, 435, 464, 564, 567–569, 591, 603, 678, 681, 682, 684, 685, 691–693, 699, 701, 702, 704, 706, 713, 716, 765, 923, 1075, 1088, 1100, 1127, 1133, 1134, 1143
maturity 899, 1016
maxim 52, 187, 249, 295, 296, 749
Mayan 391
meaning 9, 15, 52, 81, 84, 85, 88, 89, 107, 109, 111, 112, 116, 120, 121, 133, 139, 141–143, 163, 189, 199, 201, 210, 226, 252, 266–268, 275, 277, 284, 289–291, 299, 314, 320, 321, 323, 327, 329, 334, 339, 342, 350–355, 357, 359, 364, 368, 371, 374, 402, 403, 407, 409, 438, 439, 450, 451, 453, 457, 463, 488–491, 494, 502, 505, 506, 508, 517, 523, 525, 540, 542, 544, 545, 547, 550, 555, 557, 558, 573, 579, 587, 588, 601, 606, 610–612, 622, 627, 633, 642, 648, 649, 664, 669, 673, 675, 682, 689, 693, 694, 700, 713, 717, 723, 726, 732, 735, 741, 743, 746, 755, 765, 766, 769, 770, 774, 781, 789, 798, 802, 810, 811, 817, 823, 824, 849, 868, 869, 871, 890, 898, 904, 908, 911, 925, 933, 940, 942, 960, 970, 978, 979, 983, 984, 987, 991, 994, 1007, 1009–1011, 1015, 1040, 1043, 1045, 1046, 1049, 1050, 1054, 1059, 1061, 1080, 1081, 1085, 1092, 1094, 1098, 1101, 1103, 1107, 1115, 1124, 1130, 1135, 1140, 1149, 1164
mechanism 290, 291
mediator 367
medicine 1, 49, 50, 91, 135, 144, 158, 159, 257, 268, 289, 302, 339, 344, 393, 400, 401, 414, 446, 485, 572, 595, 614, 618, 622–624, 688, 691, 716, 733, 898, 932, 983, 984, 1019, 1040, 1053, 1062, 1141
memorability 71, 118, 119, 472, 484, 893, 915
memorable message 561
memorization 954, 976
memory 53, 81, 90, 92, 118, 119, 247, 272, 279, 326, 350, 483, 487, 497, 498, 500, 504, 505, 513, 561, 741, 806, 900, 901, 976, 1007–1010, 1060, 1080, 1103
men 17, 172, 248, 264, 306, 392, 630, 638, 850, 855, 858, 879, 904, 908, 945, 988, 1022, 1044, 1082, 1117, 1131, 1166
mentality 14, 21, 23, 160, 174, 213, 235, 237, 238, 271, 283, 286, 369, 425, 468, 479, 556, 559, 613, 737, 747, 781, 802,

850–852, 911, 1024, 1029, 1057, 1058, 1082, 1106, 1115
Mesopotamia 15
message 57, 214, 405, 407, 525, 561, 819, 821, 848, 857, 1014
metaphor 18, 35, 37, 41, 44, 45, 52, 55, 57, 76, 78, 84, 98, 99, 101, 103, 105, 106, 108, 120, 121, 126, 127, 137, 139, 140, 143, 154, 160, 161, 169, 170, 184, 191, 192, 194, 221, 231, 237, 240, 241, 250, 260, 262, 266, 269, 277, 279, 301, 303, 308, 312, 323, 334, 341, 342, 347, 350, 351, 355, 356, 358, 360–362, 364, 372–374, 378, 379, 397, 401, 410, 424, 430, 438, 440, 443, 448, 450, 452, 456, 457, 467, 478, 479, 487, 489, 490, 494, 498–505, 508, 511, 523, 533, 538–541, 544, 545, 550, 558, 573, 575, 576, 579, 587, 588, 592, 603, 607, 610, 611, 627, 634, 640, 652, 660, 666, 672, 681, 686, 691, 695, 702, 703, 707, 716, 718, 720, 726, 727, 736, 742, 743, 755, 756, 765, 766, 769, 772, 783, 785, 798, 799, 807–811, 815, 822–824, 833, 841, 842, 845, 846, 854–856, 859, 860, 863, 866, 867, 869, 873, 890, 891, 897, 900, 901, 919, 921, 923, 925–927, 942, 944–946, 950, 955, 967, 983–986, 989, 991, 998, 1015, 1027, 1032, 1037, 1040, 1053, 1058, 1059, 1062, 1063, 1068, 1070, 1077, 1084, 1085, 1100, 1102, 1105, 1110, 1111, 1119, 1125, 1133, 1140, 1142, 1145
metaphorization 597, 1026
metaphysics 1109, 1110
meta-linguistic 78, 121
meta-proverb 56

metonymy 312, 357, 462, 467, 587, 636, 736, 1037
Mexican 325, 817
Middle Ages 92
Minangkabau 307
mind mapping 271
minority 77
misericord 718
misogyny 6, 17, 37, 40, 146, 156, 217, 264, 293, 369, 531, 547, 585, 629–632, 638, 679, 683, 771, 784, 790, 832, 841, 858, 879, 895, 904, 945, 988, 1000, 1041, 1082, 1116, 1131, 1153, 1156, 1158–1161, 1166
missiology 189
missionary 729
modality 814
modernity 251, 523, 529, 683, 793, 856, 980, 1038, 1133
modification 222, 300, 529, 567, 568, 570, 588, 653, 736, 751, 982, 1088, 1132, 1133, 1143
modularity 518
monkey 48
Monopoly 517
moral 507, 633, 650, 665, 681
morality 32, 43–45, 188, 193, 277, 315, 476, 492, 519, 521, 560, 658, 670, 717, 738, 753, 778, 789, 836, 837, 873, 887, 888, 909, 1108, 1116
Moravian 965
mores 59
Moroccan 1116, 1124
morphology 28, 222, 567, 569
Moslem 548
Mossi 114, 953
mother 245, 662
motivation 139, 240, 311, 356–358, 364, 373, 398, 408, 424, 450, 451, 498, 539, 736, 842, 933
motto 321
mouse 93

mouth 596
multilingualism 333
Muscovite 282
music 37, 684, 693, 869
Muslim 549
myth 82, 260
mythology 1111

name 404, 567, 570, 1054
narrative 79, 93, 151, 321, 463, 465, 469, 484, 649, 699, 788, 842, 873, 913, 923, 968, 969, 1053, 1054, 1078, 1115, 1150
national character 134, 152, 263, 265, 280, 282, 285, 286, 298, 365, 404, 419, 422, 496, 584, 695, 716, 750, 773, 787, 801, 872, 881–883, 896, 905, 912, 924, 972, 1028, 1029, 1051–1053, 1064, 1095, 1121, 1127, 1128, 1144, 1169
National Socialism 244, 280, 496, 527, 677, 691, 697, 698, 702, 708
nationalism 77
nationality 394
Native American 38, 391, 684, 694, 924
native speaker 35, 335
nature 93, 410
negation 569, 570, 949
negro 1154
Nembe 7
neologism 251, 523, 529, 542
Netherlandic Proverbs 718
neurolinguistics 143, 279, 284, 741, 847, 1093, 1094
neurology 870, 1092
neurophysiology 1007
neuropsychology 257, 586, 1042
New Mexico 109
New Testament 583, 656, 658, 716, 729, 888, 1135
news 116
newspaper 464, 567–569, 591
Nigerian 513, 776
nomination 672
nonsense 403, 1037, 1133

norm 425, 429, 834, 835, 914, 916, 918, 939, 1030, 1031, 1044
number 234, 241, 850–854
nurture 93
nutrition 485, 623, 624, 984
obituary 435
obscenity 12, 18, 19, 293, 572, 601, 674, 678, 753, 774, 788, 807, 833, 945, 1053, 1073, 1074
obsoleteness 980, 1038
occupation 59, 60, 147
Old Testament 188, 656, 658, 888, 981
onomastics 404, 567, 570
ontology 1109
opinion 605
opposition 261
optimization 803, 804
orality 40, 55, 92, 109, 114, 127, 143, 182, 228, 260, 326, 391, 402, 449, 469, 533, 565, 566, 604, 606, 654, 655, 716, 728, 744, 775, 777, 789, 915, 968, 969, 993, 1047, 1078, 1083, 1084, 1121, 1152
Oriental 615
origin 41, 44, 45, 56, 71, 116, 128, 193, 221, 251, 252, 266–268, 327, 333, 423, 462, 507, 542, 581, 593, 634, 636, 657, 682, 686, 689, 693, 694, 700, 706, 713, 736, 793, 886, 923, 937, 956, 975, 983, 984, 1015, 1028, 1029, 1053–1055, 1078, 1101, 1117, 1127, 1133
Oriya 724
orthodoxy 32
ostentation 644
Ovambo 585

parable 301
paradox 9, 381, 382, 583, 608, 660, 765–767, 934, 1105
Paraguayan 638
parallelism 1013
paranoia 155

paraphrase 439, 443, 633
parasite 135
paremiography 251, 423, 427, 676, 705, 706
paremiological minimum 179, 180, 273, 415, 421, 427, 680, 690, 691, 695, 844, 934, 965, 966, 990
paremiology 114, 134, 176, 179, 213, 341, 412, 416, 418, 423, 426, 427, 510, 536, 676, 686, 687, 695, 699, 705, 706, 708, 802, 842, 843, 896, 914, 923, 984, 989, 1026, 1048, 1053, 1054, 1078, 1099, 1123, 1127, 1167
parents 324, 519, 520, 662, 670, 671, 775, 1069
parody 63, 407, 433, 434, 660, 684, 753, 857, 1073, 1074
pathology 459
patriarchy 6
pattern 33, 34, 581
peace 1110
peasant 31, 32
pedagogy 86, 195, 219, 273, 301, 449, 478, 492, 670, 671, 673, 699, 717, 772, 800, 813, 837, 861, 953, 962, 993, 1021, 1036, 1071, 1075, 1076, 1088, 1127, 1139, 1140, 1144
people 14, 576, 648
perception 111, 112, 140, 262, 410, 512, 533, 607, 642, 653, 662, 1068, 1070
performance 108, 109, 118, 119, 123, 202, 225–227, 247, 314, 324, 555, 695, 764, 1148, 1150, 1151, 1164
perlocution 695, 764
personal proverb 561
personality 59, 60, 64, 436, 437, 590, 643, 675, 878, 919, 952
personhood 248
perspective 461
persuasion 36
pessimism 584, 1169

pharmaceutics 618
philology 122, 130, 615, 699
philosophy 7, 29, 114, 161, 193, 214, 372, 405, 477, 513, 534, 553, 565, 610, 611, 613, 778, 779, 808, 887, 888, 953, 960, 1043, 1078, 1107–1110, 1130
phonetics 566
phraseography 129, 233, 236, 281, 676
phraseologism 65, 69, 70, 78, 120, 122, 125, 126, 129, 163, 184, 199, 228, 252, 255, 263, 270, 272, 279, 395, 396, 398, 408, 438–442, 444, 445, 450–452, 462, 470, 496, 509, 510, 518, 523, 524, 564, 597, 610, 626, 648, 649, 667, 668, 674, 733, 735, 736, 742, 752, 766, 791, 792, 802, 814, 815, 842, 846, 856, 859, 862, 865, 866, 879, 913, 935, 936, 940, 944, 945, 949, 950, 955, 962, 967, 969, 971, 1001, 1002, 1005, 1035, 1036, 1051, 1057, 1062, 1063, 1074, 1077, 1101, 1106, 1119, 1122, 1127, 1132, 1136, 1143, 1145, 1162
phraseology 51, 123, 124, 127–130, 195, 196, 205, 221, 232, 233, 237, 241, 246, 281, 283–286, 300, 341, 396, 399–402, 443, 479, 480, 554, 564, 567, 569, 570, 626, 635, 676, 733, 816, 850–855, 935, 936, 944, 958, 962, 1001, 1030–1032, 1058, 1137, 1138, 1167
phylacterism 907
physician 618
physiognomy 48, 471
physiology 289, 339, 344, 446
picture 501, 506, 695, 718
Pidgin English 776
planning 249
poetics 4, 35, 41–45, 92, 134, 195, 321, 356, 463, 472, 537, 566, 653, 686, 691, 705, 736,

745, 811, 816, 955, 989, 1010, 1068, 1070, 1071, 1075, 1090, 1125, 1133, 1167
poetry 135, 278, 493, 526, 588, 639, 683–685, 725, 763, 1015, 1032, 1075, 1163
polemics 85
Polish 280, 841, 865
politeness 1122
politics 16, 85, 116, 193, 244, 294, 528, 534, 565, 619, 626, 677, 685, 696, 697, 701–703, 707–716, 731, 749, 818, 857, 883, 889, 1028, 1029, 1035, 1110, 1132, 1136, 1137, 1143, 1152
polyphony 407
popularity 8, 551, 580, 659, 669, 1134
Portuguese 90, 335, 596, 865, 879, 959
postmodernism 657
postmodernity 982
poverty 185, 1052
power 56, 786, 818, 825, 1025, 1052
pragmatics 10, 109, 130, 133, 173, 196, 199, 203, 237, 246, 346, 396, 397, 463, 489, 491, 503, 537–539, 554, 573, 574, 617, 635, 636, 695, 739, 740, 936, 959, 1034, 1048, 1102, 1105, 1138, 1150, 1151
pragmatism 225–227, 249, 278, 994
preaching 656, 658
precept 981
prediction 89, 149, 230, 260, 346
prejudice 19, 38, 66, 77, 263, 280, 282, 298, 310, 365, 369, 393, 404, 419, 422, 496, 547, 585, 629, 679, 694, 695, 698, 700, 710–713, 750, 787, 790, 796, 801, 817, 832, 841, 858, 872, 879, 904, 924, 929, 945, 958, 972, 988, 1000, 1028, 1029, 1041, 1044, 1051, 1052, 1082, 1128, 1153, 1154, 1156, 1158, 1159, 1165, 1166
prescription 918, 939
prevention 91
principle 13, 187, 1004
production 108, 118–120, 123, 165, 443, 507, 599
profession 218, 294, 486, 618, 733, 892, 898, 903, 988, 1023, 1087, 1104
professor 36
progress 331
projection 46, 878, 952
propaganda 677, 697, 698, 701, 702, 708
proposition 672, 940
prostitution 146
proverb duel 658
proverb picture 695, 718
proverb type 581, 582
proverbiality 28, 35, 202, 203, 330, 507, 536, 645, 695, 719, 1068, 1070, 1071, 1090
proverbialization 556, 557, 731, 955, 956
proverbs test 20, 23, 46, 53, 58–60, 62, 64, 67, 68, 73, 75, 80, 81, 87, 97–107, 115, 118, 131, 136, 137, 148, 149, 153–155, 157, 165, 167, 168, 177, 184, 186, 191, 192, 208, 211, 212, 231, 257, 269, 288, 292, 299, 303, 308, 313, 314, 318, 319, 324, 331, 336, 340, 345, 351, 366, 368, 378, 386–390, 406, 417, 432, 436, 437, 440, 455, 458–461, 468, 474–475, 482, 483, 487, 494, 495, 498, 499, 501, 502, 509, 530, 544, 545, 550, 552, 562, 577, 586, 589, 594, 606, 607, 609, 628, 637, 642, 643, 646, 647, 663, 675, 687, 716, 740, 741, 756, 759, 762, 783, 794, 797, 812, 828–831, 839, 840, 867, 870, 884, 885, 892, 899–901, 919, 927, 928, 948, 951, 952,

964, 976–977, 996, 997, 1006–1010, 1016, 1045, 1046, 1056, 1065, 1066, 1092, 1098, 1103, 1113, 1114, 1118, 1120, 1140, 1162

prudence 917, 1089

pseudo-proverb 915, 916, 1004, 1129

psychiatry 20, 23, 67, 68, 73, 87, 94, 98–107, 115, 137, 148, 149, 153–155, 167, 168, 176, 186, 208, 288, 313, 319, 324, 380, 386–390, 406, 417, 447, 454, 458–460, 474, 475, 494, 495, 577, 589, 594, 604, 606, 628, 642, 663, 675, 741, 797, 828–831, 884, 885, 899, 919, 927, 948, 951, 964, 977, 996, 997, 1014, 1017, 1042, 1045, 1085, 1113, 1114, 1118, 1120

psychoanalysis 82, 259, 265, 267, 284, 285, 473, 493, 526, 531, 639, 641, 674, 753, 793, 886, 906, 907, 973, 1097, 1168

psycholinguistcs 487, 503, 890

psycholinguistics 76, 80, 81, 84, 90, 96, 110, 120, 121, 123, 128, 130, 136, 140–143, 157, 165, 170, 176, 177, 182, 184, 186, 190–192, 194, 195, 201, 207, 210–212, 223–227, 231, 247, 249, 250, 254, 269–272, 279, 281, 283–286, 299, 300, 308, 311–314, 317, 318, 329, 331, 336, 345, 347, 350–364, 368, 371–374, 378, 397, 417, 436–438, 440, 443, 445, 457, 461, 462, 468, 479, 482, 483, 488, 489, 497–502, 504–509, 520, 530, 538–541, 544–546, 550, 552, 562, 575, 587, 588, 598, 599, 607, 612, 627, 637, 643, 644, 646, 647, 652, 653, 721, 722, 732, 734, 743, 755–762, 772, 793, 798, 799, 803, 804, 806, 816, 822–824, 839, 840, 847, 849, 863, 864, 867, 871, 891, 892, 900, 901, 918, 919, 921, 928, 952, 962, 976, 978, 979, 998, 1003, 1007–1010, 1018, 1029, 1039, 1046, 1049, 1050, 1056, 1059–1061, 1065, 1079–1081, 1085, 1091–1094, 1098, 1103, 1140, 1155

psychology 5, 20–23, 46, 58–62, 64, 67, 68, 71, 73, 76, 80–82, 84, 87, 94, 96–107, 115, 118–120, 122, 131, 136, 137, 143–145, 148, 149, 153–155, 165, 167, 168, 176, 177, 184, 186, 190–192, 194, 197, 198, 208, 210–212, 218, 219, 224–227, 230, 231, 247, 249, 250, 265, 269, 279, 284, 285, 288, 291, 292, 295, 296, 299, 300, 303, 304, 313, 314, 317–319, 324, 329, 331, 336, 340, 344–347, 350–355, 357–364, 366, 368, 372–374, 378–380, 386–390, 406, 417, 432, 436, 437, 447, 448, 454, 455, 457–461, 468, 474, 475, 482, 483, 487–490, 494, 495, 497–509, 520, 530–532, 550, 552, 559, 562, 572, 577, 586–589, 594, 604, 606, 607, 609, 614, 627, 628, 637, 641–643, 646, 647, 651, 653, 659, 663, 664, 667, 670, 671, 675, 687, 695, 699, 705, 706, 716, 717, 721, 732, 734, 737, 741, 743, 747, 755, 794, 797–799, 812, 828–831, 839, 840, 849, 863, 867, 870, 876, 878, 881, 884, 885, 890, 891, 895, 899–901, 906, 907, 919–921, 927, 928, 948, 951, 952, 963, 964, 972, 976, 977, 991, 995–998, 1002, 1005–1010, 1016, 1017, 1021, 1024, 1042, 1045, 1059–1061, 1085, 1092, 1094, 1100, 1103, 1113, 1114, 1118, 1120, 1121, 1123, 1125, 1126, 1142, 1169

psychopathy 366
psychosemiotics 417
psychotherapy 61
Puerto Rican 177
Pulayas 532
pun 370
punishment 150

quotation 85, 202, 330, 345, 433, 457, 542, 660, 730, 857, 973, 1162

race 318, 677, 697, 698, 702, 708, 710–713
rape 1160
rationalism 1107, 1109
rationalization 643, 748
reading 197, 276, 540
realia 57, 79
reality 111, 112, 809
reasoning 9, 87, 140, 231, 385, 405, 806
recall 90, 509, 1060, 1103
reception 151, 561
reciprocity 810, 994
recognition 509, 1007–1010, 1050
recurrence 611
red hair 393, 408, 453, 471, 752
reduction 179, 982
redundancy 367, 893
regionalism 127
relationship 325
relativism 994
relevance 246
reliability 386
religion 29, 39, 55, 92, 114, 174, 188, 189, 193, 294, 322, 453, 469, 486, 548, 549, 560, 595, 600, 613, 656, 658, 670, 699, 707, 729, 738, 745, 778, 836, 906, 917, 942, 981, 1025, 1110, 1135, 1142, 1144, 1159
Renaissance 1

repertoire 10, 95, 582
repetition 35, 258, 497, 628, 793, 893, 976, 1068
reproducibility 303
reproduction 1034
reputation 248
retrieval 806
rhetoric 3, 16, 25, 63, 69, 85, 215, 216, 296, 337, 405, 430, 465, 467, 492, 529, 565, 603, 626, 665, 677, 696, 697, 701–703, 707–711, 714, 715, 739, 740, 845, 883, 1011, 1079, 1125, 1127, 1135–1137, 1141, 1142, 1150, 1152
rhyme 653
riddle 37, 82, 405, 724, 754
ritual 1122
routine formula 428, 431, 625, 954, 955, 1034
rule 425, 477, 542, 561, 888, 941, 981, 982, 1004, 1014, 1020, 1104
Rumanian 349, 641, 894, 939
Russian 16, 65, 134, 282, 330, 365, 572, 701, 754, 801, 842–844, 861, 958, 995, 1001, 1002, 1051, 1074
Rwandan 931

sanction 63
scatology 18, 259, 265, 293, 342, 572, 601, 674, 678, 753, 774, 857, 889
schizophrenia 20, 46, 67, 68, 73, 87, 94, 98–107, 131, 137, 148, 149, 153–155, 167, 208, 212, 279, 288, 324, 378–380, 386–390, 406, 417, 432, 447, 454, 458–461, 474, 475, 494, 495, 552, 577, 589, 604, 606, 607, 628, 663, 675, 797, 828–831, 884, 899, 919, 927, 951, 952, 964, 977, 996, 997, 1045, 1113, 1114, 1118, 1120

science 14, 26, 114, 135, 260, 262, 289, 291, 664, 737, 1040, 1062, 1141
science fiction 260
Scottish 750
selection 95, 803, 804
self-help book 39, 295, 296
semantics 10, 16, 18, 22, 28, 35, 51, 53, 55, 57, 90, 92, 127, 130, 143, 151, 160–162, 164, 166, 171, 173, 183, 209, 221, 222, 232, 236–240, 270, 272, 300, 312, 330, 341, 356, 362, 363, 370, 381–384, 394–396, 398, 416, 418, 420, 423, 424, 426, 441, 443, 445, 451, 467, 473, 480, 484, 491, 497, 500, 536, 538, 539, 557–559, 564, 568–570, 573–575, 602, 608, 616, 617, 634, 635, 644, 653, 666, 668, 672, 686, 687, 691, 699, 705, 716, 732, 733, 739, 740, 744, 751, 754, 757, 765, 814–816, 842, 843, 847, 859, 860, 862–864, 873, 876, 893, 897, 902, 914, 921, 923, 926, 934, 946, 955, 970, 989, 1001, 1007–1010, 1012, 1026, 1027, 1030, 1036, 1039, 1048, 1057, 1090, 1091, 1099, 1105, 1119, 1127, 1134, 1136, 1137, 1143, 1154, 1161, 1167
semiotics 11, 51, 57, 79, 133, 134, 160, 162, 169, 234, 237, 241–243, 270, 281, 384, 397, 399, 416, 418, 420, 423–426, 479, 480, 511, 536, 537, 575, 602, 616, 617, 626, 636, 645, 695, 699, 705, 842, 843, 850–854, 865, 873, 902, 930, 959, 960, 1001, 1027, 1032, 1047, 1048, 1057, 1063, 1102, 1167
sentence 80, 84, 207, 456, 635
sententious remark 1136
Sephardic 10, 600, 601
sermon 656, 658
sex 1, 12, 18, 19, 37, 57, 60, 117, 146, 217, 259, 267, 293, 294, 306, 342, 343, 392, 404, 572, 678, 753, 774, 788, 807, 833, 857, 889, 945, 1022, 1073, 1074, 1097, 1116, 1160, 1168
sexuality 572, 624, 678, 770, 774, 784, 788, 790, 807, 945, 1116
shame 452, 1117
shibboleth 13
Shona 651
Sicilian 367
sign 384, 397, 405, 416, 418, 420, 610, 626, 636
signification 396
silence 170, 596, 631, 768, 795, 947, 1112
simile 640
simple form 330, 416, 418, 420, 422, 423, 537, 602, 897, 955
slang 19, 267, 275
slave 321, 333
slavery 709–712, 909
Slavic 280, 801, 929, 974
slogan 16, 19, 26, 61, 174, 217, 244, 328, 470, 679, 691, 712, 735, 754, 876, 883, 920, 1143
Slovakian 271, 872
slur 12, 19, 38, 77, 263, 280, 282, 298, 393, 404, 419, 422, 496, 694, 695, 700, 702, 713, 787, 801, 817, 872, 924, 929, 958, 972, 1028, 1029, 1051, 1064, 1154, 1165
sociability 275
socialization 88, 215, 216, 230, 449, 662, 775, 784, 1129
society 3, 4, 8, 11, 14, 15, 17, 18, 21, 25, 27, 29, 31, 32, 47, 54, 55, 57–59, 71, 74, 83, 88, 95, 108, 113, 114, 116, 130, 132, 144, 147, 152, 156, 161, 166, 173, 185, 187, 198, 206, 220, 227, 248, 253, 256, 258, 262, 265, 278, 287, 297, 301, 305, 310, 322, 325, 332, 333, 335, 336, 342, 346, 367, 369, 375–377, 381, 382, 391, 409,

Subject Index

413, 425, 428, 444, 466, 476, 477, 486, 512, 520, 521, 525, 527, 528, 532, 534, 543, 548, 549, 551, 554, 555, 579, 584, 585, 587, 588, 590, 592, 614, 629–632, 654, 655, 657, 659, 661, 662, 665, 680, 682–685, 689, 691, 695, 703, 704, 707, 708, 710–713, 716, 719, 723, 724, 726, 727, 731, 735, 738, 754, 763, 769–771, 774, 776–778, 780–782, 786, 788, 789, 793, 796, 808, 812, 818, 819, 821, 823, 825, 834, 835, 837, 838, 855, 857, 859, 869, 874, 880, 882, 883, 887, 891, 903–905, 912, 917, 919, 921–923, 925, 931, 937, 939–943, 957, 971, 980, 985–988, 992, 995, 1000, 1004, 1021, 1023, 1028, 1029, 1031, 1033, 1035, 1044, 1045, 1048, 1055, 1058, 1066, 1067, 1083, 1084, 1086, 1087, 1095, 1104, 1110, 1112, 1116, 1121, 1122, 1125, 1128, 1131, 1139, 1142, 1145, 1146, 1150, 1152, 1154, 1158, 1160, 1161
sociolinguistics 2, 4, 129, 206, 213, 227, 336, 445, 520, 521, 535, 593, 619, 620, 623, 624, 631, 632, 644, 650, 735, 812, 822–824, 836, 837, 846, 892, 965, 967, 1025, 1033, 1044, 1067, 1122, 1146, 1154, 1160
sociology 8, 11, 21, 22, 41, 47, 83, 122, 265, 275, 287, 291, 476, 531, 534, 535, 615, 680, 699, 713, 731, 734, 763, 781, 796, 807, 808, 876, 920, 922, 980, 995, 1086, 1104, 1121, 1123, 1124
Somali 25
somatism 162, 171, 393, 394, 401, 404, 408, 446, 471, 567, 590, 594, 596, 668, 697, 742, 752, 850, 932, 960, 984, 1145
song 565
Sotho 409, 410
sound 648
South American 38
Spanish 10, 37, 38, 49, 95, 109, 146, 152, 158, 159, 177, 206, 209, 310, 473, 486, 514, 516, 600, 601, 667, 716, 859, 860, 877, 879, 881, 882, 936, 945, 989, 990, 1044, 1063, 1082, 1089, 1096
speech 2, 4, 10, 25, 27, 30, 36, 38, 56, 69, 70, 78, 109, 116, 123, 130, 133, 161, 169, 170, 173, 182, 199, 202, 204, 215, 216, 223, 254, 267, 294, 300, 316, 320, 321, 349, 376, 377, 397, 403, 452, 460, 491, 494, 538, 546, 555, 565, 582, 596, 600, 625, 626, 631, 645, 648, 661, 696, 714, 715, 728, 739, 740, 764–766, 768, 772, 774, 782, 795, 805, 808, 833–835, 869, 876, 930, 935, 936, 947, 970, 986, 987, 1011, 1030, 1034, 1036, 1048–1050, 1112, 1121, 1122, 1125, 1146, 1148, 1150, 1151, 1157
speech act 2, 10, 25, 27, 30, 36, 69, 70, 78, 109, 123, 130, 133, 161, 169, 173, 199, 202, 204, 215, 216, 254, 294, 300, 320, 321, 377, 397, 403, 452, 491, 555, 565, 582, 600, 625, 626, 645, 728, 739, 740, 764–766, 772, 774, 782, 805, 808, 833–835, 869, 876, 930, 935, 936, 970, 986, 987, 1011, 1030, 1034, 1036, 1048–1050, 1121, 1122, 1125, 1146, 1148, 1150, 1151
sports 568, 569
stability 399, 484, 792, 816, 874
statistics 35, 303, 412, 413, 421, 427, 466, 551, 580, 585, 609, 680, 720, 965, 968, 969, 978, 990, 1041, 1067–1070, 1072
stereotype 12, 19, 37, 38, 47, 66, 77, 146, 152, 156, 170, 172, 217, 245, 261, 263, 280–282,

298, 305, 310, 365, 369, 393, 396, 404, 419, 422, 471, 496, 522, 547–549, 585, 625, 629, 630, 631, 632, 638, 677, 679, 691, 694, 697–700, 702, 708, 710–713, 750, 771, 784, 787, 790, 801, 817, 832, 841, 858, 872, 876, 879, 904, 912, 924, 929, 945, 955, 958, 971, 972, 974, 988, 1000, 1012, 1023, 1028, 1029, 1041, 1044, 1051, 1058, 1064, 1082, 1087, 1095, 1102, 1116, 1117, 1121, 1128, 1131, 1153, 1154, 1156, 1158, 1159, 1161, 1165, 1166
story 502
strategy 11, 121, 132, 173, 258, 385, 405, 450, 451, 593, 726, 727, 782, 803, 804, 821, 930, 985, 1030
structure 33, 34, 41–43, 51, 52, 79, 84, 130, 134, 143, 164, 173, 181, 195, 202, 209, 232, 236, 238, 239, 259, 279, 283, 300, 309, 311, 312, 328, 330, 337, 341, 348, 367, 381–383, 396, 410, 416, 418–420, 423, 426, 436, 463, 467, 470, 479, 484, 488, 505, 536, 537, 550, 558, 564, 574, 576, 581, 583, 587, 588, 602, 616, 633, 645, 652, 666, 669, 686, 691, 694, 695, 716, 720, 733, 735, 745, 746, 751, 765, 766, 783, 806, 810, 816, 842, 843, 862, 875, 889, 893, 897, 902, 915, 916, 923, 934, 936, 938, 955, 958, 963, 970, 976, 983, 984, 986, 989, 1012, 1013, 1015, 1026, 1027, 1053, 1054, 1065, 1074, 1075, 1084, 1090, 1099, 1105, 1110, 1115, 1117, 1119, 1127, 1135, 1137, 1143, 1146, 1148, 1167
student 47, 60, 75, 80, 81, 97, 136, 200, 201, 212, 229, 271, 275, 297, 299, 308, 314, 318, 331, 336, 437, 441, 444, 468, 483, 489, 506, 517, 544, 545, 620, 637, 646, 647, 720, 721, 757, 794, 803, 804, 844, 857, 864, 868, 948, 962, 978, 990, 993, 998, 1016, 1049, 1056, 1066, 1070, 1075, 1076, 1139, 1147, 1161
stupidity 312
style 232, 481, 537, 645, 686, 730, 814, 815, 862, 897, 914, 916, 955, 959, 973, 1053, 1088, 1115, 1117, 1127
subversion 656, 658
success 255
Sumerian 15
summary 253, 254
superstition 3, 144, 266, 323, 393, 408, 453, 471, 752, 907, 1025, 1053
supervisor 892
Swahili 302, 819–821, 986
Swedish 98–107, 925, 1031
Swiss 64, 120, 121, 129, 130, 441, 570, 934, 962, 968, 969
Swiss German 120, 121, 129, 130, 441, 570, 934, 962, 968, 969
symbol 160, 161, 241, 242, 258, 284, 306, 322, 392, 393, 850, 853, 854
symbolism 237, 243, 498, 607, 742, 851, 852, 1032, 1063, 1097, 1168
symmetry 1013, 1079
synchronic 124, 130, 442
synonymy 395, 396, 488, 505
syntax 22, 28, 35, 202, 222, 300, 348, 356, 362, 363, 383, 403, 463, 472, 518, 564, 569, 570, 573, 616, 645, 746, 751, 765, 792, 816, 842, 847, 875, 893, 934, 936, 938, 961, 970, 1013, 1039, 1071, 1091, 1138, 1143
taboo 12, 1025
Talmud 595
Tamil 911
tautology 383, 384, 576

Subject Index

teaching 86, 138, 169, 175, 195, 196, 271, 273, 276, 308, 317, 415, 428, 429, 444, 449, 492, 514–517, 520, 593, 625, 673, 699, 717, 720, 772, 800, 820, 837, 844, 881, 962, 993, 1036, 1066, 1071, 1075, 1076, 1088, 1139, 1140, 1161
teenager 470, 529
terminology 127, 816
testing 20
Tetela 789
textile 718
theatre 266, 565
Themne 534
theology 469
therapy 61, 295, 296, 387, 734, 747, 919, 920, 996, 1125
thought 358, 494, 495
time 145, 201, 332, 591, 1033, 1077
Tiv 74
toothache 49
topic 254
topos 1136
tradition 3, 11, 17, 21, 27, 29, 32, 114, 161, 166, 174, 175, 178, 182, 189, 198, 216, 261, 266, 278, 297, 307, 391, 449, 484, 512, 593, 600, 654, 655, 681, 683, 728, 729, 744, 764, 813, 819, 848, 873, 874, 923, 980, 982, 1011, 1038, 1044, 1056, 1128, 1147, 1150, 1152, 1163
traditionality 35, 507, 632, 645, 686, 765
transformability 90
transformation 302, 1073
transition 254
translation 177, 330, 533, 569, 691, 692, 713, 736, 975, 1053, 1101, 1112
transmission 24, 56, 315, 384, 449, 478, 561, 566, 662, 874
truism 563
truth 7, 13, 47, 49, 58, 204, 274, 277, 307, 336, 338, 374, 381– 383, 425, 543, 555, 563, 571, 587, 605, 650, 653, 681, 687, 731, 737, 744, 809, 845, 921, 933, 940, 1014, 1015, 1040, 1056, 1104, 1146, 1149
Turkish 11, 56, 57, 248, 376, 377, 522
type 33, 34, 581, 582
typology 237, 241

Ubuntu 535
uniformity 83
univeral 232
universality 13, 162, 203, 281, 286, 426, 563, 571, 634, 636, 687, 783, 805, 809, 874, 894, 896, 1012, 1015, 1026, 1105
use 88, 95, 120, 132, 215, 216, 253, 275, 321, 331, 334, 398, 402, 425, 441, 445, 466, 480, 528, 555, 608, 610, 620, 662, 680, 699, 717, 726, 727, 789, 864, 876, 970, 985–987, 1011, 1067, 1093, 1100, 1130, 1135, 1138, 1142, 1148
utility 89
valence 570
validation 109, 485
validity 8, 23, 24, 28, 47, 54, 60, 148, 149, 204, 212, 337, 466, 563, 571, 653, 734, 737, 809, 848, 885, 932, 980, 1003, 1038, 1040, 1043, 1064
value 31, 39, 54, 59, 91, 182, 185, 189, 198, 211, 261, 278, 307, 316, 338, 349, 365, 376, 449, 466, 469, 476, 510, 519, 521, 535, 551, 552, 579, 585, 591, 596, 605, 647, 651, 659, 662, 665, 680, 722, 767, 768, 773, 775, 780, 786, 788, 795, 812, 813, 818, 820, 821, 827, 834, 835, 837, 868, 869, 873, 874, 892, 920–922, 939, 941, 947, 971, 987, 993, 995, 1012, 1055, 1056, 1096, 1147, 1157, 1158

variability 130, 141, 232, 309, 321, 399, 570, 626, 1026, 1151
variant 37, 179, 181, 222, 252, 327, 333, 371, 408, 427, 434, 443, 477, 478, 512, 523, 548, 549, 564, 581, 686, 811, 897, 937, 963, 986, 1027, 1099, 1127, 1132, 1134
variation 52, 127, 128, 150, 179, 199, 237, 300, 330, 407, 443, 484, 523, 551, 557, 657, 660, 691, 694, 875, 961, 975, 1053, 1073, 1099
verb 946
verbal dueling 565, 800
verbalization 100, 104, 106
Vermont 689, 691
veterinarian 618
Vietnamese 747, 1055
village 95, 213
violence 40
virginity 1097, 1168
virtue 670, 671
vision 262
vocabulary 53, 211
Völkertafel 1028, 1029
Vute 1011

war 685, 696, 701, 708, 709, 714, 1132
wedding 641
wellerism 15, 52, 678, 684, 989, 1053, 1054, 1127
wisdom 6, 7, 14, 24, 27, 83, 114, 178, 188, 192, 220, 274, 277, 287, 291, 295–297, 338, 377, 385, 426, 476, 507, 510, 521, 522, 528, 543, 553, 560, 578, 592, 621, 622, 624, 656–659, 662, 670, 671, 681, 683, 691, 702, 716, 717, 728, 731, 737, 744, 745, 749, 763, 770, 776, 779, 812, 837, 838, 848, 861, 862, 917, 918, 922, 930, 933, 981, 982, 993, 1005, 1015, 1043, 1083, 1104, 1110, 1115, 1126, 1127, 1129, 1130, 1135, 1141, 1147
wit 1005
wolf 243, 1111
women 6, 17, 37, 40, 62, 114, 146, 156, 170, 206, 217, 245, 248, 264, 285, 305, 310, 369, 486, 547, 585, 629–632, 638, 651, 679, 771, 790, 832, 841, 850, 855, 858, 879, 895, 904, 945, 988, 1000, 1022, 1032, 1041, 1044, 1082, 1097, 1100, 1116, 1117, 1131, 1153, 1156–1161, 1166, 1168
woodcut 718
word 141, 270, 379, 381, 404, 433–435, 597
wordplay 370, 407, 564, 568, 678, 683, 684, 802, 857, 934, 1143
work 64, 187, 218, 341, 590
world 11, 832
world-upside-down 832
worldview 14, 21, 29, 31, 32, 78, 83, 147, 156, 166, 174, 182, 185, 211, 213, 214, 223, 230, 233, 234, 238, 245, 248, 249, 259–263, 265, 267, 278, 281, 285, 286, 301, 304, 310, 316, 328, 332, 341, 345, 349, 365, 367, 376, 377, 394, 404, 452, 466, 469, 470, 473, 490, 496, 511, 513, 522, 527, 529, 532, 547, 551, 553, 559, 560, 565, 584, 585, 591, 596, 600, 615, 621, 629–632, 638, 644, 646, 647, 661, 665, 689, 693, 704, 708, 719, 722, 729, 731, 734, 735, 744, 747, 748, 750, 767, 768, 773, 784, 786, 790, 795, 796, 802, 813, 818, 825, 838, 850–853, 856, 868, 869, 873, 874, 895, 896, 904–906, 908, 911–913, 917, 923, 931, 936, 937, 942, 947, 957, 971, 974, 992, 994, 995, 1002, 1005, 1021, 1024, 1028, 1029,

1033, 1041, 1052, 1055, 1057, 1078, 1083, 1087, 1089, 1095, 1096, 1102, 1106, 1110, 1112, 1144, 1145, 1153, 1169

Xhosa 114

Yiddish 572, 644, 716, 838, 906, 1144

Yoruba 2, 30, 114, 592, 788, 790, 807, 808, 941, 992, 1157–1161

youth 470, 523, 529, 567, 735, 755, 758, 761, 775, 931, 1072

PROVERB INDEX

The proverbs and proverbial expressions (also a few quotations) listed here refer to publications concerned with individual proverb studies. They are grouped according to language and italicized keywords, and they are quoted for the most part in their original languages. All numbers refer to the entries and not to pages.

English

When *Adam* delved and Eve span, who was then the gentleman? 695

An *apple* a day keeps the doctor away, 485, 688, 691

The *apple* doesn't fall far from the tree, 692

To throw the *baby* out with the bath water, 691

Early to *bed* and early to rise, makes a man healthy, wealthy and wise, 688, 691

It is an ill *bird* that fouls its own nest, 716

To kill two *birds* with one stone, 1132

Blood, sweat, and tears, 696

To wear the *breeches*, 117, 832

The *buck* stops here, 13

Sweet *bugger* all, 267

Paddle your own *canoe*, 712

Don't count your *chickens* before they're hatched, 633

Stuff a *cold* and starve a fever, 339, 688, 691, 716

To be a *cuckold*, 117

Do unto others as you would have them do unto you, 477

Hear no *evil*, see no evil, speak no evil, 685

Good *fences* make good neighbors, 493, 526, 539, 725, 1163

Big *fish* eat little fish, 682

To put the best *foot* forward, 1101

A *friend* in need is a friend indeed, 555

Who goes drunk to bed begets but a *girl*, 1

To see through colored *glasses*, 252

The *grass* is always greener on the other side of the fence, 693, 695

It is better that ten *guilty* persons escape than that one innocent suffer, 887

Many *hands* make light work, 590

Two *heads* are better than one, 594

When you hear *hoofbeats*, think horses, not zebras, 268

To bestow (plant) a pair of *horns* upon one's husband, 306, 392

A *house* divided against itself cannot stand, 528, 703, 707, 709

To err is *human*, to forgive divine, 975

Ignorance is bliss, 1003

The only good *Indian* is a dead Indian, 694, 702

Kill 'em all and let God sort 'em out, 937

Know thyself, 1130

Break a *leg*, 266

Life is short, and the art is long, 50, 898

Whistling *maids* and crowing hens, Never come to no good end, 264

Marry in haste, repent at leisure, 531

Self-made *men*, 712

Nature passes (surpasses) nurture, 93, 649

Pecking *order*, 846

To wear the *pants*, 117, 832

A *picture* is worth a thousand words, 691

The *pitcher* (pot) goes to the well until it is broken at last, 1097, 1168

A watched *pot* never boils, 145

Prevention is better than cure, 688, 691

Spare the *rod* and spoil the child, 150

Seeing is believing, but feeling is the truth, 111, 112, 262

Small talk, 971

Speech is silver, silence is golden, 1112

Proverb Index

A rolling *stone* gathers no moss, 4, 73, 555

Different *strokes* for different folks, 657, 684

No *struggle*, no progress, 711

No *tickee*, no washee, 700, 702

The *tongue* is the enemy of the neck, 948

The Ivory *Tower*, 322

French

La *lutte* pour la vie, 26

Malin comme un *singe*, 48

German

Angriff ist die beste Verteidigung, 967

Arbeit macht frei, 244

Jdm. einen *Bären* aufbinden, 438

Blut ist dicker als Wasser, 327

Der *Deutsche* hat den Affen erfunden, 801

Über den *Geschmack* läßt sich nicht streiten, 1043

Das *Gesicht* verlieren, 171

Ein *Hahnrei* sein, 1022

Da liegt der *Hase* im Pfeffer, 438

Mehr *Licht*, 433, 434, 435

Wer *lügt*, der stiehlt, 825

Mannomann, 172

Morgenstunde hat Gold im Munde, 673

Jeder ist seines Glückes *Schmied*, 603

Jedem das *Seine*, 244

Wer nicht liebt *Wein*, Weib und Gesang, der bleibt ein Narr sein Leben lang, 683

Was du nicht *willst*, daß man dir tu, das füg auch keinem andern zu, 888, 1020

Latin

Errare *humanum* est, 975

Summum *ius*, summa iniuria, 583

Spanish

No tiene la culpa el *indio*, sino el que lo hace compadre, 817

El que *nace*…, 33, 34

Wolfgang Mieder
Strategies of Wisdom
Anglo-American and German Proverb Studies
Phraseologie und Parömiologie Band 6.
2000. 372 Seiten. Kt. ISBN 3896763024. € 25,—

This volume includes ten essays on various aspects of Anglo-American and German proverbs and proverbial expressions. The first study presents a review of modern paremiography and paremiology and also points to desiderata for future research. Two chapters deal with the use of proverbs by Lord Chesterfield and Benjamin Franklin during the eighteenth century, and three additional studies investigate the function of proverbs in the works of Charles Dickens, Abraham Lincoln, and Frederick Douglass during the nineteenth century. There is also a detailed historical review of how the German proverb "The apple doesn't fall far from the tree" found its way to the United States. Turning to the twentieth century, yet another chapter discusses the proverbial dialectics in the works of Bertolt Brecht. Finally, there are two studies concerning the proverbial manipulations in Adolf Hitlers's *Mein Kampf* and the proverbial rhetoric in Victor Klemperer's *Diaries of the Nazi Years (1933–1945)*. A detailed bibliography and a keyword index of the proverbs cited conclude the book.

G. L. Permjakovs Grammatik der sprichwörtlichen Weisheit
Herausgegeben, übersetzt und bearbeitet von **Peter Grzybek**.
2000. 199 Seiten. Kt. ISBN 3896761978. € 17,—

Mit einer deutschen Übersetzung der *Grammatik der sprichwörtlichen Weisheit* wird hier erstmals der vollständige Text dieses originellen Ansatzes zur Beschreibung und Klassifikation von Sprichwörtern des führenden Parömiologen G. L. Permjakov (1919-1983) in einer westlichen Sprache zugänglich gemacht. Der Text wird ergänzt um eine ausführliche Einleitung sowie um ein alphabetisch und ein nach Typen angeordnetes Verzeichnis aller thematischen Paare zur Beschreibung der sprichwörtlichen Semantik.

Eine Auflistung aller von Permjakov selbst klassifizierten russischen Sprichwörter (original und mit deutscher Übersetzung) sowie eine kommentierte Liste mit Klassifikationen allgemein bekannter deutscher Sprichwörter runden den gesamten Band ab.

Schneider Verlag Hohengehren
Wilhelmstr. 13; D-73666 Baltmannsweiler

Wer A sägt, muss auch B sägen

Beiträge zur Phraseologie und Sprichwortforschung aus dem Westfälischen Arbeitskreis. Hrsg. von **Dietrich Hartmann** und **Jan Wirrer**
2002. 448 Seiten. Kt. ISBN 3896765523. € 29,80

Aus dem Inhalt:
Alexander Bierich **Quellen der russischen Phraseologie des 18. Jahrhunderts** • Christoph Chlosta / Torsten Ostermann **Überlegungen zur Nutzung des Internets in der Sprichwortforschung** • Dmitrij Dobrovol'skij **Grammatik der Idiome** • Sabine Dönninghaus **Das lexikalisch-semantische Feld der Täuschung in Phraseologismen des Tschechischen** • Manfred Eikelmann **Zur historischen Pragmatik des Sprichworts im Mittelalter** • Wolfgang Eismann **Gibt es phraseologische Weltbilder?** • Stephan Elspaß **Phraseologische Gebrauchsauffälligkeiten von Sprachbenutzern** • Erla Hallsteinsdóttir **Das Verstehen unbekannter Phraseologismen in der Fremdsprache Deutsch** • Françoise Hammer **Zur Phraseologie der Reisereportagen** • Barbara Lenz **Reihenfolge-Präferenzen in Zwillingsformeln** • Barbara Lenz **Tradierte und neue Quasi-Tautologien** • Anke Levin-Steinmann **Passivbildung aus kognitiver Sicht im allgemeinen und bei Phraseologismen** • V.M. Mokienko **Prinzipien einer historisch-etymologischen Analyse der Phraseologie** • Günter Nahberger **Anmerkungen zu einer sprechakttheoretischen Analyse von Sprichwörtern** • Günter Nahberger **Welche Sprechhandlungen kann man mit Sprichwörtern vollziehen?** • Jutta Pieper **Vorkommen und Funktion von Phraseologismen in deutschen Fernseh-Talkshows** • Klaus Dieter Pilz **Vorschläge für ein Phraseolexikon der deutschen Sprache** • Ulrike Preußer **Phraseologismen in Horoskopen.** • Ulrike Preußer **Phraseologismen in populärwissenschaftlicher Literatur** • Stanislaw Prędota **Phonische Mittel bei der Bildung von Antisprichwörtern** • Peter Stolze **Die Verwendung von klassischen geflügelten Worten in der Gegenwartssprache und neue Möglichkeiten des Belegnachweises** • Silke Tappe **Zur Funktion von Mikroformeln in argumentativen Texten** • Jan Wirrer **Für eine syntaxbasierte Phraseologie** • Arne Ziegler **Zur @kronymischen Verwendung der Phraseologismen in Textsorten der Internet-Kommunikation** • Dietrich Hartmann **Am Runden Tisch in Bochum. Vorbemerkungen des Veranstalters** • Dmitrij Dobrovol'skij **Phraseologie als Datenbank** • Dietrich Hartmann **Ein Plädoyer für lexikologische Struktur und Lexikographie phraseologischer Wortschätze** • Elisabeth Piirainen **Areale Aspekte der Phraseologie** • Jan Wirrer **Phraseologie und Pragmatik**

Schneider Verlag Hohengehren
Wilhelmstr. 13; D-73666 Baltmannsweiler